Anthropocene Ecologies of Food

Anthropocene Ecologies of Food provides a detailed exploration of cross-cultural aspects of food production, culinary practices, and their ecological underpinning in culture. The authors draw connections between humans and the entire process of global food production, focusing on the broad implications these processes have within the geographical and cultural context of India. Each chapter analyzes and critiques existing agricultural/food practices, and representations of aspects of food through various media (such as film, literature, and new media) as they relate to global issues generally and Indian contexts specifically, correcting the omission of analyses focused on the Global South in virtually all of the work that has been done on "Anthropocene ecologies of food." This unique volume employs an ecocritical framework that connects food with the land, in physical and virtual communities, and the book as a whole interrogates the meanings and implications of the Anthropocene itself.

Simon C. Estok is a full professor and Senior Research Fellow at Sungkyunkwan University (South Korea's first and oldest university) and a member of the European Academy of Sciences and Arts. Estok teaches literary theory, ecocriticism, and Shakespearean literature.

S. Susan Deborah, an Assistant Professor in the Department of English at MES College of Arts and Commerce, Goa, West India, is the co-editor of *Ecodocumentaries: Critical Essays* (2016), *Ecocultural Ethics: Critical Essays* (2017), and *Culture and Media: Ecocritical Explorations* (2014).

Rayson K. Alex, an Associate Professor in the Department of Humanities and Social Sciences, Birla Institute of Technology and Science Pilani, is the secretary of tiNai and the founder and co-director of tiNai Ecofilm Festival.

Routledge Studies in World Literatures and the Environment
Series Editors: Scott Slovic and Swarnalatha Rangarajan

Mushroom Clouds
Ecocritical Approaches to Militarization and the Environment in East Asia
Edited by Simon C. Estok, Iping Liang, and Shinji Iwamasa

Dystopias and Utopias on Earth and Beyond
Feminist Ecocriticism of Science Fiction
Edited by Douglas A. Vakoch

Ecofeminist Science Fiction
International Perspectives on Gender, Ecology, and Literature
Edited by Douglas A. Vakoch

Surreal Entanglements
Essays on Jeff VanderMeer's Fiction
Edited by Louise Economides and Laura Shackelford

Narrating Nonhuman Spaces
Form, Story, and Experience Beyond Anthropocentrism
Edited by Marco Caracciolo, Marlene Karlsson Marcussen, and David Rodriguez

The Tree of Life and Arboreal Aesthetics in Early Modern Literature
Victoria Bladen

The Experience of Disaster in Early Modern English Literature
Edited by Sophie Chiari

Anthropocene Ecologies of Food
Notes from the Global South
Edited by Simon C. Estok, S. Susan Deborah, and Rayson K. Alex

For more information about this series, please visit: www.routledge.com/Routledge-Studies-in-World-Literatures-and-the-Environment/book-series/ASHER4038

Anthropocene Ecologies of Food

Notes from the Global South

Edited by Simon C. Estok,
S. Susan Deborah, and Rayson K. Alex

NEW YORK AND LONDON

First published 2022
by Routledge
605 Third Avenue, New York, NY 10158

and by Routledge
4 Park Square, Milton Park, Abingdon, Oxon, OX14 4RN

Routledge is an imprint of the Taylor & Francis Group, an informa business

Library of Congress Cataloging-in-Publication Data
A catalog record for this title has been requested

ISBN: 978-1-032-25401-2 (hbk)
ISBN: 978-1-032-25402-9 (pbk)
ISBN: 978-1-003-28297-6 (ebk)

DOI: 10.4324/9781003282976

Typeset in Sabon
by Newgen Publishing UK

To the farmers in India who fought for their rights and won their battle

To the memory of David Steven Estok (1961–2021)
לזכרו של אחי, דָּוִד

Contents

Acknowledgments ix
List of Contributors x

Introduction: Food Systems and Ecological Well-Being 1
S. SUSAN DEBORAH

PART I
Bioregion, Diversity, Food 9

1 Rice and the Anthropocene in the Southern Indian Peninsula 11
NIRMAL SELVAMONY

2 The Taste of Place: Food, Ecology, and Culture in Kodagu 36
SUBARNA DE

3 This Compost! India and the History of Global Organic Farming 57
MART A. STEWART

PART II
Intercultural Food Practices 75

4 Environmental Food Documentaries: From *Fast Food Nation* to a Popular Selection of Top 20 YouTube Videos 77
PAT BRERETON

5 *Bacalhau* in England and Goa: A Case Study of Economy, Ecology, and the Assignation of Value in the Global South, *Circa* 1472–2019 97
WILLIAM SPATES

6 The Future of Food: Trajectories in Paolo Bacigalupi's *The Windup Girl* 112
YOUNG-HYUN LEE

7 Metaphors and Metonymies of Food in Four Asian Texts 126
CHITRA SANKARAN

PART III
Crises, Disintegration, Food 139

8 Agrarian Distress and Food Sovereignty in the Anthropocene: A Reading of Namita Waikar's *The Long March* 141
P. RAJITHA VENUGOPAL

9 Dalit Food, Ecology, and Resistance 158
SAMUEL MOSES SRINIVAS KUNTAM

Afterword: Toward Shifts in Global Food Systems 180
SIMON C. ESTOK

Index 185

Acknowledgments

This book was born as the result of a conference on Food and Culture, organized in 2016. Our sincere gratitude goes out to the organizers and paper presenters of the same. We acknowledge Dr. Cidalia Bodade, the coordinator of the conference and the host institution, MES College of Arts and Commerce, Zuarinagar, Goa. We exetend our heartfelt thanks to the then head of MES College, Dr. R. B. Patil, who supported the conference proceedings and stood by the organizers at every step. We are also thankful to the organizing team, Ms. Palia Pandit, Ms. Shilpa Tanna, Ms. Saba Syed, and Ms. Rupali Kamat. From 2016, the idea of a book was brewing within us and it finally came to fruition in 2022. We are thankful to our contributors who accepted our proposal and braved deadlines and revisions as they trudged along with us on this journey. We offer our sincere gratitude to Michelle Salyga for her wisdom in seeing the potential in our proposal. Finally, we are deeply grateful to Bryony Reece, the editorial assistant at Routledge, whose patience defies description.

We are indebted to our families and friends, whose support and encouragement made our academic endeavors and projects possible.

Finally, the editors owe their gratitude to the earth which provides food for nourishment and has instilled a sense of taste and love of food and ingredients. We acknowledge the various cuisines that we have sampled over the years and offer thanks to the creators of those delicious and scrumptious meals.

Simon C. Estok, S. Susan Deborah,
and Rayson K. Alex

Contributors

Rayson K. Alex, an Associate Professor in the Department of Humanities and Social Sciences, Birla Institute of Technology and Science Pilani, K. K. Birla Goa Campus, Goa, West India, is the secretary of tiNai—previously called Organization for Studies in Literature and Environment-India (OSLE-India)—and the founder and co-director of tiNai Ecofilm Festival. Dr. Alex is also the co-editor of *Essays in Ecocriticism* (Sarup, 2007), the first anthology of Indian ecocriticism; the co-editor of *Ecodocumentaries: Critical Essays* (Palgrave Macmillan, 2016), the first anthology of Indian eco-media; and the co-editor of *Ecocultural Ethics: Critical Essays* (Lexington 2017).

Pat Brereton has been Associate Dean for Research in the Faculty of Humanities and Social Science at Dublin City University for the last five years. His books include *Hollywood Utopia: Ecology in Contemporary American Cinema* (2005), *Continuum Guide to Media Education* (2001), *Historical Dictionary of Irish Cinema* (2007) with Roddy Flynn and *Smart Cinema, DVD Add-ons and New Audience Pleasures* (2012), *Environmental Ethics and Film* (2015). He has several other book chapters and publications across a wide range of journals on various aspects of film and media culture and remains committed to developing cross-disciplinary links.

Subarna De is a Fellow at the Rachel Carson Center for Environment and Society, Ludwig Maximilian University, Munich. She researches the transformations of the environment and society, focusing on bio-regionalism and indigeneity. Her research is situated at the interface of cultural anthropology, human geography, environmental history, and environmental humanities scholarship. Her doctoral thesis (2019), funded by the Central University Doctoral Fellowship (India), focused on the environmental history and ecological practices of Indian coffee plantations and was supported with a research stay at Queen's University, Belfast, UK.

S. Susan Deborah, an Assistant Professor in the Department of English at MES College of Arts and Commerce, Goa, West India, is the co-editor of *Ecodocumentaries: Critical Essays* (Palgrave Macmillan, 2016), *Ecocultural Ethics: Critical Essays* (Lexington, 2017) and *Culture and Media: Ecocritical Explorations* (Cambridge Scholars Publishing, 2014), the first anthology of Indian eco-media. She is the recipient of the Association for the Study of Literature and Environment-USA (ASLE-USA) Media Subvention Grant, and her areas of specialty and expertise match precisely those covered by the book under consideration: food studies, eco-media, and ecocriticism.

Simon C. Estok is a full professor and Senior Research Fellow at Sungkyunkwan University (South Korea's first and oldest university) and a member of the European Academy of Sciences and Arts. Estok teaches literary theory, ecocriticism, and Shakespearean literature. His award-winning book *Ecocriticism and Shakespeare: Reading Ecophobia* appeared in 2011 (reprinted 2014), and he is co-editor of five books: *Anthropocene Ecologies of Food* (Routledge), *Mushroom Clouds: Ecological Approaches to Militarization and the Environment in East Asia* (Routledge, 2021), *Landscape, Seascape, and the Eco-Spatial Imagination* (Routledge, 2016), *International Perspectives in Feminist Ecocriticism* (Routledge, 2013), and *East Asian Ecocriticisms* (Macmillan, 2013). His latest book is the much-anticipated *The Ecophobia Hypothesis* (Routledge, 2018; reprinted with errata as paperback in 2020). Estok has published extensively on ecocriticism and Shakespeare in journals such as *PMLA*, *Mosaic*, *Configurations*, *English Studies in Canada*, and others. He is currently working on a book about slime in the Western cultural and literary imagination.

Samuel Moses Srinivas Kuntam, Assistant Professor, Department of English (Self Financing Stream) at Madras Christian College, Chennai, is the co-Director of tiNai Ecofilm Festival (www.teff.in). His areas of interest include ecocriticism, Dalit studies, and postcolonial criticism.

Young-hyun Lee teaches at Sungkyunkwan University in Seoul, South Korea. Her publications of translated books include *Do You Know The "Comfort Women" of the Imperial Japanese Military?* (2017), *Truth: Problems for Peace (2017)*, and 나의 첫여름 (*My First Summer in the Sierra*), which Lee co-translated with Dr. Won-Chung Kim in 2008. Lee recently received twice a one-year research award from the National Research Foundation, to be held at Kangwon University for the academic years 2018–2019 and 2019–2020. She is the author of the scholarly articles: "Food Ethics and GMOs in Margaret Atwood's *Oryx and Crake* and Paolo Bacigalupi's *The Windup Girl*" (published in *Mushroom Clouds: Ecocritical Approaches to Militarization and the Environment in East Asia, 2021)*, which Simon Estok, Iping Liang, and Shinji Iwamasa co-edited, and was published in Routledge; "Trans-corporeality, Climate Change, and *My Year of Meats*," *Neohelicon* 47 (A&HCI, 2020); "인류세환경론과 타자성 재고: 여성과 유색인

종, 자연의 동인으로서의 물성인식" ("Reconsidered Anthropocene Environmentalism and Otherness: Recognition of Materiality of Women, People of Color, and Nature as Agent"), *Literature and Environment* 19.4 (2020); "Food Transformation Technology in Paolo Bacigalupi's *The Windup Girl* and What it Means for Us," *Kritika Kultura* 33/34 (A&HCI, 2019); "The Different Representation of Suffering in the Two Versions of *The Vegetarian*," *CLCWeb* 21.5 (A&HCI, 2019); and "A Study of *The Man with the Compound Eyes on Climate Change*, Plastics, and Body" (forthcoming). Her research interests lie primarily in the area of environmental humanities, cli-fi (climate fiction), and translation.

Chitra Sankaran, Associate Professor, Department of English Language & Literature, National University of Singapore, researches and publishes in ecocriticism, Asian fiction, and postcolonial and feminist theory. She edited a special issue on ASEAN ecocriticism for *The Journal of Ecocriticism* (2018). She published, with Suny, *History, Narrative and Testimony in Amitav Ghosh's Fiction* (2012). Her other publications include monographs, edited volumes on Asian literatures, book chapters and articles in internationally refereed journals, including *Journal of Commonwealth Literature*, *ARIEL*, *Australian Feminist Studies*, and *Critical Asian Studies*. She has contributed to *Oxford History of the Novel in English* (OHNE). She is currently working on ecofeminism in South and Southeast Asian fiction. She is the founding-president of ASLE-ASEAN.

Nirmal Selvamony is an Indian academician and scholar. He retired as Professor and Head of the Department of English Studies and Dean of the School of Social Sciences and Humanities in Central University of Tamil Nadu. His major interests include literary theory, ecocriticism, ecotheory, music, and drama. He is the current president of *tiNai* (formerly, OSLE-India).

William Spates received his D.Phil. in Renaissance literature at the University of Saint Andrews, Scotland, in 2005. He taught at Shorter University, Auburn University, Haverford College, Eastern Mediterranean University (North Cyprus), the Baha'I Institute of Higher Education (Iran), Qatar University, and Birla Institute of Technology and Science, Pilani (Goa Campus) in India before taking on his current role as an associate professor of English and department chair at Georgia Military College. He has published essays and book reviews in *Clio, Notes and Queries, Theatre Journal, Shakespeare Bulletin, Sixteenth Century Journal, DQR Studies in Literature,* and Ashgate's *Literary and Scientific Cultures of Early Modernity* series.

Mart A. Stewart was a forester in his first career, working in the mountains of the American West. He now teaches courses in environmental and cultural history at Western Washington University, and is also an affiliate professor in Huxley College of the Environment at the University. He completed his Fulbright Senior Scholarship at BITS Pilani-Goa in India. Stewart was researching the development of environmental history as a field of scholarship in India. He is the author or editor of many books, essays, and articles on the environmental history of the US South and on the Mekong Delta, including *What Nature Suffers to Grow: Life, Labor, and Landscape on the Georgia Coast, 1680–1920* (1996), and many essays and articles, and co-editor of *Environmental Change and Agricultural Sustainability in the Mekong Delta* (2011). He is now working on a project on the environmental history of food. Professor Stewart is also one of the Series Editors of "Flows, Migrations, and Exchanges" published by the University of North Carolina Press.

P. Rajitha Venugopal teaches as Assistant Professor at FLAME University, Pune, India. She completed her doctoral research from the Department of English, Jamia Millia Islamia, on the writings of contemporary American author Barbara Kingsolver. Her M.Phil. research, from the same department, was a study on the short stories of Narayan, the first published Adivasi writer in Malayalam literature. She has presented papers at national and international seminars and has also contributed to journals and edited volumes, particularly in the area of ecocriticism. Previously she has worked as guest faculty in FLAME University, Jamia Millia Islamia, and Institute of Home Economics, Delhi University, and as Project Fellow (Special Assistance Program, under Department Research Support, a research grant offered by the University Grants Commission) in the Department of English, Jamia Millia Islamia. Her areas of interests are environmental narratives, postcolonial studies, contemporary Indian writing in English and translations, Dalit and Adivasi narratives, and Kerala studies.

Introduction

Food Systems and Ecological Well-Being

S. Susan Deborah

"Food systems represent the nexus between human health and environmental well-being," (1) comment Fanzo et al. in their essay, "Eating our way through the Anthropocene," and their observation cannot be truer because food, food systems, and food practices are pertinent to the understanding of the politics of food cultures in the Anthropocene. While I write this, the farmers in Northern India of the Global South have been protesting the passing of three bills by the Indian Government; while the media has been largely covering the epidemic, the protesting farmers continue to do so in order to address their livelihood and an important concern for every person – food and the related food systems. At the time of writing it has been one year, one month, two weeks, and six days since the protest began and, still it shows no signs of waning. The protest has become a grave concern in the construction of *naturecultures* (see Donna Haraway[1]) because of the interconnectedness of food to every aspect of life and living. The farmers' concern is the government's apathy towards their demands and siding with the big corporate firms. Bilal Kuchay of *Al Jazeera* writes:

> Once accounting for a third of India's gross domestic product (GDP), the agricultural sector now makes only 15 percent of India's $2.9 trillion economy. More than half of the country's farmers are in debt, with 20,638 dying by suicide due to debt and crop failures in 2018 and 2019, according to India's National Crime Records Bureau.
>
> (Kuchay)

While protests as these largely color the Global South, it is no surprise that the Anthropocene has paved the way for struggles as these. The essays in *Anthropocene Ecologies* focus on the diverse issues that plague the Global South and elsewhere. The various positions in this volume bring together the theoretical frameworks from the areas of ecocritical studies and food studies employing interdisciplinary approaches and methodologies to understand eco-food studies. The following issues connecting both areas, thus, become important: (1) how food connects culture to the environment; (2) how local and global foods can transform cultures

DOI: 10.4324/9781003282976-1

and ecologies; and (3) how food controls the power systems that manage/ manipulate societies, political systems, and ecosystems. Understanding these personal-cum-collective ethical positions as rooted in culture and daily life is a type of union between theory and praxis, as Lawrence Buell terms it, the "spirit of environmental praxis."[2] While on one hand, food is quite intimate and personal, it also segues into the political—the farmers' protest which is still fomenting in India, one of the important countries from the Global South, is a fitting example of the same. Ecocriticism which combines personal ethos with the political by critiquing classism, racism, anti-Semitism, sexism, speciesism, homophobia, and ecophobia provides a strong theoretical framework for eco-food studies, which is the focus of *Anthropocene Ecologies of Food* with a spotlight on the Global South.

Anthropocene Ecologies also addresses concerns and positions that have different perspectives in the Global South and Global North. I remember having a conversation on vegetarianism and meat eating with a colleague from the Global North who questioned my fondness for eating meat. While I could understand where his question came from, it is important to understand that meat eating in India is connected to the livelihoods of people—what Joan Martinez-Alier calls "environmentalism of the poor."[3] Since the communities are closely tied to their land, the food systems demand eating beef, which is an easily available and cost-effective source of protein. While the Global North articulates a strong position in what Tony Weis calls "meatification,"[4] the Global South is fighting against homogeneity of food habits across diverse cultures and communities that have their own peculiar food habits, which in most cases connect them to their land and local region. The exploitation of certain communities on the basis of food to maintain the hierarchy shows how food and caste politics are closely connected. Samuel Moses Srinivas Kuntam in his essay in this volume discusses this issue.

Connecting ethics, food practices, and communities, Peter Singer and Jim Mason open the debate in their 2006 volume, *The Way We Eat: Why Our Food Choices Matter*,[5] which largely looks at the American diet across sections of classes. The attorney and the philosopher duo voice their concerns against the meat industry, which is one of the largest causes of climate change in the Global North, with the Global South also slowly following suit. Certain other notable works among the many in the field of food studies are Raj Patel's compelling volume, *Stuffed and Starved: The Hidden Battle for the World Food System* (2008),[6] which looks at the paradox of food in the current scenario where, in spite of increased production of food, the number of people who are overweight is higher than the people who are hungry. Patel's argument that "the stuffed and starved are linked together through the chains of food production" is undeniably crucial to the study of food, its production and consumption. Given the context of the Anthropocene, Patel's volume addresses many concerns across the global countries of the South and North. Ken Albala's *Routledge International Handbook of Food Studies*[7] (2013) brings together diverse disciplines in the social sciences and humanities and explores the myriad aspects of food, food systems, foodways, and eating habits predominantly from the Global North. The volume cuts across disciplines such as Anthropology, Gender Studies, History, Sociology, and other such, with each scholar bringing to the table an approach peculiar to their specific field. The handbook offers a comprehensive study into the multi-dimensional approaches that could be employed to the field of food studies. While it cannot be denied that any reading of food and related topics cannot escape discussing land issues, ethics, and the big corporates that largely control food systems, ecocritical studies connects food to the ecological well-being of the land and its various inhabitants. The uniqueness of combining the disciplines of ecocritical studies and food studies is an upcoming area which is largely growing in popularity among scholars who evince an interest in theorizing food. Estok in "An Introduction to 'Ecocritical Approaches to Food and Literature in East Asia': The Special Cluster" opines that "Theorizing food's under-theorization in ecocriticism increasingly means looking at practice, at meat and vegetables, and at what their production represents both for natural and for human environments" (Estok 683). Ecocriticism by placing equal thrust on natural as well as human environments asks complex questions about food preferences, fads, eating habits, bioregional eating, impure food amidst issues of vegetarianism, veganism, meatarianism, and other such. The 2012 Interdisciplinary Studies in Literature and Environment[8] special cluster which provides insights into the East Asian part of the Global South has many commonalities with the present volume which looks into the South Asian counterpart of the Global South.

Anthropocene Ecologies of Food explores cross-cultural aspects of food production, culinary practices, and their ecological underpinning in culture. The authors draw connections between humans and the entire process of food production within the broad geographical and cultural context of India, analyzing and critiquing existing agricultural/food practices, and representations of aspects of food through various media, such as film, literature, and new media. The essays often employ an ecocritical framework to connect food with the land, in a physical or virtual community.

Organized into three parts, namely, Bioregion, Diversity, Food; Intercultural Food Practices; and Crises, Disintegration, Food, the volume of essays from Indian and international food and ecocriticism scholars discusses the socio-political and cultural manifestations of food towards the construction of a global Indian identity.

The first part covers place-based food and food systems. In the opening paragraphs of her essay, "Coming Home to Eat: Re-Imagining Place in the Age of Global Climate Change" (2009), Joni Adamson raises pertinent questions on local places and consumption of food produced within 20 miles of the place (Adamson 3). Essays in this section, by arguing for a food system which is native and suitable to the terrain, try to engage with the questions raised by Adamson. Place-based narratives find an important space in the Global South where the concept of "one true place" is still largely followed and preserved. While one could argue that the context of the local has largely altered with globalization, there are many communities and families who still live in the same place as their ancestors. The context of two essays is South India while one essay looks at a local practice which is followed in a place thousands of miles away. The essays could be read as responses to mitigate the rising concerns caused by the effects of bulk production, monoculture, and the introduction of new systems of food production. The collection opens with Nirmal Selvamony's "Rice and the Anthropocene in the Southern Indian Peninsula," which argues that restoration of food diversity is necessary in order to end rice monoculture and monism, as well as the Anthropocene they have engendered especially in the southern Indian peninsula. To ensure the ecological well-being of the land and the Anthropocene, Selvamony opines that "no time should be lost in reviving the heterarchic and diverse food practices of the tiṇai societies." Focusing on the Kodagu community of Karnataka, Subarna De in her essay, "The Taste of Place: Understanding the Bioregional Food System in Kodagu," analyzes how the bioregional food system practiced in the coffee plantations of Kodagu (the indigenous name of Coorg), responds to the Anthropocene in the Global South. Reading Kavery Nambisan's *The Scent of Pepper* (1996) and Sarita Mandanna's *Tiger Hills* (2010), De's essay demonstrates how bioregional eating in Kodagu determines the culture of the place providing a bioregional identity to the Kodava people. Mart A. Stewart's "This Compost!" takes up the history of compost—as recipe, material reality, and feat of imagination – and places the development of the Indore Method by Sir Albert Howard in the early nineteenth century in a British agricultural research station in Indore. Stewart, while critiquing the process of compost making in the Global North, traces the method to a city in the Global South—Indore in the state of Madhya Pradesh in India. The essay looks into the method as a no-nonsense cornerstone to the modern organic agriculture and gardening sector of the food economy. While suitably crediting the Global South for the ingenious techniques, Stewart's essay thrusts forward the need for small and local technologies and expertise, echoing E.F. Schumacher's words, "Wisdom demands a new orientation of science and technology toward the organic, the gentle, the elegant and beautiful."[9]

The second part—Intercultural Food Practices—discusses the socio-economic ramifications of food across diverse countries and media. The section looks at the context of food which has diversified from its place of origin across the globe due to globalization and emerging technologies and trends. Simple food belonging to a small locale transforms into a celebrated delicacy thanks to the growing popularity of social media and food bloggers. The section engages with not only transformation of local food into global ones but also the modification of existing food items through genetic interventions. Pat Brereton's focus is on the food practices of the Global North via the medium of documentaries. His essay, "Popular Food Documentaries: Online Affordances and Environmental Literacy across the Globe" explores "how contemporary environmental documentaries ... help foreground a range of cautionary tales around the importance of sustainable modes of food production, waste, and (over)consumption." In "Bacalhau in England and Goa: A Case Study of Economy, Ecology, and the Assignation of Value in the Global South, Circa 1472–2019," William Spates takes up the case of a North Atlantic species of salt cod and traces its transformation from a much-maligned staple of the poor into a highly valued delicacy. Central to Spates' argument is the "complex linkages between cod as a North Atlantic species and a global commodity from the North Atlantic through the perspective of early modern texts from Europe and Goa." Young-hyun Lee in "Food Transformation Technology in Paolo Bacigalupi's *The Windup Girl* and What It Means for Us" is a reading of the American biopunk writer Paolo Bacigalupi's *The Windup Girl* (2009), a futuristic novel set in Thailand. The fictitious novel quite aptly resonates the problems caused by genetically modified organisms and large corporations like Vedanta and Monsanto in the era of the Anthropocene. Lee's reading demonstrates how "food issues are one of the most urgent problems human beings face" with "unknown dangers of food transformation technology by the profit-driven monopolistic multinational companies." While the plot of the novel is an imaginary one, the brutal truths that bring out the connection between food, food systems, and the life of humans is quite close to the existing issues in the countries of the Global South. The last essay of this section, titled, "Metaphors and Metonymies of Food in Four Asian Texts," by Chitra Sankaran, examines four contemporary texts from the Global South—India, Singapore, and the Philippines—that are themed around the making and eating of food, exemplifying the diverse cultural connotations that are linked to the idea of nourishment and how these varied cultures contribute to or challenge ideas that revolve around the cooking, eating, and even wasting of food.

While the first two sections discus the context, need for diversity, and intercultural aspects of food and food systems, the third part looks at the rise of conflict over the increasing problems that plague the cultivation, production, and consumption of food. Food in this section is seen as a powerful political weapon which has to be given its due importance. Titled, Crises, Disintegration, Food, the section explores how a rupture in the food system causes unrest and conflict, leading to resistance and disintegration of the ecological well-being of the land and people. Both writers explore texts that focus on the local issues of food and resistance in the Indian scenario. P. Rajitha Venugopal's "Agrarian Distress and Food Sovereignty in the Anthropocene: A Reading of Namita Waikar's

The Long March" is an analysis into the issue of farmers' struggle in the Vidharba region of Maharashtra. The region notorious for farmers' suicides has been gaining media attention for diverse reasons. P. Sainath, popular journalist and author of *Everybody Loves a Good Drought*,[10] opines that the farmers' mass suicides "now go[es] far beyond an agrarian crisis, becoming a societal or even civilisational crisis" (Sainath). Venugopal argues that while multinational industrial agribusinesses enjoy massive profits, small farmers struggle with modernized agriculture and neoliberal policies, thereby disproportionately suffering socio-economic–ecological consequences. The essay presents some of the concerns that occur in Young-hyun Lee's "Food Transformation Technology ..." While Venugopal's text draws from real-life issues in the western state of India, Lee's text draws from real-life instances, albeit set in a futuristic imaginary world. Both these texts, although fictionalized, address the pressing concerns that prevail in the Anthropocene. Samuel Moses Srinivas Kuntam's "Dalit Food, Ecology, and Resistance," through narratives by Dalit (a lower-caste community in India) writers, explores hierarchy and resistance in food practices and rituals. Considered the bottom of the pyramid, the people of the Dalit community are shunned by the upper-caste communities for their food practices. This connection of food and hierarchy finds a stark contrast in Carol J. Adams' 1990 iconic food volume, *The Sexual Politics of Meat*, where she states, "People with power have always eaten meat," referring to the aristocratic families of Europe. Adams further extrapolates, "The sexism in meat-eating recapitulates the class distinctions with an added twist: a mythology permeates all classes that meat is a masculine food and meat eating a male activity.[11]"Adams' views speak of the Global North's predilection with food where she connects gender, class, and meat eating, whereas the Global South also connects meat to issues of class (more of caste rather) by attaching the label of impurity to certain communities which consume meat (more specifically, beef). Since the occupation of the Dalits is closely connected to the slaughter of cows, beef is their staple food; the cow is considered holy by the Brahmins and the meat-eating lower castes are often humiliated for their food habits. Matters of purity and unclean food habits color the dissent between the communities. Moses argues that food, landscape, and caste are inextricably interwoven, contributing to the continuation of the caste system in present-day twenty-first-century India.

The roots for *Anthropocene Ecologies* sprang from a conference organized by the MES College of Arts and Commerce, Goa, on food in February 2016, titled, "The Culture of Food: Literature and Society." The conference saw papers from across disciplines and countries spread across three days. Live cooking, food sampling, and a host of discussions centering on food, food systems, and the environment, made the organizers envision a volume which could collect the plethora of ideas and arguments that would bring together diverse disciplines and their outlook on food. While the editors could not glean many papers from the conference, the idea was communicated and papers were invited from scholars whose work fell in line with the volume's perspectives. The volume, while devoting a major part to issues from the Global South (India, Thailand), also touches upon similar issues in the UK and US.

As food continues to nourish our hearts and heads, we hope and believe that the issues presented in this volume will inspire and engage scholars, activists, students, and sections of the public to understand that food is both personal as well as a political tool which largely determines the well-being of the *oikos* in the era of the Anthropocene.

Notes

1 Haraway, Donna Jeanne. *The Companion Species Manifesto: Dogs, People, and Significant Otherness*. Vol. 1. Chicago: Prickly Paradigm Press, 2003.
2 See Buell, Lawrence. *The Environmental Imagination: Thoreau, Nature Writing and the Foundation of American Culture*. Boston: Harvard University Press, 1995.
3 See Martinez-Alier, Joan. *The Environmentalism of the Poor: A Study of Ecological Conflicts and Valuation*. Edward Elgar Publishing, 2003.
4 See Weis, Tony. "Confronting meatification." *Green Meat* (2020): 29–42.
5 See Singer, Peter, Jim Mason, and Rick Adamson. *The Way We Eat: Why Our Food Choices Matter*. Emmaus, PA: Rodale, 2006.
6 See Patel, Raj. *Stuffed and Starved: The Hidden Battle for the World Food System*. Melville House, 2008.
7 See Albala, Ken, ed. *Routledge International Handbook of Food Studies*. Routledge, 2013.
8 *Interdisciplinary Studies in Literature and Environment* 19.4 (2012).
9 Schumacher, Ernst Friedrich. *Small is Beautiful: A Study of Economics as if People Mattered*. Random House, 2011.
10 Sainath, Palagummi. *Everybody Loves a Good Drought: Stories From India's Poorest Districts*. Vol. 10. Penguin Books India, 1996.
11 Adams, Carol J. *The Sexual Politics of Meat: A Feminist-Vegetarian Critical Theory*. United Kingdom: Continuum, 1990.

References

Adamson, Joni. "Coming home to eat: Re-imagining place in the age of global climate change." *Tamkang Review* 39.2 (2009).

Buell, Lawrence. *The Environmental Imagination: Thoreau, Nature Writing and the Foundation of American Culture*. Harvard University Press, 1995.

Estok, Simon C. "An introduction to 'Ecocritical Approaches to Food and Literature in East Asia': The special cluster." *Interdisciplinary Studies in Literature and Environment* 19.4 (2012): 681–690.

Fanzo, Jessica, Amelia Hood, and Claire Davis. "Eating our way through the Anthropocene." *Physiology & Behavior* 222 (2020): 112929.

Kuchay, Bilal. "Indian farmers remain defiant, a year after 'black laws' passed." *Al Jazeera* 20 Sep., 2021. www.aljazeera.com/news/2021/9/20/india-farmers-a-year-of-farm-laws-agriculture. Accessed 23 Sep., 2021.

Sainath, P. "It's more than an agrarian crisis." *The Hindu* 24 June, 2019. www.thehindu.com/news/national/kerala/its-more-than-an-agrarian-crisis-p-sainath/article28122414.ece. Accessed 23 Sep., 2021.

Part I

Bioregion, Diversity, Food

1 Rice and the Anthropocene in the Southern Indian Peninsula

Nirmal Selvamony

The Anthropocene is the epoch when humans have had decisive negative impacts on the earth and its atmosphere. In the southern Indian peninsula, such an impact resulted from the rise of a civilization that depended to a great extent on a rice monoculture and monopoly, which also disrupted the age-old diversity in food practices nurtured by the pre-Anthropocene *tiṇai* societies of India. This chapter will argue that unless food diversity (as in *tiṇai* society) is restored, the Anthropocene in the southern Indian peninsula will continue.

There seem to be three basic approaches to the Anthropocene: neutral, anthropotreptic (Gk. *anthropos*, human + *trepein*, to turn) or human-oriented, and allotreptic (Gk. *allos*, other + *trepein*, to turn) or other-oriented.[1] The neutral approach to the Anthropocene is that of a scientist who does not evaluate but only describes.[2] Non-scientists (scholars of human and social sciences), on the other hand, rely on scientific description while focusing on the implications of the Anthropocene. Such an approach is likely to be either exclusively from a human point of view (anthropocentric) or from an inclusive, empathic one of a human who also seeks to view the problematic epoch through the eyes of entities other than humans. While an "anthropotreptic" approach to the Anthropocene considers it only in relation to humans, an "allotreptic" one regards it in relation to both humans and entities other than humans.

The "anthropos" in the term anthropotreptic could represent either a human collective (Ackerman 305–310; Schwagerl 224–227) or a human-made system, such as capitalism (Angus 19–23). Allotreptic accounts of the epoch approach it either through the eyes of a particular discipline or through those of more than one. Despite its focus on history, it is possible to read Dipesh Chakrabarty's essay "The Climate of History: Four Theses" as an allotreptic one because it exhorts historians to see humans as a species rather than as "mankind," "a species dependent on other species for its own existence " (219). Amitav Ghosh's *The Great Derangement*, which explores the relationship between fiction and climate change in a narrative style, is also an allotreptic text as it speaks of the possibility of the rediscovery of human "kinship with other beings" as an alternative to "the isolation in which humanity was trapped in the

DOI: 10.4324/9781003282976-3

time of its derangement" (217). The volume edited by Hackett, Kunard and Stahel, *Anthropocene*, on the other hand, is a multidisciplinary presentation on the impact of the epoch, not only on humans, but on other life forms as well. Bruno Latour's allotreptic approach to the Anthropocene is ontological rather than theoretical. His *Down To Earth* argues for a new understanding of co-agency of humans and entities other than humans. To him both are agents who are not so much subject and object in a relationship as agential nodes in a network:

> If the composition of the air we breathe depends on living beings, the atmosphere is no longer simply the environment in which living beings are located and in which they evolve; it is, in part, a result of their actions. In other words, there are not organisms on one side and an environment on the other, but a coproduction by both. Agencies are redistributed.
>
> (76)

Although anthropotreptic thinkers are of varied hues, prominent among them are the apocalyptic jeremiahs and the optimists (Angus 78–88; Schwagerl 226–227). The proponents of the allotreptic viewpoint are equally diverse, but they are all usually radically critical of the Anthropocene. This chapter positions itself in the company of the latter, although its radical criticism is not necessarily a jeremiad against the epoch. As the subject under discussion is rice, and the Anthropocene is only its context, this chapter does not probe deeply into the latter but merely provides sufficient information to understand why we need to end the Anthropocene and usher in a new epoch (Selvamony, "From the Anthropocene …" 115–130).

Paul Crutzen named the present epoch the Anthropocene because he found scientific evidence to assert that humans have had the greatest impact on the earth and its atmosphere since the Industrial Revolution. The synthesis of new chemicals was a novelty of the eighteenth century,[3] but an increase in the concentration of carbon dioxide, methane, and nitrous oxide in the atmosphere (Kritee et al. 9720–9725), and the use of fossil fuel, were not; they preceded the Industrial Revolution (Steffen, Crutzen, and MacNeill 615). If excessive human impact on the earth's systems did predate this period, the scale, speed, and quality of the impact were less than they are today. In other words, although excessive human interference with the earth's systems differs in kind and degree both before and after the Industrial Revolution, it does predate the event. A typical example of excessive human interference is deforestation, which is inexorably linked with topsoil erosion. Scholars have shown how topsoil erosion led to the decline of civilizations (Dale and Carter; Montgomery; Norris), which could not support themselves as they had adversely affected the ecosystems that nurtured them (Harrison 57). According to Brett Bowden, the relationship between civilization and the ecosystems is

> not so different from the dialectical relationship between civilization and war: the higher the level of civilization, the greater the exploitation of nature; the greater the exploitation of nature, the more civilization progresses. But as with civilization and war, this relationship cannot go on forever: natural resource extraction and exploitation is not a bottomless pit, but rather is finite and can only support so many people for so long.
>
> (12)

While the societies of the hunter–gatherers lasted more than 80,000 years, the civilizations of state societies could not be sustained beyond a few thousand years (Dale and Carter Chapter 1). Soon the rot sets in and triggers their decline even when they manage to last longer.

Although historians do not speak of the kingdom of cōḻar as a civilization, it could well be one on all counts. It was a state society which had urban centers, full-time specialists not involved in agriculture, social classes, surplus food, monuments, abundant evidence for art, music, and literature, extensive domestic and international trade, and well-developed irrigational technology (*paṭṭiṉappālai* 283–284; Nilakanta Sastri 30–99; Selvamony, "The Cries of Water"; Violatti). karikālaṉ,[4] the most outstanding king of the early phase of this civilization, had already built urban centers and "the oldest water-diversion structure in the world" (Bijker 111), and produced surplus rice by irrigating as many as 69,000 acres of wetland (Martin). In the medieval period, this civilization lasted for 1,500 years and reached its zenith during the time of the emperors Rajarajan I (985–1014) and Rajendran I (1014–1044). Irrigated rice agriculture, which sustained the civilization of cōlar, ultimately turned out to be its nemesis and, what is more, commenced the Anthropocene in southern peninsular India.[5]

The Anthropocene that Crutzen describes (2006) is global; however, the "Early Anthropocene" (Selvamony, "From the Anthropocene …" 116) prior to the Industrial Revolution did not adversely affect all humans and non-humans uniformly throughout the world. Each civilization impacted the earth and its atmosphere in its own way and formed, shall we say, "Anthropocene pockets." True, some human activities necessary for state formation may have had non-localized effects. For example, paddy monoculture released greenhouse gases into the atmosphere (Sudarmanian et al. 4116–4120) but it did not alter the atmosphere in the way in which the societies of the Industrial Revolution did. In the words of Steffen, Crutzen, and McNeill,

> Preindustrial societies could and did modify coastal and terrestrial ecosystems but they did not have the numbers, social and economic organization, or technologies needed to equal or dominate the great forces of Nature in magnitude or rate. Their impacts remained largely

> local and transitory, well within the bounds of the natural variability of the environment.
>
> (615)

If such localized impact is characteristic of an "Early Anthropocene," then it was evident in the Indus Valley by 2500 BCE, in the Gangetic plain in the first millennium BCE, and in the southern tip of the Indian peninsula only during the reign of karikālan̲.

Unlike state society, industrial society had a far greater impact on the forces of nature, inaugurating the fully fledged Anthropocene. If steam power is what ushered in this epoch in 1784 (Crutzen 13), then nuclear power did far more damage in 1945, initiating a distinct phase unparalleled in the history of the earth. The third phase of the Anthropocene or the "Late Anthropocene" (Selvamony, "From the Anthropocene…" 116) is also the period of the Great Acceleration when humans not only released the monstrous energy of the atom for destructive purposes but also impacted both human society and the earth systems dramatically.

In the southern peninsula of India, the Early Anthropocene is inextricably connected with state formation and irrigated rice cultivation. Prior to the discussion of rice cultivation and consumption, some preliminary observations on the diverse food practices in the different ecoregions, called *tiṇaikaḷ*, of this peninsula are in order.

Food Heterarchy

The food of the people of the *tiṇaikaḷ* (*kur̲iñci*, *mullai*, *pālai*, *marutam*, and *neytal*), before the emergence of state society, consisted of almost everything that was edible in the *tiṇai*—meat of all animals, including fish and seafood, all kinds of plant food, and beverages[6] supplemented with, mostly, bartered food from another *tiṇai*. Readiness to consume anything edible ensured food diversity (namaccivāyam 8–22),[7] which effectively deterred the predominance of a single staple, or "food monism."

While people in all the *tiṇaikaḷ* consumed meat, the ways in which each procured it differed. If *vēṭṭuvar* lived by hunting (*pur̲anān̲ūr̲u* 13: 1), *valaiñar* (*maturaikkāñci* 255–256), *valaivar* (*aiṅkur̲unūr̲u* 180: 2), and some *pāṇar* (*aiṅkur̲unūr̲u* 48: 1) fished with nets, while other *pāṇar* (*perumpāṇār̲r̲uppaṭai* 284–285; *akanān̲ūr̲u* 216: 1; *aiṅkur̲unūr̲u* 111: 1–2), *pāṭunar* (*akanān̲ūr̲u* 196: 1–4), and *vin̲aiñar* (*akanān̲ūr̲u* 186: 1–5) fished with hooks and foraged (*akanān̲ūr̲u* 81: 1–3). Besides fish, veal was also a favorite meat of the *pāṇar* (*nar̲r̲iṇai* 310: 9). Before cultivation became the normative occupation of *marutam*, the people of this *tiṇai* hunted (*akanān̲ūr̲u* 196: 4; *kur̲untokai* 258: 4–6) or gathered (*akanān̲ūr̲u* 116: 1–2) their food. Even those who were called *uḻavar* (or those who ploughed the land) hunted animals for their meat (*pur̲anān̲ūr̲u* 395: 2–5), demonstrating that they were foragers before they relied entirely on cultivation.[8] Cultural anthropology also avers that "gathering, hunting and fishing existed long before herding or cultivation" (Herskovits 124–125; Singaravelu 23). Though Graeber and Wengrow contest this "original sequence," their arguments problematize rather than invalidate it (446–455).

Despite evidence of primitive cultivation, such as slash and burn in the mountains and scrubland, and horticulture in the scrubland and the riverine plains, the *tiṇai* people seem to have relied, to a large extent, on food from the wild.[9] In short, food was predominantly gathered and hunted rather than cultivated in the pre-state society of the southern peninsula. This is true of the tribal people who continue to practice the lifestyle of the *tiṇai* people. For example, the present-day Bhil[10] tribe in Gujarat consumes ninety-five different foods, of which only thirty-seven are cultivated and three domesticated, the remaining being either gathered or hunted (Bhattacharjee et al. 217). Three-fourths of the food of the Dravidian tribe, the Kondh, in Odisha, is sourced directly from the forest (Mahapatra) without resorting to cultivation. It is no surprise that the tribal people do not take to cultivation unless they are forced to because they know there are numerous wild plants and animals in the forest that are edible. The Onge on the Andaman Islands is a tribe that did not practice cultivation in any form (Randhawa 96) until the 1970s, because until then their way of life had not been disrupted by any external forces, whereas the Tamil *tiṇai* people were foraging and practicing primitive cultivation in the *caṅkam* age. However, *caṅkam* literature reveals an earlier *tiṇai* way of life, namely, foraging, which was gradually abandoned, even as the poets were documenting it. While it is quite easy to see in *caṅkam* literature only the transitional surface stratum of the *tiṇai* way of life, which was rapidly acquiring the features of sedentarism, it takes quite a bit of effort to peer beneath the surface and see the buried stratum of a lifestyle based on foraging. Here, we see not one single Tamil food culture but five different ones. Diversity in food culture was possible because the people of the *tiṇai* knew which animals and plants were edible in their own *tiṇai*. Recent ethnobiological studies have put all these *tiṇai* people together under the rubric of "tribal," and have come up with interesting statistical data pertaining to their food culture. According to one such study, out of the 45,000 species of wild plants in India, about 3,900 are used by tribal people as food, including 145 roots and tubers, 521 leafy vegetables, 101 bulbs and flowers, and 647 fruits (Rai and Nath).

Among all the plant foods, *nel* is often singled out as the most important.[11] In the words of Singaravelu,

> the most important cereal would seem to have been paddy-rice, for it was not only the most nourishing but also it could be made into a kind of beer known as *tōppi* ... The classical Tamil poetry has evidence to show that rice-paddy in one form or the other was widely distributed in various regions of the ancient Tamil country.
>
> (26)

It is hard to believe that just one cereal from among hundreds of plant foods available in a *tiṇai* could monopolize and become a "food monarch." Those who patronize such food imperialism must take into account the multiple meanings of the words related to paddy-rice: *nel*, *ari*/*arici*, and *cōṟu*. *nel* was a generic name for the seed of grasses including bamboo (*vetiriṉ nel*, *puṟanāṉūṟu* 109: 4; *kuṟuntokai* 42: 7; *kaḻai vaḷar nel*, *malaipaṭukaṭām* 180; *akanāṉūṟu* 107: 7) and paddy (*cennel*, *akanāṉūṟu* 303: 12; *veṇṇel*, *akanāṉūṟu* 236: 4).

Like *nel*, *ari* or *arici* or husked grain was also the common name, not only for the grain of paddy (*peruñc cennelliṉ terikoḷ arici*, *perump āṇāṟṟuppaṭai* 473–474), but also for *tiṉai* (TL), *varaku* (*akanāṉūṟu* 394: 3), *vēy*, a species of bamboo (*vēykoḷ arici*, *malaipaṭukaṭām* 435), and a kind of grass seed (*allip paṭūum pul*, *puṟanāṉūṟu* 248: 5, avvai turaicāmi commentary).

Even the term, *cōṟu*, which means pith (*tāḻaic cōṟu*, *kuṟuntokai* 335: 5), and the cooked grain of different species of bamboo, millet, and paddy (*puṟanāṉūṟu* 61: 5), was not restricted to cooked rice. The derivative *peruñcōṟu* offers insights into the role of rice in *tiṇai* society. It was an offering of cooked meat and cereal (*naṟṟiṇai* 281: 6; not unlike modern *biriyani*) made to the ancestor (makātēvaṉ 25) and, in this respect, it could well be a ritual celebrating *kula teyvam* (clan deity). Besides the ancestral spirit being, other minor spirit beings also, supposedly, participated in this ritual (*akanāṉūṟu* 233: 10). We learn that before the human celebrants partook of the food, the crows were fed. Although the crows are natural beings, they were (and are) believed to be representatives of the ancestors (*naṟṟiṇai* 281: 4–6, comm. piṉṉattūr nārāyaṇacāmi; *naṟṟiṇai* 367: 1–6; *patiṟṟuppattu* 30: 33–44; *tolkāppiyam* III. 2.8. comm. nacciṉārkkiṉiyar).

As a part of the *puṟam* domain of *tiṇai*, it was a ritual performed on the eve of combat (*tolkāppiyam* III. 2.8) when the chieftain or king offered a "sumptuous feast" (*akanāṉūṟu* 233: 7–9) to his soldiers, presumably with the intention of invoking the blessing of the ancestor of the clan that was contemplating combat. As *cōṟu* meant cooked grain of cereal grasses, like millet and paddy, *peruñcōṟu* could have originally been made from the staple cereal of the respective *tiṇai*.

Evidently, *nel*, *arici*, and *cōṟu* were common terms for unhusked, husked, and cooked forms of millet and paddy. Their meanings are context-dependent. Therefore, they did not denote only paddy, nor was paddy the staple food even in *marutam tiṇai* (Sivathamby 69). Evidently, the indigenous inhabitants of *marutam tiṇai* gathered rice from the wild (*akanāṉūṟu* 116: 1–2; Jenks; Marton 29) along with the other food they foraged. In *neytal tiṇai* also, rice was gathered from the wild (*aiṅkuṟunūṟu* 190: 1–2; *naṟṟiṇai* 195: 6–8). If wild rice first occurred in the eastern coast of India, as Sharma argues,[12] rice consumption could have originated in *neytal* before it was domesticated in *marutam*. Further, the *tiṇai* people seem to have eaten raw but ground grains before they consumed them in their cooked form (Singaravelu 26). Raw ground millet mixed with honey seems to have been a favorite with the people of *kuriñci*. Grains were also dried on rocks before they were eaten (*kuṟuntokai* 335: 2; *naṟṟiṇai* 344: 11–12; *paṭṭiṉappālai* 22; Singaravelu 26–27).[13] *tuṭavar* (*tōṭar*/Toda) of *nīlakiri* (Nilgris) seem to have consumed raw food until very recently (kuṇacēkaraṉ 15).

To say that a community subsisted on a particular food item is to say that each enjoyed an intimate kinship with the land and understood its natural cycles, rhythms, and resonances. Hunting or gathering was not a mere occupation but a vocation, a response to the call of the land. Unlike the residents of kāvirippūmpaṭṭiṉam, who had come together as if congregating for a festival (*paṭṭiṉappālai* 213–218; cf. Cremona 272) from several places in order to make a living, native *tiṇai* communities lived-in-place (Berg and Dasmann 217–220) in their respective *tiṇai*. People who stood in convivial relationship to each other in a state society like kāvirippūmpaṭṭiṉam owned, bought, and sold food, whereas those who enjoyed kinship relations in *tiṇai* society found or bartered food. In the former, the food was ranked by means of its exchange value and, therefore, homoarchic (or rigidly ranked in one way; Bondarenko 8), whereas in the latter, it was heterarchic because its value was unranked and context-dependent (Crumley 3; Venkata Subramanian 36). This is particularly evident in the most primitive form of barter wherein the value of the article exchanged was not predetermined but depended on the need of the parties who bartered. For example, the dwellers of *pālai* bartered (captured) milch animals for toddy (*perumpāṇāṟṟuppaṭai* 141). By this primitive economic logic, a buffalo was more valuable than gold (*perumpāṇāṟṟuppaṭai* 164–165).

Food Hierarchy

The absence of a predetermined value of entities ensured a relationship between people and their world that was complex, both egalitarian and dominant at the same time. Such a relationship was not unlike kinship. But when dominance prevailed over equality without eliminating the latter, relations among the members of the *tiṇai* community were "hierarchic." In other words, the network of relations in a hierarchic *tiṇai* or *nayak koṭuntiṇai* (literally, flexibly bent *tiṇai*) is ranked but it is only a temporary state of affairs (Bondarenko 8; Crumley 2–4).

At this stage, both foraging and cultivation coexisted. While hunters employed trained dogs to find food (*puṟanāṉūṟu* 33: 1–2), shepherds lived off their domesticated animals, and cultivators who ploughed their fields and lived in big houses harvested *veṇṇel* (*puṟanāṉūṟu* 33: 4–6). *pāṇar* foraged for their food and bartered *varāl* and *keṭiṟu* fish for *veṇṇel* (*aiṅkuṟunūṟu* 48: 1–3), and *perumpayiṟu* (*aiṅkuṟunūṟu* 47: 1–3) from the *marutam* people because they did not practice any form of cultivation. However, foraging and the food obtained by foraging, to some extent, contributed, eventually, to the hierarchization of the social status of these people.

Hierarchic relations are also evident in temporary domestication. When humans benefited from some wild plants and animals, they partially domesticated them. In the patches of land where plants other than paddy grew, they sowed and harvested paddy (*naṟṟiṇai* 190: 5–6). They probably isolated some wild buffalos for their milk and meat. The food that partial domestication yielded was special and gained importance because it was available whenever it was needed.

Soon, the partially domesticated food became the principal food of the *tinai* where it was available. With proper domestication of cereal grass, millet became the principal food in *kuṟiñci* and *mullai*, and rice in *marutam* (vēṅkaṭacāmi, *uṇavu nūl* 13).[14] Although humans knew about the edibility of meat even during the Pleistocene period, they did not regard it as a principal food. Later, they ascribed that status to cereal because it was the least individuated, that is, null food category, like the null morpheme in linguistics. With maximal neutral properties, the principal food grain allows the properties of the other food categories, like meat and vegetables, to stand out. Cooked millet and rice are principal foods because they allow the other foodstuffs to become dominant. A principal food is consumed in greater quantity, not because it is tastier than the subsidiary meat or vegetables, but because it is more tasteless than them.

The concept of the principal food contributes to the hierarchization of food, a type of praxis and structure similar to the structure of the society in which such food practice is found. But the relationship between the principal and other foods is more like the relationship between background and foreground than like that between the stratified social groups (like castes) of a state society.

Food plays a decisive role in the redefinition of labor in the state society. As it is no longer duty or social obligation but a remunerable or tradable entity, it is defined in terms of food. Hence, the wage (*kūli*, *akanāṉūṟu* 301: 4–5) for remunerable work is food grain (*kūlam*).[15] As cereal grass was not the principal food in *neytal*, salt became the wage standard there. Reportedly, only grain (*kūlam*) served as a wage or *kūli* up until the 1960s when (primitive) industrialization of Indian agriculture put an end to this long-lasting practice with the introduction of cash (Kumar-Range 57; Stephen 105). While *kūli* lasted, it was the most valuable wage standard in all *tiṇaikaḷ* except *neytal*. According to James C. Scott, cereal grains were preferred to legumes, tubers, and starch plants for purposes of state administration because the former have better state-adapted qualities such as visibility, divisibility, accessibility, storability, transportability, and "rationability" (Chapter 4). By privileging, however temporarily, one food over the others, the remunerative system (*kūli*) of the state was not unlike the structure of the hierarchic state in which such an economic practice existed.

Rice Homoarchy

The flexibly ranked hierarchic state soon turned into a *nayamil koṭuntiṇai* (literally, an inflexibly bent *tiṇai*), a rigidly stratified one (Scott, Chapter 5). Such a state is based on a system, which, according to Bondarenko, is not a hierarchy but a homoarchy (Selvamony, "Vernacular..." 194). In a hierarchic system, the relata could shift positions, making the ranking flexible. But a homoarchic system does not allow for any shuffling of positions. For example, the principal food of a single *tiṇai* now becomes the most important one in all *tiṇaikaḷ*—culturally and economically.

Rice became the principal food of *marutam* when wild rice was fully domesticated. Now it was cultivated on a separate patch of land (*aiṅkuṟunūṟu* 27: 1; *puṟanāṉūṟu* 209: 2; 391: 21). Recently, the carbonized paddy, which was discovered in a burial urn at civakalai in Tamil Nadu, was dated to 1155 BCE (Sundararaju). On the basis of this archaeological evidence, we may surmise that paddy was probably cultivated along the banks of porunai or tāmiraparaṇi river from the twelfth century BCE onwards. But this does not necessarily mean that paddy was so widely cultivated as to supersede other foodstuffs and alter the dietary patterns of the people of the peninsula in much the same way as it was from the time of karikālaṉ. Around this time, paddy-rice became the dominant food grain (Nilakanta Sastri 89; paramēcuvari 86); it was the only acceptable cereal for making *peruñcōṟu*, and it became the wage standard in all *tiṇaikaḷ* except *neytal*. In the latter, salt continued to be the wage standard. Therefore, both paddy and salt were treated as equivalent standards (*akanāṉūṟu* 140: 7). This is evident in the new word, *campaḷam*, which replaced the earlier one, *kūli*. Literally, *campaḷam* means paddy and salt (*campu*, variant of *campā*, a (preferred) variety of paddy + *aḷam*, salt = *campaḷam*, paddy and salt, salary; see Eng. salary, from Lat. *sal*, salt; iḷaṅkumaraṉ 110; Kumar-Range 62; *pāvāṇar* 22; Sundaram and Mohanasundaram 68–73). The fact that salt was given along with *campā* paddy shows that *campaḷam* was the wage standard of state society, not *tiṇai* society. Paddy may be a welcome wage for an inhabitant of *neytal tiṇai* but not salt. *campā* paddy and salt were considered the standard wage for all because rice had already become the staple grain and salt had become a necessary food ingredient for people of all *tiṇaikaḷ*.

The importance of rice led to the creation of settlements around the areas where it was cultivated (*akanāṉūṟu* 201: 12–13; 220: 13, 18; 6: 5; 96: 13–14; 166: 4; *puṟanāṉūṟu* 24: 22; 379: 6; 385: 9; turai araṅkacāmi 306). One of the phrases a poet uses to describe one such settlement, namely, "the village of superior variety of paddy" (*uyar nelliṉ ūr*, *maturaikkāñci* 87–88) shows two things: the preeminence of paddy among other food items, as well as the superiority of a particular variety of paddy. This variety is *cāli*, and the village named after it is known both as nellūr and cāliyūr (commentary of perumaḻaippulavar).

Contesting the predominance of paddy, the poet mōcikīraṉār sang: *nellum uyiraṉṟē nīrum uyiraṉṟē/maṉṉaṉ uyirttē malartalai yulakam* (*puṟanāṉūṟu* 186: 1–2) [Neither is paddy life nor is water/For the wide world, the king is life]. The term *nel* has attained semantic restriction because it now denotes only paddy and nothing else, as it did before. In other words, *nel* is rigidly ranked now in relation to the other food items. There is restriction not only of semantics and food but also of the definition of the state. Earlier, the principal constituents of the state were rain, water bodies, mountain, and fort (*tirukkuṟaḷ* 737), but now it is paddy cultivation, as the following song of a medieval poet tells us:

> As the field bund rises, rises water,
> As water rises, rises paddy,
> As paddy rises, rise the people,
> As people rise, does the scepter,
> As the scepter rises, does the king.
> (author's translation)
>
> [*varappuyara nīr uyarum,*
> *nīr uyara nel uyarum,*
> *nel uyarak kuṭi uyarum,*
> *kuṭi uyarak kōl uyarum,*
> *kōl uyark kō uyarum.*]

Avowedly, the poet is compelled to attribute the king precedence over paddy because extensive paddy cultivation has been instrumental in the formation of the state.

The dominance of paddy-rice was possible through monoculture, which changed the heterarchic ecosystem of the land of cōḻar into a homoarchic one.[16] In other words, the basic structure of the praxis—monocultural agriculture or monarchic political culture—of the *nayamil koṭuntiṇai* is rigid hierarchy (Shiva 1–4). By inflexibly subordinating political opposition, monarchic politics could practice monocultural agriculture and project it as if it were the best option for the well-being of the state. This was inevitable, as the "Early Tamil monarchic kingdoms were located in the major rice producing areas" (Sivathamby 51). Such ideology and politics sustained the homoarchic state that built itself upon the anthropocenic political economy of karikālaṉ.

Rice Homeoarchy

In order to strengthen and expand his kingdom, karikālaṉ launched an ambitious project of extensive irrigated paddy cultivation in the peninsula around 300 BCE (vēlāyutam and cīṉivācaṉ 15). By taking advantage of the largest river, kāviri, which had been flowing through his kingdom since 2300 BCE (Deivanayagam 652–660; Ramasamy et al. 1611; Thirumalai 100–104), karikālaṉ built *kallaṇai* in order to divert water "from the river bed into channels that watered widespread paddy fields" (Bijker 111; Deivanayagam and Paranthaman 70; Ludden 21; Martin), which could produce a thousand *kalam* or 28,300 kilos of paddy per *vēli* (6.5 acres; Robb et al. 207; *porunarāṟṟuppaṭai* 245–48; *puṟanāṉūṟu* 391: 21) in the wetlands of the delta, probably irrigated by the veṇṇāṟu and kāviri (Jayaraman).[17] Although we do not know how many *vēlikaḷ* were brought under the plough by karikālaṉ, we would not be far off the mark if we surmised that a good part of present-day Tiruvarur and Nagappattinam districts were irrigated by *kallaṇai* (Jayaraman).

The wealth his state produced was traded with distant lands and to facilitate trade, he shifted his capital from the inland town of uṟaiyūr to the port town of kāvirippūmpaṭṭiṉam (*paṭṭiṉappālai* 283–86; vēṅkaṭacāmi, *paḻankālat tamiḻar vāṇikam*; "*caṅka kālattuk* kāvirippūmpaṭṭiṉam"; pārttacārati; vēṅkaṭarāma ayyar). This town became the center of pre-medieval Tamil trade with other nations, such as īḻam (Sri Lanka) and kāḻakam (Myanmar) (*paṭṭiṉappālai* 191; cf. Mukund ix). With the revenue raised from rice production and trade, karikālaṉ established a kingdom that asserted its hegemony over his rivals, pāṇṭiyar and cērar, in the southern peninsula and also over northern India. His kingdom laid the foundations for the medieval Asian empire of cōḻar. The role of rice in the making of the continental polity of cōḻar cannot be underestimated.

Anthropocenic state society cannot be described adequately by means of the existing notions of hierarchy and homoarchy. Both presume ranking among the relata and, therefore, the persistence of more than one relatum in the mode of relationship at any given point of time. But a state is a type of relationship in which one relatum assumes greater power than the others and seeks to oust and eliminate the other relata. Although the ranked relational mode (either in its hierarchic or homoarchic form) is the given one, it soon yields to a condition of unranking through elimination. Theoretically, a state could be a ranked relational system but, practically, it is a system already erasing ranking.

Such a relational mode in which one of the relata seeks to eliminate the other(s), may be called "homeoarchy." The key idea here is power, evident in the Greek root word, *-arkhia*, or rule, from which the English form, *-archic* derives. The initial element "homeo" qualifies this power as that "of the same kind." The different modes of power of humans and non-humans evident in heterarchic primal society are now reduced to a single mode—that of the humans. In other words, different agential modes of power now concentrate on a single agent, leaving the other agents powerless and non-dominant. As the riverine plain was the dominant agricultural ecoregion in the homeoarchic state, the other non-dominant ecoregions were "invisibilized." If agriculture dominated gathering and hunting in the homoarchic state, the latter almost disappeared from the homeoarchic state.

karikālaṉ's homeoarchic rice kingdom was built on land acquired by eliminating forests and scrubland (*paṭṭiṉappālai* 283). In other words, he used nature (rice) to eliminate nature (forest). While the state he built relied entirely on river water that flowed from the mountains of kuṭaku (Kodagu), he persisted in cutting down the forests necessary to cause rain. He inaugurated large-scale monoculture and established food homogeneity in the southern peninsula. Rice is now seen more as culture than as nature. As culture it was hominized even when it fed the monarch's elephants (*patikam* of the third decad of *patiṟṟuppattu*) because the elephants were, after all, weapons of war (Trautman 50–70), no longer natural and wild beings. Denaturization of nature is tantamount to elimination of the nature of nature.

Rice monoculture sought to eliminate not only nature but also the supernatural. Destruction of forest land meant destruction of the habitat of the *tiṇai* people and their ancestral spirit beings that dwelt in those habitats. Even as rice monoculture destroyed heterarchic foods of all habitats (collectively called *kāṭu*) other than *nāṭu* to create the food of the inhabitants of *nāṭu*, the rice state discarded the diverse clan deities (*kula teyvaṅkaḷ*) and the *tiṇai* deity (*vēntaṉ*) to create the monotheos, a *perunteyvam* (major deity) of the state, namely, viṇṇavar kōmāṉ (*cilap.* I.5.240), later called intiraṉ.

Homeoarchic state is inseparable from homeoarchic food. The latter was possible only in the wetlands because only in this land could humans control food production maximally. The dry land depended on rainfall, over which pre-modern humans had no control. Therefore, the poet kuṭapulaviyaṉār counseled king pāṇṭiyaṉ neṭuñceḻiyaṉ that even if a vast territory of dry land were under the rule of a king, it would not serve his purpose unless he had access to adequate quantities of water (*puṟanāṉūṟu* 18: 23–25). A monarch's most compelling desire is to expand his territory and become the sole ruler of the whole world (*oru ni ākal vēṇṭiṉum*, *puṟanāṉūṟu* 18: 15) by defeating all opponents. The relationship between a sole ruler and the other rulers is neither hierarchy nor unchangeable ranked relations, called homoarchy, but homeoarchy, in which opposition is eliminated. To achieve his purpose of homeoarchic rule, the monarch should, according to kuṭapulaviyaṉār, ensure a perennial supply of water required to produce food by storing water in low-lying areas (*puṟanāṉūṟu* 18: 27–30). kuṭapulaviyaṉār's strategy was adopted to the greatest advantage only in the kingdom of cōḻar when karikālaṉ built *kallaṇai* (Sivathamby 54, 69). With perennial water supply (through irrigation), karikālaṉ could also produce food perennially.

Of all the food crops that could be raised by irrigated cultivation, paddy proved to be the best choice because rice had already become the staple in northern India, especially in the Gangetic plain. According to the Allchins, "the cultivation of rice was a feature of the rise of the Ganges civilization" (1993, 265). As the Tamil monarchs, traders, scholars, and probably others had some acquaintance with northern India, Ganges civilization could have served as a model for karikālan̲, who himself undertook a successful expedition to northern India (Nilakanta Sastri 36). In the formation of his state, the contribution of the Indus Valley people, who had migrated southward at the time of the decline of Indus culture (Gurumurthy 108; makātēvan̲ 9–10, 15), and other migrants from Gujarat and the regions adjoining the Ganges and Yamuna, must have been significant (makātēvan̲ 9–10). The immigrants could have played their own part in the rise of the three monarchies, the iron-based civilization, and the Megalithic Age in the southern peninsula (makātēvan̲ 9–10; Sivathamby 52). Further, the Brahmins who came to the peninsula from the Gangetic plains could have also championed the cause of rice monism (Allchin & Allchin 1996, 315, 356; 1993, 265). Although they were basically pastoralists who relished milk and dairy products, they had already grown accustomed to rice on the Gangetic plains and tried to emulate vegetarianism, teetotalism, scholarly pursuits, and several other cultural practices of the Jains (Selvamony, "*tiNai*" 45; "Is Homing Spiritual Praxis?"). Therefore, they could have impressed upon the rulers in the peninsula why the gods should be fed rice and milk rather than meat, toddy, and other foodstuffs. Until paddy-rice and dairy became the main diet of the gods, the particular variety of *nel* (cereal grass seed of millet or paddy) available in a given ecoregion was used in worship. For example, in the scrubland, millet grain (generically, *nel*) and jasmine flowers (*mullai*) were offered to the gods (*mullaippāṭṭu* 8; *neṭunalvāṭai* 43). In the mountains, old women who performed the ritual called *kaṭṭu* used *nel* of bamboo or cane (*nar̲r̲iṇai* 288: 6).

But Aryanization of the food culture of the southern peninsula was effectively achieved by the tabooing of meat in mainstream religious rituals. Meat prohibition in rituals discriminated against indigenous food and spiritual traditions. Effectively, alien Aryan scrubland culture hybridized with riverine rice culture overwhelmed the native cultural diversity of different ecoregions. Ludden puts it in the following manner: "Tamils turned the watery lowlands depicted in the *caṅkam* verse into irrigated, paddy-growing centers of civilization, ordered according to Brahmanical ideology and around deity worship in temples" (181; Stein 69). For example, millet could not substitute paddy-rice in *peruñcōr̲u* any more because the latter had already eliminated the worthiness of millet as ritual food. The high point of Gramscian hegemony is evident in the consensus with regard to the rice-centricity of Tamil culture. Rice-centered Tamil identity was already in the making during karikālan̲'s time, but it found loud articulation in the time of his successors—namely, the medieval cōl̲ar, who offered rice to their gods first when the fields were ready for harvest (*putiyitu/putiyīṭu*, Subramaniam 1467; "History and Origin of Pongal Festival"). This practice could explain why *poṅkal* is a rice-centered harvest festival and why it has, as the typical Tamil festival, marginalized the festivals and identities of other *tiṇaikaḷ*.

The rice-centered festival was given special privileges by the medieval cōḻar because *nel* was the major food mentioned in the medieval temple inscriptions of South India, and this shows how it sustained the economy of the South Indian temple (Swaminathan 140, 148, 150, 153, 155–156; paramēcuvari 88). It determined the importance of wetland necessary for temple maintenance. By being the central economic resource of temple maintenance, *nel*, the most crucial homeoarchic cereal, determined the rice-centered culture of the peninsula.

In the shaping of riverine rice culture, the contribution of Aryan immigrants was of no small importance. The Aryan preference for rice was encouraged by the local rulers who made tax-free land gifts, called Brahmadeya, to Brahmins. The Brahmadeya was often located near an irrigation facility because it was predominantly wetland for raising paddy (Stein 141–172). A ruler of the land of cērar, celvakkaṭuṅkō vāḻiyātaṉ, gifted, for the worship of māya vaṇṇaṉ, a settlement called ōkantūr where a variety of paddy called *ōttira nel*, used in ritual (*patikam* of the seventh decad of *patiṟṟuppattu*) was grown. The alternative name of this variety of paddy, *irācāṉṉam*, betrays the prestige paddy, in general, and *ōttira nel*, in particular, enjoyed in Aryanized rituals in the Tamil countryside. The former variety, according to Balasubramanian, was consumed mainly by rich people (53).

Rice-producing wetland also supported cattle for their milk and ghee, major ingredients in temple rituals along with rice. Although the royal text would say the land was gifted to the god, in reality, the beneficiaries were privileged humans. In this way, the local rulers perpetuated the hegemony of the rice–dairy culture that suppressed indigenous food diversity. This strange coalition of rice and dairy patronized one element from *marutam* and another from *mullai* and suppressed the other foods like meat of *mullai, kuṟiñci, pālai,* and *marutam*, millets of *mullai,* and seafood of *neytal*.

Neo-*tiṇai*cene

By eliminating other cereal grasses and greenery, rice is on a path to self-destruction. Today, the forested area in the Cauvery Delta Zone Districts (Thanjavur, Thiruvarur, and Nagapattinam) is only 24.19% ("TN Districtwise Profile").[18] Rice monoculture has shrunk and impoverished the kāviri delta over the years. A major concern of the South Indian economy today is the fact that the delta has shrunk by twenty percent and deteriorated into wasteland thirteen-fold (Janakarajan; Shaji). Due to lack of water in the river, the delta itself has disappeared, resulting in the ingression of seawater and salination of arable land (Janakarajan). As the dams upstream have blocked the free flow of sediment into the delta, the soil has been considerably impoverished by an acute decrease in sedimentary deposits. Due to siltation in the dams, their storage capacity has decreased progressively (Shaji). In Papanasan Taluk of Thanjavur district, in the last twenty-five years, paddy land has been used for cultivating other crops or left fallow, resulting in the shrinking of the average net sown area for paddy (Punithavathi and Baskaran 4).

In short, land and water, which favored the emergence of rice as the principal cereal two millennia ago, now, in the epoch of the Anthropocene, have been degraded to such an extent that the very production of rice is jeopardized. Rice has proven to be the enemy of rice. Scientifically developed new varieties of rice have only eliminated their indigenous counterparts. In Richharia's words,

> The neglect of the bulk of indigenous varieties is one of the main causes of stagnation in rice productivity in India, on the whole, except in some selected areas where inputs and facilities are available in abundance. The exclusive dependence on High Yielding Varieties (HYVs) with the exotic dwarfing gene has not only brought about genetic uniformity but also vulnerability to diseases and pests. It is, therefore, self-evident, that the only way to promote improvements in rice productivity in the long run is to maintain and utilize genetic diversity existing in the indigenous rice cultivars.
>
> (Krishnan and Ghosal 28)

The propagation of the genetically modified varieties of paddy has proved detrimental to the habitat of paddy itself. The toxic chemicals in pesticides, weedicides, and fungicides necessary to sustain the artificial varieties have degraded land and water. As the soil becomes "addicted" to fertilizers, it needs increased quantities of fertilizers, which only further impoverish and contaminate the soil. The intensive chemical agriculture initiated by the Green Revolution of the 1960s (Sriram 174–199) has invigorated the rice Anthropocene inaugurated by karikālaṉ.

As long as the goal is rice monism, the monocultural crop will suppress food diversity (Wahlqvist 304–308), which in turn will undermine cultural and natural diversity (Selvamony, "Monistic Elimination of Nature"). Suppression of diversity and heterarchy will result in homeoarchy, which involves overexploitation of Nature, greater detrimental impact on the earth, and the persistence of the Anthropocene. Therefore, purposeful reversal of the present "rice crisis" requires making conditions favorable for ending rice monism and the Anthropocene. Rice monism cannot be separated from food monism and, ultimately, from the supremacy of *marutam* (which amounts to *tiṇai* monism) and its way of life. Overvaluation of *marutam* meant disrupting its original heterarchic relation between humans and the ecosystem in order to facilitate the commencement of the Anthropocene. The anthropocenic *marutam* way of life thrived on rice monism, only to degrade the very sources sustaining it.

Rice monism is another name for food fundamentalism (Pretty 46). Often fundamentalism cohabits with destructive violence. It will be profitable to study how rice monism contributes to negative violence.

To effectively end the epoch of rice monism, the people of the southern Indian peninsula need to acknowledge the primordiality and necessity of the opposite of fundamentalism, namely, diversity in food indigenous to each *tiṇai*, so that they can usher in the *tiṇai*cene that preceded the Holocene. But the *tiṇai*cene that succeeds the Anthropocene can only be Neo-*tiṇai*cene or *tiṇai*cene with appropriate modifications, which do not disrupt the basic nature of the *tiṇai*. The dawning of the Neo-*tiṇai*cene can only occur with the restoration of *tiṇai* food diversity.

Notes

1 The author's neologisms, "anthropotreptic" and "allotreptic," are modeled on the already existing word, "protreptic," which means "intended to persuade" (Gk. *pro*, before + *trepein*, to turn = protreptic).

2 Scientists can only describe the Anthropocene by enumerating its characteristics. From select data, the scientist constructs (about the epoch) finding(s) that can only be quantitative, not qualitative. The modern, western scientific method would allow the scientist to specify the quantity of carbon in the atmosphere but not go into its implications for the wellbeing of humans and entities other than humans. Therefore, we can turn to the scientists for knowledge about what the Anthropocene is, but not for an understanding of its implications for all life forms. The disciplines of the non-scientists allow them to engage methodically with the implications of the Anthropocene while relying on the description provided by the scientists. Dismissal of science on the part of non-scientists is only at the cost of their credibility. But science (including climate science), on the contrary, can afford to ignore the humanities and social sciences with no loss of credibility on its part, and this justifies the avoidance of discussion of the implications of the Anthropocene in vintage science. This means discussion of the implications of the Anthropocene (even when a non-scientist attempts to rely on scientific findings regarding the Anthropocene) can only be "non-scientific" (to the scientist), however academically rigorous it is. For this reason, the non-scientist does not refrain from relying on science either.

3 Except for the medieval alchemic experiments in the transmutation of metals, the first modern scientific attempt at synthesizing the first synthetic organometallic compound, cacodyl oxide, is that of Grassicourt in 1757 (just six years prior to the invention of the steam engine by Watt and Boulton).

4 karikālaṉ is the most prominent king of a Tamil dynasty called "Early cōḻar," whose capital was uṟaiyūr, which is now a part of the city, Tiruchirappalli, that stands on the southern banks of the river kaviri. Scholars are not agreed on the dates for karikālaṉ. According to vēlāyutam and cīṉivācaṉ (15), he ruled the Tamil country around 300 BCE. See also cuppiramaṇiya āccāriyār, ulakanāta piḷḷai, and nirañcaṉātēvi.

5 Although the focus of this chapter is on the rice culture of cōḻar, the Anthropocene discussed here is that of the entire southern peninsula. Stein (4) explains the link between cōḻar and the southern peninsula in the following manner: "the Chola period is a necessary starting point for any longitudinal interest in the agrarian system of the Tamil plain and its extension into the interior upland of modern Salem, Coimbatore, portions of the Arcots, and major portions of the Karnataka plateau and the Andhra plain."

6 Meat as food: *puṟanāṉūṟu* 113:1; 379:8; *malaipaṭukaṭām* 175, 176, 508; *kuṟuntokai* 169: 4; *naṟṟiṇai* 120:5; *akanāṉūṟu* 216: 1-4, *perumpāṇāṟṟuppaṭai* 256; 340–345; *cirupāṇāṟṟuppaṭai* 156–163, 177, 194–195; *porunarāṟṟuppaṭai* 217; *aiṅkuṟunūṟu*, 364: 1.

Plant food: *puṟanāṉūṟu* 225: 1–3; 335: 5, 399: 1–12, 16; *aiṅkuṟunūṟu* 51: 3; *puṟanāṉūṟu* 109: 4; *malaipaṭukaṭām* 115, 121, 425–426; *aiṅkuṟunūṟu* 58: 1; *kuṟiñcippāṭṭu* 204–206; *perumpāṇāṟṟuppaṭai* 192–195, 254.

Beverages: *puṟanāṉūṟu* 114: 4; *maturaikkāñci* 137; 23; *akanāṉūṟu* 216: 3, 184: 14, 394: 11; *kuṟiñcippāṭṭu* 188–189; *perumpāṇāṟṟuppaṭai* 156–160, 280–281; *naṟṟiṇai* 168: 2–5; 38: 1–3.

7 Food diversity, in this chapter, denotes variedness of food at the intra-*tiṇai* as well as inter-*tiṇai* levels, which is the opposite of monism rather than uniformity in food. Food monism is based on the idea of a “staple” or basic food. For example, rice as a staple food is an example of food monism. Food uniformity, on the other hand, refers to sameness in the production and consumption of food, which is not the issue problematized in this chapter because food that is diverse can be uniformly produced and consumed for a long time. Food diversity and self-sufficiency in food are not incompatible goals at all. A *tiṇai* can, in principle, continue to be both diverse and self-sufficient with regard to food. What is more, barter, collective production, and public sharing of food need not be perceived as threats to both diversity and self-sufficiency in food. Barter in *tiṇaikaḷ*, we might presume, precedes the buying and selling of food either in its raw or cooked form. Again, food was also shared on public occasions, as the term *uṇṭāṭṭu* (*tolkāppiyam* III.2.3: 8) indicates. Now, does this refer to sharing what is available within a single *tiṇai* or from more than one? If the latter, then *uṇṭāṭṭu*, like barter, makes food from a *tiṇai* other than one's own, available. Further, when food was consumed in public, it was produced collectively. Even collective food production may not be sufficient reason, as Stephen (109) argues, to contest either food self-sufficiency or diversity in *tiṇai*.

8 Just as primitive cultivation and foraging coexisted cheek by jowl, specialization and non-specialization of avocation were also in evidence in *tiṇai*. The singers or *pāṭunar* and the musicians or *pāṇar* were also hunter–gatherers. Even in the state societies we meet up with *pāṇar* who continue to hunt and gather food like their hunter–gatherer ancestors.

9 In *kuriñci*, they hunted wild animals such as wild boar (*puṟanāṉūṟu* 152: 3–4), porcupine (*puṟanāṉūṟu* 374: 11), monitor lizard (*puṟanāṉūṟu* 152: 5), and deer (*puṟanāṉūṟu* 198: 9; 152: 25–26), gathered the grains of bamboo (*malaipaṭukaṭām* 435) and millet (*maturaikkāñci* 291), and wild honey (*naṟṟiṇai* 168: 2–5; *kuṟuntokai* 39: 7–9), and harvested the roots of *vaḷḷi* (*Dioscorea sativa*; Singaravelu 25), ginger, and turmeric (*maturaikkāñci* 287–289). Even today, millet, rather than rice, is the staple food of the hill tribe called *malaiyāḷi* of the kalvarāyaṉ hills of tamiḻ nāṭu (kiruṭṭiṉamūrtti 190, viii), and of the Dravidian tribe of Koya living on the borders of Andhra and Odisha (Misra).

In *mullai* they hunted deer (*pulvāy*, *akanāṉūṟu* 284: 10) and hare (*puṟanāṉūṟu* 34: 11; 396: 17–18) and gathered termites (*akanāṉūṟu* 394: 4–5) and several plant foods: the grains of kodo millet (*akanāṉūṟu* 394: 3), pearl millet (*peru mpāṇāṟṟuppaṭai* 166–168), vegetables like horse gram (*puṟanāṉūṟu* 105: 5),

Indian beans (*puṟanāṉūṟu* 215: 1–5), tamarind (*akanāṉūṟu* 311: 10–11), fruits such as *kaḷā* (*akanāṉūṟu* 394: 1) and wood-apple (*akanāṉūṟu* 394: 1). They consumed goat curd (*akanāṉūṟu* 394: 2), cow ghee (*akanāṉūṟu* 394: 6), milk (*akanāṉūṟu* 394: 11), buttermilk (*perumpāṇāṟṟuppaṭai* 156–160), and honey from *Pongamia glabra* (*puṟanāṉūṟu* 34: 10) and enjoyed their share of toddy too (*ariyal*, *akanāṉūṟu* 184: 14) (muttucāmi 92–95).

pālai dwellers hunted wild boar (*perumpāṇāṟṟuppaṭai* 110), hare (*perum pāṇāṟṟuppaṭai* 115), and monitor lizards (*perumpāṇāṟṟuppaṭai* 132). They netted red-wattled lapwings (*naṟṟiṇai* 212: 1–2) and probably other birds too. They scrounged the meat left over by predatory animals (*akanāṉūṟu* 107: 4–5; *naṟṟiṇai* 43: 3–5), gathered the grains of bamboo (*akanāṉūṟu* 107: 7), *pullarici* (*perumpāṇāṟṟuppaṭai* 94), gooseberries (*akanāṉūṟu* 54: 15), and wood-apples (*naṟṟiṇai* 12: 1; 24:2), and found water in the bark of *ukā* trees (*kuṟuntokai* 274: 1–6).

marutam people hunted land turtles (*aiṅkuṟunūṟu* 81: 1–2; *naṟṟiṇai* 280: 6), freshwater snails (*nantu*, *naṟṟiṇai* 280: 7), freshwater shrimps (*akanāṉūṟu* 96: 1), freshwater fish (*akanāṉūṟu* 196: 2; *naṟṟiṇai* 120: 5), and veal (*naṟṟiṇai* 310: 9). They gathered wild rice that grew among lotus and hairy water lilies (*akanāṉūṟu* 116: 1–2), vegetables like bitter gourd (*akanāṉūṟu* 156: 5), red beans (*aiṅkuṟunūṟu* 47: 3), black-gram (*akanāṉūṟu* 86: 1), tamarind (*aiṅkuṟunūṟu* 51: 3), and sugarcane (*aiṅkuṟunūṟu* 55: 1; 65: 1), and fruits such as mangoes (*aiṅkuṟunūṟu* 61: 1) and *pirappaṅkaṉi* (*akanāṉūṟu* 196: 6). They enjoyed beverages like *naṟavu* (*akanāṉūṟu* 96: 1) and *ariyal* (*kuṟuntokai* 258: 4–5).

The people of *neytal* hunted sharks (*naṟṟiṇai* 111: 6–7; 199: 5–6) and hammerheads (*kuṟuntokai* 304: 4; *naṟṟiṇai* 207: 6–8), the apex predators of the ocean, as well as several other sea animals: prawns (*naṟṟiṇai* 111: 1–2), crabs (*ciṟupāṇāṟṟuppaṭai* 194–195), oysters (*akanāṉūṟu* 280: 11–14), and pearl oysters (*naṟṟiṇai* 87: 6–7). From the backwaters they caught fish such as mackerel (*akanāṉūṟu* 60: 1–4; 3–6) and catfish (*aiṅkuṟunūṟu* 167: 1–2). Palmyrah was the primary source of their vegetable food: the endosperm of the green fruit, the fruit, and the edible sprout from the seed (*puṟanāṉūṟu* 225: 1–5); they also drank a beverage made out of its fruit (*paṭṭiṉappālai* 89; *naṟṟiṇai* 38: 1–3) besides the alcoholic drinks, *tēṟal* (*naṟṟiṇai* 388: 7–9) and *ariyal* (*perumpāṇāṟṟuppaṭai* 280-281). The fruit of the Malabar plum was also a favorite with them (*naṟṟiṇai* 35: 1–7).

10 While scholars agree on the Tamil origin of the name of the tribe, Bhil (*vil*, bow; Naik 14–15; "Bhil"), they may not if one contested the Indo-Aryan affinity of Bhil language. In fact, a thorough relook at the linguistic affinity of Indian languages is necessary for a better understanding of the Indian subcontinent.

11 For the frequency of occurrence of the term *nel* and related terms in *caṅkam* texts, see mātaiyaṉ (25), and for the properties of rice, see campanta mutaliyār. For a history of rice, see Smith and Dilday; Sharma; Marton; for wild rice, see Oka 1974; 1988; Morishima; for black rice, see Carney; Kushwaha.

12 Sharma (4) is of the opinion that the Asian rice species, *Oryza rufipogon* and *Oryza nivara*, grew wildly on the eastern coast of India. He also observes that people must have harvested rice from these species for centuries before

they domesticated them. Sharma, Oka (1974; 1988), and Morishima are of the view that the upland species, *Oryza nivara*, was first domesticated in "present-day Chhattisgarh, western Orissa, Jharkhand, and eastern Uttar Pradesh" (Sharma 5) before it was grown on the Gangetic plains. Although the irrigated cultivation of rice began in the southern Indian peninsula only by 300 BCE, the people of the peninsula had been familiar with rice from very early times. The Greeks borrowed the word for rice from Tamil rather than from any other language because rice or *arici* (which yielded the Greek *Oryza*) was "introduced from India into Europe and it cannot be doubted that we have here the Tamil word *arisi*, rice deprived of the husk, this being the condition in which rice was then, as now, brought up in India for exportation to Europe" (Caldwell 91). It must also be pointed out that *arici* (*akanāṉūṟu* 107: 7) is a variant of the Tamil word, *ari* (*malaipaṭukaṭām* 180), which is probably the earlier word for rice in Tamil. In the Kanyakumari district and in Malayalam, rice is commonly referred to as *ari* (as in the *puttari* ritual of the tribe, *ūrāḷi*, paḻaniccāmai 115–120) rather than *arici* and it has been pointed out by scholars that archaic Tamil words (like *tāḻkkōl*, meaning "key") enjoy currency in those parts of the peninsula rather than anywhere else. It may be pertinent to note that indigenous people in North America also gathered wild rice (Herskovits 148; Jenks).

13 Singaravelu (339) observes that the Tamil word for food, *uṇavu*, derives from the practice of drying cereals and meat, two important food categories, before consuming them. He derives *uṇavu* from the verbal root, *uṇ*-, which, to him, means "parch" or "burn." But, according to Gnana Prakasar, the verbal root means "to put inside," "draw in" (339).

14 It is unfortunate that the notion of cereal being the principal food is not historicized by Tamil scholars; see vēṅkaṭacāmi, *uṇavu nūl* 13.

15 Krishnan and Ghosal (26) point out that the *Jataka*s speak of paddy as payable as wages to a domestic and agricultural worker and as tax to the king; see also *taṇṭulanāli Jataka*.

16 The concept of homoarchy may be profitably compared with Pretty's notion of "monoscape." He speaks of monoscape "as a kind of fundamentalism because it suggests that there is only one way, and no others can be correct. Monoscapes are dysfunctional systems. They are good at one thing, but people do not much care for them. In truth, monoscape is less valuable than it appears, largely because value is captured and claimed by a small number of stakeholders ... By contrast, a polycultural approach accepts differences and the value of the whole" (46).

17 During the time of parāntakaṉ I (907–955 ACE; vēlāyutam), two *vēlikaḷ* yielded 300 *kalaṅkaḷ* of paddy in a growing season, and later, when uttama cōḻaṉ ruled (970–985 ACE; vēlāyutam), three *vēlikaḷ* produced 710 *kalaṅkaḷ* in a year (paramēcuvari 85).

18 Forest cover in Cauvery Delta Zone (Districts):

Name of District	*Geog. Area* (in sq. km)	*Forest* (in sq. km)
Thanjavur	3,415	436(12.77%)
Thiruvarur	2,716	59 (2.17%)
Nagapattinam	2,140	198 (9.25%)
Total	8,271	693(24.19%)

References

Ackerman, Dianne. *The Human Age: The World Shaped By Us*. Headline Publishing Group, 2014.

Allchin, Bridget, and Raymond Allchin. *The Birth of Indian Civilization: India and Pakistan before 500 BC*. Penguin Books, 1993.

Allchin, Bridget, and Raymond Allchin. *The Rise of Civilization in India and Pakistan*. Cambridge University Press, 1996.

Angus, Ian. *Facing the Anthropocene: Fossil Capitalism and the Crisis of the Earth System*. AAKAR Books, 2017.

Balasubramanian, P. "Economy of the Tamils in Sangam Age." *Economic Heritage of the Tamils*, edited by Annie Thomas. International Institute of Tamil Studies, 2007, pp. 53–8.

Berg, Peter, and Raymond F. Dasmann. "Reinhabiting California." *Reinhabiting a Separate Country: A Bioregional Anthology of Northern California*, edited by Peter Berg. Planet Drum Foundation, 1978.

Bhattacharjee, Lalita, Gopa Kothari, Vidya Priya, and Biplab K. Nandi. "The Bhil Food System: Links to Food Security, Nutrition, and Health." *Food and Agriculture Organization of the United Nations*, www.fao.org/tempref/docrep/fao/012/i0370e/i0370e11.pdf.

"Bhil." Tribal Research and Training Institute, Tribal Development Department, Government of Gujarat, https://trti.gujarat.gov.in/bhil.

Bijker, W. E. "Dikes and Dams, Thick with Politics." *Isis*, vol. 98, no. 1, 2007, pp. 109–23.

Bondarenko, D. M. *Homoarchy: A Principle of Culture's Organization: The 13th–19th Centuries Benin Kingdom as a Non-State Supercomplex Society*. KomKniga, 2006, p. 8, www.researchgate.net/publication/220033080_Homoarchy_A_Principle_of_Culture%27s_Organization_The_13th_-_19th_Centuries_Benin_Kingdom_as_a_Non-State_Supercomplex_Society.

Bowden, Brett. "Civilization and its Consequences." *Oxford Handbooks Online*, Feb. 2016, www.oxfordhandbooks.com/view/10.1093/oxfordhb/9780199935307.001.0001/oxfordhb-9780199935307-e-30.

Caldwell, Rt. Rev. Robert. *A Comparative Grammar of the Dravidian or South Indian Family of Languages*. University of Madras, rpt., 1976.

campanta mutaliyār. *cātāraṇa uṇavupporuḷkaḷiṉ kuṇaṅkaḷ* [Qualities of ordinary foods]. 1948.

Carney, Judith A. *Black Rice: The African Origins of Rice Cultivation in the Americas*. Harvard University Press, 2001.

Chakrabarty, Dipesh. "The Climate of History: Four Theses." *University of Victoria*, Winter 2009, www.law.uvic.ca/demcon/2013%20readings/Chakrabarty%20-%20Climate%20of%20History.pdf.

cilappatikāram (*cilap.*). Research notes by u. vē cāminātaiyar. ṭākṭar u. vē. cāminātaiyar, 1978.

Cremona, Vicki Ann. *Carnival and Power: Play and Politics in a Crown Colony*. Palgrave Macmillan, 2018, https://link.springer.com/content/pdf/bbm%3A978-3-319-70656-6%2F1.pdf.

Crumley, Carole L. "Heterarchy and the Analysis of Complex Societies." *AnthroSource*, Jan. 1995, www.researchgate.net/publication/227664129_Heterarchy_and_the_Analysis_of_Complex_Societies.

Crutzen, Paul. "The Anthropocene." *Springer Link*, 2006, https://link.springer.com/chapter/10.1007/3-540-26590-2_3.

cuppiramaṇiya āccāriyār, ve. cu. *karikālar mūvar* [Three persons named karikālaṉ]. aruḷ patippakam, 2011.

Dale, Tom, and Vernon Gill Carter. *Topsoil and Civilization*. University of Oklahoma Press, 1955, https://soilandhealth.org/copyrighted-book/topsoil-and-civilization/.

Deivanayagam, G. "Pre-history of River Kaveri." *Historical Heritage of the Tamils*, edited by S. V. Subramanian and K. D. Thirunavukkarasu. International Institute of Tamil Studies, 2010, pp. 652–9.

Deivanayagam, G., and R. Paranthaman. *Kallanai Kaveri*. akanī veḷiyīṭu, 2012.

Ghosh, Amitav. *The Great Derangement*. Penguin Books, 2016.

Gnana Prakasar, S. *An Etymological and Comparative Lexicon of the Tamil Language*. International Institute of Tamil Studies, 1999.

Graeber, David, and David Wengrow. *The Dawn of Everything: A New History of Humanity*. Allen Lane, 2021.

Gurumurthy, S. "Harappa and Tamil Culture." *Historical Heritage of the Tamils*, edited by S. V. Subramanian and K. D. Thirunavukkarasu. International Institute of Tamil Studies, 2010, pp. 104–13.

Hackett, Sophie, Andrea Kunard, and Urs Stahel, editors. *Anthropocene: Burtynsky, Baichwal, de Pencier*. Goose Lane Editions, 2018.

Harrison, Robert Pogue. *Forests: The Shadow of Civilization*. University of California Press, 1993.

Herskovits, Melville J. *Cultural Anthropology*. IBH Publishing, 1974.

"History and Origin of Pongal Festival." https://festivals.awesomeji.com/pongal/pongal-history.html.

iḷaṅkumaraṉ. *tēvanēyap pāvāṇariṉ collāyvukaḷ* [Word Studies by tēvanēyap pāvāṇar]. ulakat tamiḻārāycci niṟuvaṉam [International Institute of Tamil Studies], 1985.

Janakarajan, S. "Cauvery Faces Manifold Threats in Tamil Nadu," www.downtoearth.org.in/blog/water/cauvery-faces-manifold-threats-in-tamil-nadu-65896.

Jayaraman. "The Delta Region." Lecture. Department of English Studies, Central University of Tamil Nadu, 17 Oct. 2014.

Jenks, A. E. "The Wild Rice Gatherers of the Upper Lakes." *Bureau of American Ethnology*, 19th Annual Report, 1900, pp. 1019–137.

kiruṭṭiṉamūrtti, ko. *kalvarāyaṉ malai makkaḷ* [The people of kalvarāyaṉ hills]. teṉṉārkkāṭu māvaṭṭa āṭcit talaivar veḷiyīṭu, 1992.

Krishnan, Omkhar, and Anjali Ghosal. *Rice: A Study of Literature and Navadanya's Field Experience in Traditional Rice Cultivation*. Navdanya, 1995.

Kritee, Kritee, et al. "High Nitrous Oxide Fluxes from Rice Indicates the Need to Manage Water for Both Long-[Term] and Short-Term Climate Impacts." *Proceedings of the National Academy of Sciences of the United States of America*, vol. 115, no. 39, 25 Sep. 2018, pp. 9720–5, www.pnas.org/content/115/39/9720.

Kumar-Range, Shubh. *Like Paddy in Rock: Local Institutions and Gender Roles in Kolli Hills*. M. S. Swaminathan Research Foundation, 2001.

kuṇacēkaraē, kē. ē. *tamiḻaka malaiyiṉa makkaḷ* [Mountain people of Tamil Nadu]. New Century Book House, 1994.

Kushwaha, U. K. S. *Black Rice: Research, History and Development*. Springer International Publishing, 2016.

Latour, Bruno. *Down To Earth: Politics in the New Climatic Regime*. Translated by Catherine Porter. Polity, 2018.

Ludden, David. *Peasant History in South India*. 2nd ed. Oxford University Press, 1993.

Mahapatra, Basudev. "How Tribal People in Odisha are using Forest Food to keep Malnutrition at Bay." *Huff Post*, 20 Dec. 2017, www.huffingtonpost.in/village-square/how-tribes-in-odisha-are-using-forest-food-to-keep-malnutrition-at-bay_a_23305039/.

makātēvan̠, airāvatam. *cintuveḷip paṇpāṭum caṅka ilakkiyamum* [Indus Valley civilization and *caṅkam* literature]. cemmoḻit tamiḻāyvu mattiya nir̠uvan̠am (Central Institute of Classical Tamil), 2010.

Martin, Rebecca. "Grand Anicut." *Online Historical Database of Civil Infrastructure*, www.thecivilengineer.org/online-historical-database-of-civil-infrastructure/item/382-kallanai-dam-grand-anicut.

Marton, Renee. *Rice: A Global History*. Reaktion Books, 2014.

mātaiyan̠, pe. *caṅka ilakkiyattil vēḷāṇ camutāyam* [Agricultural society in *caṅkam* literature]. 2nd ed. New Century Book House, 2010.

Misra, Snigdha. "Food Culture of Koya Tribe." *Tribal Tribune*, vol. 1, 2018, www.etribaltribune.com/index.php/volume-1/mv1i4/food-culture-of-koya-tribe.

Montgomery, David R. *Dirt: The Erosion of Civilizations*. University of California Press, 2007.

Morishima, H. "Wild plants and domestication." *Biology of Rice*, edited by S. Tsunoda and N. Takahashi. Elsevier, 1984, pp. 3–30.

Mukund, Kanakalatha. *The World of the Tamil Merchant: Pioneers of International Trade*. Penguin Random House, 2012.

muttucāmi, a. *caṅka ilakkiyattil āyar* [Shepherds in *caṅkam* literature]. irāṇi patippakam, 1993.

Naik, T. B. *The Bhils: A Study*. Bharatiya Adimjati Sevak Sangh, 1956, http://ignca.gov.in/Asi_data/5304.pdf.

namaccivāyam, cē. *tamiḻar uṇavu* [Food of the Tamil people]. International Institute of Tamil Studies, 1981.

Nilakanta Sastri, K. A. *The Colas*. University of Madras, 1984.

nirañcan̠ātēvi, ra. *karikāl cōḻan̠*. vikaṭan̠ piracuram, 2012.

Norris, Richard. "Exploring the Environmental Impact of Ancient Civilizations." *Scripps Institution of Oceanography*, 1 Mar. 2017, http://scrippsscholars.ucsd.edu/rnorris/announcements/exploring-environmental-impact-ancient-civilizations.

Oka, H. I. *Origin of Cultivated Rice*. Japan Scientific Society Press, 1988.

———. "Experimental Studies on the Origin of Cultivated Rice." *Genetics*, vol. 78, 1974, pp. 475–86.

paḻan̠iccāmai, mā. *keraḷa ūrāḷip paḻaṅkuṭikaḷin̠ vaḻakkār̠r̠iyal* [The folklore of *ūrāḷikaḷ* of Kerala]. tirukkur̠aḷ patippakam, 2009.

paramēcuvari, po. "*cōḻar kālattu uṇavu*" [Food in the age of cōḻar]. *tamiḻar uṇavu* [Food of the Tamil people], edited by Bhakthavatsala Bharathi. kālaccuvaṭu patippakam, 2011, pp. 82–100.

pārttacārati, nā. "pūmpukār nakar" [pūmpukār town]. *paḻantamiḻar kaṭṭaṭak kalaiyum nakaramaippum* [Ancient Tamil architecture and town planning]. tamiḻp puttakālaiyam, 1992, pp. 155–80.

pāvāṇar, tēvanēyap. *collārāyccik kaṭṭuraikaḷ* [Etymological essays]. South India Saiva Siddhanta Works Publishing Society Tinnevely, 1956.

Pretty, Jules. *Agri-Culture: Reconnecting People, Land and Nature*. Earthscan, 2002.

Punithavathi, J. and R. Baskaran. "Changes in the Cropping Pattern, Crop Concentration, Agricultural Efficiency in Papanasam Taluk, Thanjavur District, Tamil Nadu, India." *Recent Research in Science and Technology*, vol. 2, no. 5, 2010, pp. 1–7, https://updatepublishing.com/journal/index.php/rrst/article/view/430.

Rai, Rajiv, and Vijendra Nath. "The Role of Ethnic and Indigenous People of India and their Culture in the Conservation of Biodiversity." www.fao.org/3/xii/0186-a1.htm.

Ramasamy, S. M., J. Saravanavel, M. G. Yadava, and Rengaswamy Ramesh. "Radiocarbon Dating of Some Palaeochannels in Tamil Nadu and their Significance." *Current Science*, vol. 91, no. 12, Dec. 2006, pp. 1609–13.

Randhawa, M. S. *A History of Agriculture in India*, vol. 1: *Beginning to 12th Century*. Indian Council of Agricultural Research, 1980.

Robb, Peter, Kaoru Sugihara, and Haruka Yanagisawa, editors. *Local Agrarian Societies in Colonial India: Japanese Perspectives*. Curzon Press, 1996.

Schwagerl, Christian. *The Anthropocene: The Human Era and How it Shapes Our Planet*. Synergetic Press, 2014.

Scott, James C. *Against the Grain: A Deep History of the Earliest States*. Yale University Press, 2017, https://astudygroup.files.wordpress.com/2018/01/against-the-grain_-a-deep-histo-james-c-scott.pdf.

Selvamony, Nirmal. "Is Homing Spiritual Praxis?" *Pragmatism, Spirituality and Society*, edited by Ananta Kumar Giri. Palgrave Macmillan, 2021, 275–296.

———. "Vernacular as Homoarchic Mode of Existence." *South Asian Review*, vol. 41, no. 2, 2020, pp. 194–6, https://doi.org/10.1080/02759527.2020.1725225.

———. "Monistic Elimination of Nature." International Conference on "The Wider Significance of Nature," organized by the Forum on Contemporary Theory at Ravenshaw University, Cuttack, Odisha, 20–23 Dec. 2015, unpublished paper.

———. "From the Anthropocene to the Neo-*tiṇai*cene." *Humanities Circle*, vol. 3, no. 2, Winter 2015, pp. 115–30.

———. "The Cries of Water." *Interactions*, Sep. 2014, https://lilainteractions.in/dividing-waters/.

———. "*tiNai* in Primal and Stratified Societies." *Indian Journal of Ecocriticism*, vol. 1, no. 1, 2008, pp. 38–48.

Shaji, K. A. "Kaveri Delta: Shrinking Area and Decreasing Farm Productivity Hit South India's Agricultural Backbone." *Firstpost*, 2020, www.firstpost.com/long-reads/kaveri-delta-shrinking-area-and-decreasing-farm-productivity-hit-south-indias-agricultural-backbone-6371071.html.

Sharma, S. D., editor. *Rice: Origin, Antiquity and History*. CRC Press, 2010, https://doi.org/10.1201/EBK1578086801.

Shiva, Vandana. "Monocultures of the Mind." *Trumpeter*, 1993, http://trumpeter.athabascau.ca/index.php/trumpet/article/viewFile/358/563.

Singaravelu, S. *Social Life of the Tamils: The Classical Period*. International Institute of Tamil Studies, 2001.

Sivathamby, Karthigesu. *Studies in Ancient Tamil Society: Economy, Society and State Formation*. New Century Book House, 1998.

Smith, C. Wayne, and Robert H. Dilday. *Rice: Origin, History, Technology, and Production*. Wiley, 2003.

Srinivasan, T. M. "Agricultural Practices as Gleaned from Tamil Literature." *Indian Journal of History of Science*, vol. 51, no. 2, 2016, pp. 167–89, www.researchgate.net/publication/304660257_Agricultural_Practices_as_Gleaned_from_the_Tamil_Literature_of_the_Sangam_Age.

Sriram, Sangeetha. *pacumaip puraṭciyiṉ katai* (The Story of Green Revolution). kālaccuvaṭu Publications, 2012.

Steffen, Will, Paul J. Crutzen, and John R. McNeill. "The Anthropocene: Are Humans Now Overwhelming the Great Forces of Nature?" *Ambio*, vol. 36, no. 8, Dec. 2007, pp. 614–21, www.pik-potsdam.de/news/public-events/archiv/alter-net/former-ss/2007/05-09.2007/steffen/literature/ambi-36-08-06_614_621.pdf.

Stein, Burton. *Peasant State and Society in Medieval South India*. Oxford University Press, 1994.

Stephen, G. "*caṅka ilakkiyattil nāṭṭār uṇavu*" [Rural food in *caṅkam* literature]. *tamiḻar uṇavu* [Food of the Tamil people], edited by Bhakthavatsala Bharathi. kālaccuvaṭu patippakam, 2011, pp. 101–13.

Subramaniam, T. N., editor. *South Indian Temple Inscriptions*, vol. 3, part 2. Government Oriental Manuscripts Library, 1957.

Sudarmanian, N. S., S. Pazhanivelan, K. P. Raghunath, and S. Panneerselvam. "Estimation of Methane Emission from Rice Fields Using Static Closed Chamber Technique in Tiruchirapalli District." *International Journal of Chemical Studies*, vol. 7, no. 3, 2019, pp. 4116–20, www.chemijournal.com/archives/2019/vol7issue3/PartBO/7-3-473-129.pdf.

Sundaram, R. M., and V. Mohanasundaram. "Barter System in Ancient Tamil Nadu." *Economic Heritage of the Tamils*, edited by Annie Thomas. International Institute of Tamil Studies, 2007, pp. 68–73.

Sundararaju, V. "The Porunai in Sangam Literature: A River of Wealth, Power and Antiquity." *DownToEarth*. September 21, 2021. www.downtoearth.org.in/blog/environment/the-porunai-in-sangam-literature-a-river-of-wealth-power-and-antiquity-79131.

Swaminathan, K. D. *Early South Indian Temple Architecture: Study of Tiruvalisvaram Inscriptions*. CBH Publications, 1990.

taṇṭulanāli Jataka, no. 5. [The Jataka], vol. 1, 1895, *Sacred Texts*. Translated by Robert Chalmers, www.sacred-texts.com/bud/j1/j1008.htm.

Thirumalai, R. "Economic Aspects in Irrigation Methods." *Economic History of the Tamils*, edited by Annie Thomas. International Institute of Tamil Studies, 2007, pp. 99–104.

tirukkuṟaḷ, http://library.bjp.org/jspui/bitstream/123456789/1494/1/Thirukkural%20English%20Translation%20-%20G.U.%20Pope.pdf.

"TN Districtwise Profile," *Government of Tamil Nadu Forest Department*, www.forests.tn.gov.in/pages/view/tn-districtwise-profile.

Trautman, Thomas. *Elephants and Kings: An Environmental History*. Ashoka University, 2015.

turai araṅkacāmi, mo. a. *caṅka kālac ciṟappup peyarkaḷ* [Personal names of *caṅkam* age]. 2nd ed. pāri nilaiyam, 1980.

ulakanāta piḷḷai, el. *mutalām karikālaṉ eṉkiṟa cōlaṉ karikāl peruvaḷattāṉaip paṟṟiya ārāycci*. [Study of karikālaṉ I, aka cōlaṉ karikāl peruvaḷattāṉ]. lāli elektrik accukkūṭam, 1913, www.tamilvu.org/library/nationalized/scholars/pdf/history/choozhan_karikaar_peruvalattaan.pdf.

vēlāyutam, pē.ka. & pa. cīṉivācaṉ. *caṅkakāla maṉṉar varicai* [Timeline of *caṅkam* kings]: *āyvuk kuṟippukaḷuṭaṉ* [with research notes]. pārati nūlakam, 1997.
vēṅkaṭacāmi, mayilai cīṉi. *uṇavu nūl* [Book on food]. taṭākam, 2017.
———. "*caṅka kālattuk* kāvirippūmpaṭṭiṉam" [kāvirippūmpaṭṭiṉam during *caṅkam* age]. *caṅkakālattu varalāṟṟu āyvukaḷ* [Historical researches on the age of *caṅkam*], vol. 1. em. veṟṟiyaraci, 2001, pp. 157–82.
———. *paḻaṅkālat tamiḻar vāṇikam* [Ancient Tamil trade]. 3rd ed. New Century Book House, 1990.
vēṅkaṭarāma ayyar, C. P. "kāvirippūmpaṭṭiṉam." *Town Planning in Ancient Dekkan*. 1916, pp. 80–97.
Venkata Subramanian, T. K. *Environment and Urbanisation in Early Tamilakam*. Tamil University, 1988.
Violatti, Cristian. "Civilization." *Ancient History Encyclopedia*, www.ancient.eu/civilization/.
Wahlqvist, M. L. "Regional Food Diversity and Human Health." *Asia Pacific Journal of Clinical Nutrition*, vol. 12, no. 3, 2003, pp. 304–8, http://apjcn.nhri.org.tw/server/APJCN/12/3/304.pdf.
For the following Tamil texts, see www.projectmadurai.org,

aiṅkuṟunūṟu,
akanāṉūṟu,
cirupāṇāṟṟuppaṭai,
kalittokai,
kuṟiñcippāṭṭu,
kuṟuntokai,
malaipaṭukaṭām,
maturaikkāñci,
mullaippāṭṭu,
naṟṟiṇai,
neṭunalvāṭai,
paripāṭal,
patiṟṟuppattu,
paṭṭiṉappālai,
perumpāṇāṟṟuppaṭai,
porunarāṟṟuppaṭai,
puṟanāṉūṟu,
tirumurukāṟṟuppaṭai,
tolkāppiyam.

2 The Taste of Place

Food, Ecology, and Culture in Kodagu

Subarna De

Introduction

Food has become part of a growing global discussion. In their introduction to the third edition of *Food and Culture: A Reader* (2013), food critics Carole Counihan and Penny Van Esterik commend the growing genre of food studies because of its interdisciplinarity: "This field resists separating biological from cultural, individual from society, and local from global culture" (1). Simon Estok observes that theorizing food within the environmental humanities domain increasingly means looking "at meat and vegetables, and at what their production represents both for natural and for human environments" (681). A significant inquiry within bioregional studies aims to understand how food connects people to place and culture and revives the lost ecology of place. This chapter demonstrates how literature can help in understanding bioregional eating and the role of native species in producing place-based identity through a reading of Kavery Nambisan's[1] *The Scent of Pepper* (1996) and Sarita Mandanna's[2] *Tiger Hills* (2010), works that are set in a particular place (Kodagu) and that depict particular epochs (approximately, the mid-nineteenth to mid-twentieth centuries).

The Scent of Pepper begins around 1855 and ends with the uprising that led to Indian independence. The novel, which is mostly set in Athur in Kodagu, presents the colonial history of the propagation of coffee in Kodagu through its description of how Nanji, a strong-headed dominant female persona, manages the Kaleyanda household, her in-laws' house, the family's paddy fields, and the coffee plantations. Significantly, the novel shows that the Kodava people, influenced by the European coffee planters, invested a significant amount in coffee as well as in their traditional paddy. *Tiger Hills* spans from 1878 to 1936, narrating the life story of Devi, the seventh child of a woman named Muthavva. Devi was a strong-headed Kodava woman who was married to her childhood friend Devanna. Even in their childhood, Devi and Devanna were greatly influenced by the ecology of Kodagu. Tayi (Devi's grandmother) and Thimmaya (Devi's father) had a spiritual attachment to land. The novel depicts the influence of the Europeans—who did not have such a spiritual

DOI: 10.4324/9781003282976-4

attachment—on the Kodava people and the change in Devi's attitude regarding land after coming into possession of one hundred acres of an untended coffee plantation.

This chapter probes the two novels' depictions of how specific plant species and their qualities have become intricately woven into the social fabric of place and community. The central aim is to investigate how inextricable food practices, plant life, and bioregional identity mesh together to define the bioregional food system and the bioregion itself. These two literary examples, which narrate the personae's lived-in experiences across four generations, show how the food, ecology, and culture of the place have contributed to the development of a bioregional identity in Kodagu.

Anthropocene Geographies of the Kodagu Bioregion

Kodagu[3] is a wet mountainous region of approximately 4,102 square kilometers located on the eastern slopes of the Western Ghats in Karnataka, India (Chisholm 91–92; Richter 1). The region, which is the source of the prominent watershed Tala Kaveri, has moist black alluvial soil and rich biodiversity (Richter 3–4). Kodagu has faced the adverse effects of the Anthropocene since the colonial establishment of coffee plantations.[4] In Kodagu, the consequences of the Anthropocene are evident in the massive deforestation and the introduction of non-native cash crop species. In 1854, European colonizers began to burn the vast forested mountain slopes of Kodagu, thereby introducing the practice of coffee monoculture[5] and continuous cultivation[6] (Gadgil and Guha 125; Mandanna 222; Nambisan 57). These practices led to erosion of the topsoil and a massive loss of native plant and animal species (Pretty 40; Proctor 229; Venkatesh et al. 281). The colonizers introduced the non-native coffee *Coffea arabica/robust* to Kodagu from Ceylon (Mandanna 222; McCook 177–78; Nambisan 57; Richter 24–25, 81, 95),[7] which, according to Peter Berg and Raymond F. Dasmann, exemplifies the "invader mentality" (217).[8] Berg and Dasmann argue that invaders remove "one species or native people after another to make a living" for themselves (217). The introduction of non-native crops restricts the reproduction, growth, and cultivation of indigenous plant species.

Altogether, the colonial interference brought an immense loss of biodiversity, threatening Kodagu's ecosystem and transforming the place into an injured land.[9] In pre-colonial times, the Kodava people were primarily hunter–gatherers rooted in the region's topographies—its hills, rivers, forests, and land—which formed the bedrock of their ethnic and cultural diversity. From a bioregional perspective, the Kodava people had been living-in-place, a bioregional concept that means "following the necessities and pleasures of life as they are uniquely presented by a particular site, and evolving ways to ensure long-term occupancy of that site" (Berg and Dasmann 217). The destruction of the forests during the colonial period threatened the traditional Kodava lifestyle: their food, culture, and ecology. Even worse, the late nineteenth century saw the Kodava people gradually embrace the colonial tradition of cultivating coffee in large tracts of land. As described in both *The Scent of Pepper* and *Tiger Hills*, the Kodava people had originally been hunter–gatherers who were turned into coffee planters. During the late nineteenth century, Kodagu became the ideal destination of choice for Europeans. The extended practice of monoculture, continuous cultivation, and replacement of native plant species with non-native coffee resulted in agricultural consumerism and ecological instability in the Kodagu region. From a bioregional perspective, extensive human interference brings a[10] potential threat of land injury, which necessitates reinhabitation, or "learning to live-in-place in an area that has been disrupted and injured through past exploitation" (Berg and Dasmann 217). To counter the looming ecological crisis, the Kodava people started growing native crops on coffee plantations at the beginning of the twentieth century, transforming Kodagu into a sustainable coffee plantation region in the Global South. Today, having revived the distinct nature and culture of place and community, Kodagu is the fifth-largest coffee-producing destination in the world and a global biodiversity hotspot in South Asia. The ecological initiative of the people of Kodagu shows that edible plants native to Kodagu are not a mere part of local economic and social practices but rather play a critical role in shaping these practices. Probing this reinhabitory approach, this chapter expands on "bioregional eating" (Estok 682), the bioregional food system (the geography and ecology of food production and consumption), and bioregional identity, showing how the native species have gradually evolved as significant ecological and social markers of place and community, simultaneously producing a place-based identity for the Kodava reinhabitors.

What is Bioregional Eating?

Simon Estok uses the term "bioregional eating" in a simple assertion: "bioregional eating is a good thing" (682), without expanding on what it means.[11] In a discussion of how food defines place-based culture when contextualizing Portland, Oregon, Gary Snyder explains that "maize, rice, reindeer, sweet potato—these indicate places and cultures" (49). Further, in a discussion of the Sacramento Valley bioregion as a "lifeplace," Robert L. Thayer posits a question about "how humans have related to [plants] and sustainably extracted their living from them and how they might do so in the future" (35). He even identifies the indigenous communities according to their eating habits—for example, "the indigenous acorn-eating peoples in central California" and "the salmon eaters of the Pacific Northwest" (35–36). Drawing upon Snyder's and Thayer's concept of place-based eating, we can understand "bioregional eating" as referring to eating practices that depend entirely on the ingredients that are naturally available in the bioregion. The concept of a bioregion "refers both to geographical terrain and a terrain of consciousness—to a place and the ideas that have developed about how to live in that place" (Berg and Dasmann 218). In the case of Kodagu, the Kodava people identify themselves with the place. They develop "ideas" to "live-in-place" and "reinhabit" Kodagu. For example, the Kodava people cook their daily meals from the native species available in abundance in the region. *Tiger Hills* provides an instance of this in its depiction of the children Devi and Devanna enjoying catching crabs from the crab stream and bringing them home for Devi's grandmother, Tayi, to cook crab chutney (Mandanna 19, 64, 225, 449). Similarly, *The Scent of Pepper* describes the enthusiasm of Boluka, Nanji's help, for catching crabs in the evening: "mushrooms or bamboo shoots or the tiny koile meenu [fresh water fish] from the waterlogged paddy fields," which he takes home for his wife to cook (Nambisan 36, 39). Further instances showing that the Kodava people know their land and find pleasure in surviving on local animals and plants for their food include the first pick of mushrooms after the thunder showers, which were very delicate and the favorite of Boju (Nanji's brother-in-law), and celebrating the harvest festival.

Knowing the availability of fruits, vegetables, crops, and meat requires knowing the land, which, as Kirkpatrick Sale puts it, is "becoming conscious" about learning the land (44). Finding crabs and fish in waterlogged paddy fields shows that the Kodava people know their land well, which Sale sees as a necessary part of bioregional living (42–44). The waterways, fields, and forests become the natural provider of necessities such as fish, crabs, mushrooms, paddy and other crops, fruits, and vegetables, as well as pleasures such as fishing, catching crabs, and consuming meat and plant-based food. Catching fish and crabs and collecting mushrooms, fruits, and vegetables from the fields, streams, and forests are practices that endorse Sale's advice to "becom[e] conscious" about the ecological and geographical features of the land (44), Thayer's idea of creating a "lifeplace" (66–67), and Berg and Dasmann's idea of creating a "terrain of consciousness" (218), and this makes Kodagu a bioregion. In the introduction to *The Bioregional Imagination* (2012), Tom Lynch, Cheryll Glotfelty, and Karla Armbruster outline the basic principles of bioregional literary criticism and specifically state that anything related to a bioregion is a part of "bioregional discourse" (6).

Understanding the term "bioregional eating" as it relates to the native eating practices in Kodagu has important implications for matters of globalization and multiculturalism. Bioregional eating does not encourage cultural diversity and multiculturalism, because these practices open the possibility of non-native crop cultivation, resulting in topsoil erosion and infused food habits. Bioregional eating signifies a departure from multiculturalism[12] and focuses primarily on the traditional culture specific to the region. It is therefore essential to categorize bioregional eating as the consumption of "native" species, rather than use words such as "local," "ethnic," or "rural," which do not address the scientific and ecological aspects of the species but instead largely stress cultural diversity and aspects of multiculturalism that are present in the place-based food.[13]

"Native" is an appropriate term when considering "bioregional eating" because it refers to plants and animal species that occur naturally in the region and do not cause any harm to the environment. In other words, native species support long-term survival. Throughout this chapter, "native" refers to the edible plant and animal species abundantly available in the Kodagu region. A native plant species "occurs naturally in a particular region, state, ecosystem, and habitat without direct or indirect human actions" (Guiaşu 11; Morse et al. 12). According to Snyder and Thayer, native species indicate places, determine the bioregional culture, and support life continuity (Snyder 49; Thayer 36). Madhav Gadgil and Ramachandra Guha note that indigenous people who lived in the forests and the surrounding area relied on these forests for "fuel, fodder, construction timber or industrial raw material" (148). In this connection, Nambisan observes that for a long time, the Jenu Kurubas,[14] the forest-dwelling Kodava people, depended on the Kundathbottu[15] forests (199): "They went to the forest near Kundathbottu to see the Jenu Kurubas gather honey from the giant hives on athi trees [*Ficus racemose*, also known as Indian fig tree]" (36). This shows how the Kodava people collected their food from their immediate natural surroundings, as their ancestral hunter–gatherers did.

Bioregional eating does not always take the form of a hunter–gatherer diet. Gary Paul Nabhan considers the primordial hunter–gatherer type of diet as an ancestral diet, "one that ignores ethnicity in exchange for a sense of antiquity" (38–39). He believes that "eating your way back to your roots" (39) means eating mostly "raw forms" of a broad "variety of fresh fruits, flowers, leaves, and bulbs" (40). The collaborative practice of collecting food from the streams and forests is an integral part of bioregional eating. However, bioregional eating largely differs from Nabhan's concept of ancestral diet. In Kodagu, bioregional eating involves preparing traditional delicacies from native plant species, the use of spices such as cardamom and black pepper (cultivated in the bioregion without causing any damage to the soil), and consumption of specific animals such as fish, pork, and boar meat, which are naturally available through the primordial practice of hunting in the wild. Mandanna describes the evenings as being alive with the smells of cooked food: "The moon rose high over the village green as liquor flowed freely and cauldrons of wild boar, chicken, mutton, vegetable and egg curries were hauled from the open-air kitchens" (11). Here, food represents the cultural imagination of the Kodava community. Nambisan and Mandanna do not dwell in much detail on traditional Kodava recipes. However, in the course of their narratives, they refer to many traditional Kodagu dishes and their preparation from ingredients that are abundantly available in the region. Kodava food has evolved as a significant ecological and social marker of place and community because it is available from the land's natural life-supporting systems (Berg and Dasmann 219–220). Although neither novel describes recipes, both depict how specific plant and animal species and their qualities have become intricately woven into the social fabric. In this process, bioregional eating drives away the food politics founded on globalization and processed food and evolves as more than merely a desideratum, an object of desire and appetite.

For the Kodava people, bioregional eating is a lived-in experience with distinct intrinsic values because of the native resources. The intrinsic value of bioregional eating is that it creates a sense of interconnectedness between the human and the non-human and between native and non-native species. *The Scent of Pepper* and *Tiger Hills*, both of which are set in the colonial period, fictionalize the transformation of the coffee plantations into resource grounds for Kodagu that are filled with native species. Devi's plantation, Tiger Hills, was filled with "orderly rows of shade trees—orange, jackfruit and silver oak" where "frogs croaked from the damp grass around the estate pond" (Mandanna 230), which transformed the Kambeymada coffee plantation into a site of rich biodiversity. The coffee plantations of the Kaleyanda family in *The Scent of Pepper* have similar narratives of biodiversity and native resources, with a stream flowing through their estate: Nanji's son Subbu "scooped up a handful of sardines" from the stream inside their plantation, and Nanji "judged the freshness of the fish from the smell that wafted across the stream" (Nambisan 34). The edible plants and animals native to Kodagu are not just a part of regional economic and social practices but rather play critical roles in shaping them, constituting Berg and Dasmann's "geographic terrain" and "terrain of consciousness" (218).

Although the non-native coffee crop is the main economic engine of the Kodagu region, the narratives of the plantations in both novels follow an indigenous farming strategy—namely, the initiation of biodiverse farming of native species, such as pepper, cardamom, and citrus fruits. Estelle Biénabe argues that the "agro-forestry systems" (as she calls them) that result from growing native trees within the coffee plantations are characteristic features of the Kodagu region and that they "contribute greatly to Coorg's [the Anglicized name of Kodagu] image," providing a cultural identity for the local Kodava coffee-growers (240). In the Global South, where Indonesia, Vietnam, Brazil, Mexico, Thailand, and the Philippines also have coffee estates, the coffee estates of the Kodagu region are the only example of coffee growing extensively under the shade of native trees within coffee plantations.[16] The planting of native trees has converted the coffee plantations into mini-forests that help restore the damage caused by monoculture plantations and continuous coffee cultivation since 1854. In this way, coffee has become a bioregional crop in Kodagu. This is also depicted in *Tiger Hills*, where Devanna explained to Devi that "as years passed, the initial advantage of virgin soil had been eroded" (Mandanna 227). He said that the European planters had followed Ceylon's coffee plantations too closely and hence made a severe error in Kodagu because the "coffee in Kodagu was exposed to too much sunlight" (Mandanna 227). Devanna proposed that growing coffee under native shade trees would help recover the forests of their childhood and would also produce enough coffee (Mandanna 227). Growing native plants on the estates is the Kodava way of responding to deforestation and colonial coffee cultivation. This introduces species assimilation on coffee plantations to provide enough shade to the coffee bushes. The reinhabitory approach of growing coffee under native shade trees makes the coffee plantations of Kodagu bioregional. Prominent native shade trees on the coffee plantations include jackfruit,[17] mango,[18] and orange[19] (Mandanna 223–230). Along with shade trees, paddy, cardamom, and pepper, there are other common native trees that every Kodava household grows in their backyard and estates. This ecological practice helps the Kodava people reinhabit their land and identify themselves with the Kodagu bioregion. Even today, coffee is grown under native shade trees in Kodagu. Regrowing forests on plantations is a bioregional response to the unsustainable practice of coffee monoculture.

Growing coffee under native shade trees was a significant turning point in environmental history, restricting the adverse effects of land-use changes, restoring the bioregion's lost ecology, maintaining the topsoil that enables long-term survival, and providing the resources of native crops and other ingredients for daily survival. Regrowing native species on the coffee plantations has also enhanced the cultural rootedness of the Kodava community because the native species are part of their daily diet and vital ingredients of the grand feast held by Kodava community members during the Kodagu festivals of Puthari (the harvest festival) and Kailpodh (the festival of weapons). In this way, the growth of native species on the plantations contributes to the practice of bioregional eating. To this extent, bioregional eating enables the community's long-term survival without causing any damage to Kodagu land.

It is evident that bioregional eating, then, is a concept within bioregional discourse that is rooted in place and addresses Kodagu's regional, ecological, and cultural identity. As a process, bioregional eating is a product of the bioregional food system that involves cultivation of native species, making food from such species, and regularly consuming that food as daily meals and during festivals.

Bioregional Ecologies of Food

Bioregional eating, the core structure supporting a bioregional way of life, evolves as a holistic process. The bioregional food system creates an increased awareness of the links between the consumption of food and the production of native species. These linkages create bioregional identity and bioregional culture. "Bioregional culture" refers to the communal practices that determine daily life in the bioregion, and bioregional identity refers to the strong sense of place that develops with the lived-in experiences of living-in-place or reinhabiting the bioregion. The narratives in *Tiger Hills* and *The Scent of Pepper* that describe the Kodava peoples' relationship between nature and culture show how inextricably native species, people, food, ecology, and culture intertwine to create a bioregional lifeway. Throughout *Tiger Hills*, Mandanna explains how the characters are rooted in Kodagu's ecology. Seeing the paddy growing and herons skimming the crab pool, Devi remembers that on the peak of the Bhagamandala hills, Machu said to her, "These are my roots" (378). Here the place's ecology became Machu's roots. The vivid descriptions of the kitchen gardens filled with native vegetable patches (Mandanna 270) also define the native ecology. In *The Scent of Pepper*, Nanji's father-in-law, Rao Bahadur, gave his son a sprawling bungalow with "one-hundred and twelve acres of newly-planted coffee" (10), where Nanji planted bitter lemon, mango trees, and areca palms among the coffee plants (8). Nambisan describes Nanji's experiments in planting native pepper along with coffee on their plantation (33) and that she found the process rewarding enough to continue with more native planting (33–34). Nanji also used the spice from the pepper vines in her coffee plantations as a "carminative, a digestant," and mixed it with honey for soothing sore throats (33). E. N. Anderson argues that foods that cause a burning sensation, like ginger, black pepper, alcohol, and chilli, heat the body and are therefore suitable for medicinal use (143). Using native species from the plantations to cure the seasonal ailments of the Kodava people adds to their daily lived-in experiences of connecting with nature. Other such examples include economic extraction of quinine from cinchona bark (*Cinchona succirubra*) to cure Devi's mother's malaria (Mandanna 65), and crushing black peppercorn into powder and mixing it with tiger's milk (collected from the forest) to prepare an ointment to cure Nanji's youngest son Subbu's crippled legs (Nambisan 38). Anderson recognizes that local diet therapy is used worldwide (141) and argues that it adds "meaning and significance" to place and community (140). The nexus between the traditional knowledge of native plants, growing native plants on the coffee estates, and using them as necessary ingredients to cure seasonal and severe diseases shows how indigenous ecologies have shaped lived-in experiences in Kodagu.

The Kodava community also celebrates cultural practices that are strongly connected with the cultivation of paddy, which is the traditional crop and the region's staple diet. Reverend Gundert Richter documents in his 1870 *Gazetteer of Coorg* (87) that the Kodava people have small acreages of paddy fields in the valleys and foothills where they cultivate the large-grained rice ("Dodda-batta"), a more refined variety ("Sanna-batta"), a type of parched rice ("Kalame"), and red rice ("Késari"). Mandanna opens her novel *Tiger Hills* on a clear day in July during the sowing season.[20] In the sowing season, "before the completion of the largest field an open space of about 10 feet wide is left throughout the whole length" (Richter 89). The Kodava people arrange races "in the freshly ploughed, waterlogged paddy fields" (Mandanna 35) to entertain themselves before finishing the laborious sowing activity. This cultural phenomenon is peculiar to the highland Kodava community's practice of paddy cultivation. Mandanna refers to the race in the paddy fields during the sowing season as a part of traditional Kodava agricultural practice. With participants drawn from the farmers and their families, this race expresses food's symbolic power to convey meaning, linked tightly to the ethnographic evidence of using native species and food resources as a means of communication.

Overall, the paddy integrates the lived-in experiences of the Kodava people and their indigenous lifeway. The Kodava women weave straw mats from the paddy crops' dried leftovers after the harvest (Nambisan 225). Straw mats are an essential part of the Kodava food system and culture; both Kodava hosts and guests sit on straw mats for daily meals. The straw mats have become cultural symbols of creativity, festivity, community, ecology, and nature, and also contribute to the waste management process of paddy cultivation, an integral aspect of the bioregional lifeway. In "Reinhabiting California," Berg and Dasmann emphasize the need to process cut trees without producing any waste (218–219). From an economic perspective, they suggest making "crafts that use every part of the tree" (218–219). Craftwork, they continue, would "make maximum use of the materials while employing a greater number of regional people" (219). The Kodava people also craft other articles from dried grains and leftover paddy crops after the harvest. Using straw, dried rice grains, a deer's horn, and wood from a fallen tree, the Kodava people can create various wall-hanging crafts. In her book *In Service of the Wild* (1995), Stephanie Mills observes that waste management can be "ways of sophisticating old-style household and neighborhood frugality" (18–19). This cultural phenomenon of using agricultural waste to produce aesthetic objects adds social meaning to the Kodagu culture and signifies their rootedness in nature. The communal practice of reusing agricultural waste in making handicrafts also contributes to an understanding of the Kodagu bioregional identity that demonstrates their concern about maintaining a sustainable lifeway. This craftwork, born from the agricultural waste of the paddy crop, forms an essential aspect of the bioregional food system. The native paddy, including the waste, is both living and food to the Kodava people, and the paddy, overall, reflects on their sense of place and rootedness in their traditional belief system. Additionally, the paddy cultivation introduces a long-term sustainable lifeway by producing minimal waste and using every part of the resource. As Berg and Dasmann observe, the making of these crafts involves regional people. The practice facilitates small-scale businesses based on the land and the food of the region. The small-scale economic strategies aim to evolve "ways to ensure long-term occupancy of the site" and help in achieving "sufficiency" (Berg and Dasmann 217).

According to Berg and Dasmann, "sufficiency" is an essential concept in bioregional living, as it reduces ecological destruction by using and maintaining natural resources. Sufficiency consists of maintaining and using "natural life-system continuities" for long-term living (Berg and Dasmann 219). The natural life-systems of water, soil, and forests "create conditions of abundance in the region," but these need proper maintenance along with the practices of "enjoying them and using them to live" (Berg and Dasmann 219). An instance of "sufficiency" occurs in *Tiger Hills* when Mandanna narrates the economic benefits of the high yield of the native paddy crop: "The paddy that year was so bountiful that Thimmaya [Devi's father] was able to buy two milch cows with the gold it fetched him" (10). The paddy crop harvest in Kodagu is a time to rejoice because it brings food, prosperity, and happiness. A bountiful production of the paddy crop enhances the Kodagu bioregion economy on two levels: for "home consumption and for exportation to the Malabar Coast" (Richter 86). Altogether, paddy cultivation helps to maintain sufficiency and forms an integral part of the Kodagu bioregional culture.

Puthari, the harvest festival associated with paddy cultivation, reflects the lived-in experience of the Kodava community and contributes to defining their bioregional way of life. During Puthari, everyone begins to "practice the songs and dances for this all-important festival of new rice" (Nambisan 188). The rituals, songs, and dances performed during the celebration of the harvesting and sowing of the paddy crop—or any other indigenous agricultural practice—contribute to the culture of the place. Discussing how plants represent the soil of a place and how crops represent the food and culture of the society living-in-place, Gary Snyder asserts that "local song and dance" are indicators of the traditional culture (49–50). In the Kodagu context, the festive dancing and rejoicing practices during Puthari showcase the cultural forms of the Kodava people and enable the human and non-human to interact with each other and with place. The songs and dances therefore form an integral part of the Kodava lifeway that focuses on the interconnectedness between the human and the non-human and helps identify the reinhabitors with their homeplace. Here, to quote David Kaplan, "food and culture define one another" (3). A week before Puthari, households begin preparing delicious foods from native ingredients that are available in abundance in the Kodagu bioregion. Nambisan describes this festive mood in great detail:

> Puthari was drawing near. A week before the full moon a pig was slaughtered, the pork fried, topped with six inches of its own fat and stored in jars; a sack of jaggery was boiled with powdered rice and grated coconut, flavoured with cardamom, and the sticky mixture made into Puthari laddus [sweets]; bunches of bananas hung above the fireplace in the kitchen to ripen just in time to mash it into thambuttoo on Puthari day.
>
> (108)

Here also, along with indigenous rituals, the celebrations include a grand feast. The native crops from the forests and plantations and boars', pigs', and hens' meat cook into traditional Kodava food. During the feast, the meat consumed is not produced by farming[21] but is rather collected through ritualistic slaughtering[22] and hunting of wild animals.

In Kodagu, hunting is a traditional practice, associated with honor and the ecology of the region. In *Tiger Hills*, Mandanna describes the Nari Mangala, the mock-tiger-wedding of the hunter with the hunted tiger, and describes how the Kodava community treats a tiger hunter with respect and honor (45–49). In this ritual, the hunter marries the dead tiger, and the family of the tiger hunter organizes a grand feast to celebrate his victory with the nearby villages. According to Kodagu tradition, the tiger hunter grows a gala mesa, a long thick mustache, which symbolizes chivalry and honor (Mandanna 45–49). The people celebrate the first day of the hunting season with the festival of Kailpodh, which is "also known as Kailmuhurtha, a festival of arms celebrated every year on [the] 3rd [of] September" (De 126). During Kailpodh, the Kodava people venerate the rusted ancestral guns that their forebears took on hunting expeditions and worship them with exceptional traditional food and offerings (Accavva et al. 31; De 127). The Kodava community performs various sacred rituals before setting out for the hunt and returning with the dead animals (Accavva et al. 31). Thus, hunting is associated with the sacred and forms an integral part of Kodava culture, food, and daily livelihood.

Founded on animistic ideology, hunting, meat, food, and traditional festivals are all closely related to the Kodava peoples' daily bioregional life. During hunting, the forests represent nature, the space for non-humans. The Kodava people perform sacred rituals to evoke the spirits and pay homage to the souls of non-humans before killing them. Animism is a philosophical and religious concept founded on a belief in the existence of "multiple spirits" (Rooney 135). In the Kodagu bioregional context, the hunter, the hunted, and veneration of the weapons used to hunt wild animals all reciprocate the belief in the sacred and provide evidence of animism. Rane Willerslev argues in *Soul Hunters* (2007) that humans exist in a "betwixt-and-between state" where they represent the souls of both animals and humans (165). Hunter worship[23] is a traditional belief that helps the hunter's soul to reincarnate so that he[24] can perform feats that he otherwise would not be able to do, such as seducing an animal and killing it. Hunters are thus both human and also the animal they kill because in the process of becoming a hunter, feelings of anxiety cause the hunters to lose their human self (Willerslev 189). Given this belief system, the primordial Kodava society considers both the hunter and the hunted honorable and hunting a sacred practice. Hunting is thus also an integral part of the bioregional food system because it reconnects the Kodava reinhabitors to their traditional belief system, food, ecology, and culture.

Indigenous hunting connects profoundly with the ecology, food habits, and regional festivities in Kodagu, and consequently the concepts of sacredness and animism are essential to the bioregional parameters of place-based eating. To link the concepts of sacredness and animism with bioregional living, it is vital to refer to Istvan Praet, who sees hunting as an invitation and makes a clear distinction between the prey and the dead animal (72). In Kodagu, before being hunted down, the "prey" symbolizes the game of chase; but the "dead animal" is sacred because, upon the return from hunting, the Kodava family members worship it. Meat, which is a part of the hunted/dead animal, is the product of the hunting and hence part of the sacred. Thus, the traditional Kodagu cuisine uses meat as a symbol of festivity and honor. The communal practice of meat consumption helps in reviving lost traditions, as the flesh of the hunted animal that is cooked during rituals connects the Kodava reinhabitors to their roots. Through this process, meat has become an essential part of bioregional eating.

In summary, the meat and the crop have gradually evolved as ritualistic and symbolic foods that celebrate and revive the Kodagu community's beliefs and practices. Because it includes the sacred, bioregional eating also serves a greater purpose of dissipating class hierarchies. Mandanna describes how Kodava families gather together to prepare grand meals to celebrate Puthari by roasting the meat on the fire (199). The preparation of the festive food reflects on the integrative communal values of the Kodagu society. The participation of Poleya women (a lower subdivision of the Kodava) as "[they] ground up white rice into powder" (199) reveals how Kodagu food making neutralizes class hierarchies. Also, on the auspicious night of the full moon, the Poleya people, the Yerava people (another subdivision of the Kodagu community), and the families of their masters would go to the paddy fields together and cut the first ripe sheaves, crying "Poli, poli, poli deva ...," a song of rejoicing, praising their ancestral lord and the protector of the Universe (Nambisan 109, 172). The inclusive participation of the Kodava people in the prime ceremony of the harvest festival reciprocates the togetherness and harmony prevalent among the community members. Evoking the ancestral lord and singing praises and prayers together, irrespective of class hierarchies, demonstrates how paddy binds the community together.

Paddy thus serves the Kodava people as more than the main food of bioregional eating. It connects the community to their ancestors, and in this process, it creates a sense of place—namely, the Kodagu bioregion and their bioregional culture. After offering "the best food and liquor to the gods and ancestors," the Kodava people set off firecrackers and bring some ripe sheaves home "to tie to the doors and bedposts" (Nambisan 109). Offering "the best food and liquor to the gods and ancestors" (Nambisan 109) during Puthari constitutes a negotiation between the people, their food and natural surroundings, and a sense of the sacred, which Elina Helander-Renvall refers to as forming a cultural circle with humans and non-humans (44, 49). Both *The Scent of Pepper* and *Tiger Hills* depict the traditional Kodava culture as being concerned with food and festivals involving the sacred, with the sacred forming a crucial element in the Kodagu way of life. After completing all of the rituals, the men would drink country liquor, preferably toddy,[25] and sing and dance to celebrate the joy of harvesting their native paddy crop. As a result, paddy has become a cultural determinant[26] of the place. In the Kodagu bioregion, paddy cultivation helps to recover from ecological, geographical, and cultural loss in three ways. First, it retains the soil's moisture and helps in restoring and maintaining the topsoil. Second, as paddy is the staple diet of the region, it contributes to maintaining self-sufficiency. Third, it celebrates bioregional eating alongside the revival of traditional culture through the races during the sowing season and the harvest festival of Puthari and its great feasts. Thus, paddy cultivation reflects the bioregional identity of the Kodava reinhabitors as they identify with place and its rituals, plants, geography, natural environment, and tradition.

Another essential native ingredient in traditional Kodava delicacies is cardamom. K. P. Prabhakaran Nair writes that cardamom is the "Queen of Species" that belongs to the genus *Elettaria* and traces its origin to southern India (109). The Kodava people grow massive amounts of the spice within the coffee plantations in Kodagu, and it flavors almost every cooked dish mentioned in *The Scent of Pepper* and *Tiger Hills*. Richter notes that "the cardamom plant (*Elettaria cardamomum*) grows spontaneously in the evergreen forests" (91). During February and March, preparations for cultivating a cardamom forest within the coffee plantations begin (92). The cardamom plant has a perennial stem that grows up to a height of nine feet and is "enveloped in the sheaths of the 1 to 2 feet long" leaves; it takes almost three years for the plant to bear fruit (92). In April, racemes bearing the capsules that ripen in September or October (92–93) shoot out from the ground. The Kodava people consider a cardamom jungle to be a mine of wealth (91). Almost every Kodava household plants cardamom within its coffee estate to balance the economy when the prices for coffee go down. Mandanna describes Devi noticing that "the cardamom prices were the highest they had been in six years," so that selling cardamom could ease her financial burdens (10). David Cleveland states that the main purpose of a human livelihood is to continue living our individual and social lives with the support of the environment, including food production (72). It is more important to initiate food production supporting the environment than to consume food produced with the environment's support. The roots of cardamom contain a large amount of potassium, iron, and aluminum oxides (Krishnakumar and Potty 130). These oxides firmly fix soluble phosphates into insoluble ones and enhance the soil's mineral content (Krishnakumar and Potty 131). Thus, cardamom cultivation restores the soil and is a prominent example of sustainable agriculture. Here, sustainable "implies a long, relatively comfortable future" (Cleveland 72). Sustainability, or long-term living, is an integral part of the bioregional way of life, as it promotes perennial appeal. In the context of food, cardamom is primarily a flavoring ingredient that appeals to the sense of taste and smell. It has become a social marker of Kodava festive food and an essential element of sensual composition that transforms Kodava cooking into an art form that appeases the human senses. Taken together, cardamom enhances the sense of place and is therefore a bioregional component of Kodava food and agriculture.

Black pepper is another native crop that unites the senses in Kodagu. Black pepper is a climbing plant that is found in abundance within coffee plantations in the bioregion. As mentioned earlier, Nanji experimented with pepper in the family plantation. The Maplahs, a tribe from the adjacent state (Kerala), had advised Nanji to grow black pepper in her estate (Nambisan 35). They told Nanji that Kodagu—"with its heavy rain, months of dry weather, and abundant shade—was ideal for pepper cultivation" (35). Nanji's education by the Maplahs about the ideal weather conditions for cultivating the native pepper recalls Kirkpatrick Sale's idea of knowing the land by "becoming conscious" of "what kind of soil is best for celery" and learning "when to set out tomatoes" and "where blueberries thrive" (44). Nanji experimented with a couple of vines planted around the shade trees on her estate (35). Black pepper climbs other native shade trees, such as jackfruit and sandalwood.[27] As already noted, this method of growing native trees on the plantations encourages coffee growth under the shade of the canopy trees. Pepper encourages mid-level canopy growth, which houses various animals and insects and also allows moss to grow underneath. In this way, growing native pepper on the plantations has contributed to recovering Kodagu's lost biodiversity: "The knife grinder beetles began to drum their feet on the trees, heralding the dusk. A buzzing, a sawing, hundreds upon hundreds of them, in the plantation" (Mandanna 437). In addition, pepper is a vital seasoning for bioregional eating in Kodagu. For example, Nanji seasoned her fried pork with the first crop from her vines. Gradually, she learned the requisites for cultivating the native pepper and coffee together "near every tree in a five-acre clearing of robusta" (Nambisan 35). Describing pepper cultivation, Nambisan writes about how the Kodava people began clearing away coffee plants and cultivating pepper instead. Like the cardamom plant, pepper balances the bioregional economy and maintains the topsoil. Replacement of the non-native robusta with the native pepper species foregrounds Nanji's bioregional identity. She represents the Kodava people in following a particular culture within the bioregion. The practice of growing native species in the Kodagu bioregion offers a bioregional culture that is an integral part of the bioregional food system.

Food and Bioregional Culture

Beyond producing and consuming native crops, the bioregional food system also revives traditional Kodagu customs, which becomes evident in Devi and her father's trip to Talakavery (the source of the Cauvery river) in the Bhagamandala mountain range (Mandanna 80). They carried "smoked boar and pickled wild mushrooms" as gifts for the relatives whose "homes lay along the way" (Mandanna 80). Similarly, when Devanna's mother left her in-laws' house to stay at her father's home permanently, "Pallada Nayak [Devanna's maternal grandfather] hurried with two of his sons to the Kambeymada home carrying five sacks of fragrant red kesari rice, a cartload of plantains, [and] two haunches of salted venison" (Mandanna 14). And when Nanji's father was sick, Nanji presented him with what he loved most: "sugarcane, steamed koovale puttoo wrapped in banana leaves" and "a jar of pork-and-bamboo pickle and a pot of salted venison" (Nambisan 105). This practice of sharing native food among friends and family constitutes "an essential aspect of eating together," which identifies the culture of place (Montanari 97), and in Kodagu, this reflects how culture is rooted in the taste of place and in the native species. To this end, bioregional eating calls for eating together and forms an inclusive culture that is an integral part of the Kodava lifeway: "[Devi's grandmother, Tayi] would exchange weighty baskets of plantains from the grove behind the house for still-slithering sardines" (Mandanna 13), and the "local Kuruba tribes offered to buy the fish in exchange for partridge and rabbit" from the Maplahs who entered Kodagu at Makutta (Nambisan 33). The Maplahs entered the region in order to trade fish for native fruits and crops. Every Maplah knew that Nanji exchanged bananas for fish, and they walked through Virajpet and Gonicoppa to Athur where Nanji lived (Nambisan 33–35). Even the Yerava people exchanged two bunches of rasa and three of poo bale (bananas) for a basket of fish, and "the sardines were then carried straight to the kitchen to be cleaned and cooked, half into curry and half as a dry-fry" (Nambisan 34). This communal practice of bartering strengthened the socioeconomic relationships and significantly contributed to maintaining bioregional sufficiency. Likely, the Kodava lifeway shared similarities with bioregional culture. In Snyder's words, "food sources … reflect society and its productive arrangements" (49). The practice of sharing native crops adds social meaning to place and culture at large, providing a bioregional identity for the Kodava people.

Conclusion

The history of bioregional eating and its sociocultural milieu remains a continuing story in the Kodagu bioregion, moving between the native resource grounds within the coffee plantations, the stretching paddy fields, and the remaining steep forests of the Western Ghats that still exist, albeit sparsely. From a holistic viewpoint, there are still potential reasons to believe that bioregional eating defines the taste of place, configures native eating practices, and enhances the human perception and understanding of food, ecology, and the culture of place. In particular, native food production promotes the indigenous/sustainable methods of coffee cultivation and agricultural practices in Kodagu. The collaborative practices involve togetherness in growing and cultivating native crops on plantations, collecting and hunting native species within natural resources such as watersheds and forests, cooking them during festivities, sharing them with fellow community members, and eating together. These cultural practices define the bioregional food system and the bioregion itself.

Notes

1 Kavery Nambisan, a prominent Indian novelist writing on social issues, is a doctor by profession. She was born in Palangala village in south Kodagu and works as Chief Medical Officer for Tata Coffee in Kodagu.
2 Sarita Mandanna, a Kodagu by birth, is an investment banker and a private equity professional living in Toronto, Canada. She has two novels to her credit, *Tiger Hills* and *Good Hope Road* (2014). *Tiger Hills*, which is set in Kodagu, has been translated into fourteen languages worldwide, including Hebrew, Italian, French, and Chinese, and was longlisted for the 2011 Man Asian Literary Prize.
3 The Kodagu region has a distinct culture that differs from that of adjacent regions. Kodagu has a colonial history of coffee plantations that significantly destroyed its biodiversity to a great extent. In the pre-colonial era, the Kodava people were generally hunter–gatherers. Colonization threatened their traditional culture, which had been rooted in the ecology of the region. Gradually, the Kodava people became coffee planters and agriculturalists. For further reference, see Chisholm; "History;" Kodagu District Profile; Neilson; Proctor; Richter.
4 As coined by Paul Crutzen and Eugene Stoermer, the "Anthropocene" refers to the current geological epoch in which human activities have been the dominant force transforming the surface of the Earth. For further details, see Ehlers et al.; Adams.
5 "Monoculture" refers to the growing of one crop variety on a vast acreage. Monoculture destroys diversity and alternatives and decentralizes the control of production and consumption. See Shiva; Wirzba.
6 "Continuous cultivation" refers to the year-round cultivation of multiple crops or a single crop to produce a high yield. Continuous cultivation causes the degradation of topsoil and loss of soil moisture (see Berg and Dasmann).
7 Before coffee was introduced in Kodagu, Ceylon had, since the mid seventeenth century, been the top coffee-growing country in the world. Beginning in 1872, Ceylon's coffee production seriously dropped because of the leaf disease (also known as leaf rust) caused by the fungus *Hemileia vastatrix*. This disease spread rapidly throughout Ceylon. Coffee production in Ceylon

eventually died in 1879. From 1874 onwards, the Europeans searched for an alternative place to establish coffee plantations, and they finally learned about Kodagu in southern India. Geographically, Kodagu's dark-soiled mountainous region bears a resemblance to the mountainous region of Ceylon, with an elevation of about 1,800 feet above sea level. For further details, see Abbay; McCook; Mendis; Proctor; Richter; Wenzlhuemer.

8 Berg and Dasmann speak of the "invader mentality" because, according to them, a settler community often includes invaders.

9 Piece of land is considered injured when it has been subjected to extensive human exploitation resulting in topographical changes that threaten the ecosystem of the place and cause an immense loss of biodiversity. Natural causes of land injury include floods, droughts, earthquakes, and tsunamis. Among the man-made causes, deforestation is one prime reason for land injury.

10 "Agricultural consumerism" here refers to both the huge need for crop production for mass consumption and the agricultural wastes produced by industrial agriculture (see Robbins).

11 This chapter borrows the term "bioregional eating" from Estok.

12 "Multiculturalism" as used here is a descriptive term for understanding the diversity within a society. This philosophical concept endorses the assimilation and integration of minor cultures within the dominant culture of the society. This does not mean that members of and immigrants from each group or community cannot practice their distinctive culture within the dominant community (see Modood). In the Kodagu context, the people reinhabit their own land, practice their own culture, and eat their traditional food. Bioregional eating in Kodagu does not involve fusion cooking (i.e., cooking methods borrowed from different cultures), which means that bioregional eating is not multicultural.

13 When talking about bioregional living, invader or settler culture becomes an essential part of the reinhabitory community (Berg and Dasmann 217). The use of such words as "local," "ethnic," and "rural" in this context is therefore confusing. The question must arise as to which takes precedence: the traditional community living-in-place or the invader/settler community reinhabiting the bioregion? Even "local" and "rural" include food species introduced by long-term invaders/settlers who became reinhabitors.

14 The Jenu Kurubas are a tribal community who lived in the mountain forests of the Nilgiris in Karnataka. In the Kannada language, "Jenu" means honey. The Jenu Kurubas gathered honey from the hives in the forests and sold it to the towns for a living. Over time, they moved out of the forests and now mainly live in the Mysore district of Karnataka (see Pradeep and Kalicharan).

15 Kundathbottu, which is known for its lush green valleys, lies in the foothills of the Brahmagiri mountain range in Karnataka.

16 In the Kodagu bioregion, coffee is an invasive species. Coffee cultivation has also had an effect on the topsoil; however, coffee is currently grown under the shade of trees that are native species. This has converted the coffee plantations into mini-forests that are restoring the topsoil, making coffee bioregional.

17 Jackfruit originated in the rain forests of the Western Ghats of India. It spread early on to other parts of India, Southeast Asia, the East Indies, and ultimately the Philippines. It is often planted in central and eastern Africa and is

fairly popular in Brazil and Surinam. In Kodagu, because of the soil and climatic conditions, it can grow to an enormous size (see Popenoe).

18 The mango is native to southern Asia, especially eastern India. There are two common types of mango, one from India and the other from the Philippines and Southeast Asia. In Kodagu, the Indian species grows in abundance. It has bursts of bright red new growth that are subject to mildew and bears monoembryonic fruit with intense color and a regular form (see Gangolly et al.).

19 This is the Indian wild orange variety, found abundantly in the Kodagu region. It originated in north-eastern India and the Indochina region. After 1450, it was also carried to Mediterranean areas by Italian traders and later, in 1500, around the world by Portuguese navigators (see Morton and Dowling; Samson).

20 Ploughing precedes the sowing season. The ploughing of rice commences in April and May, with the first rain showers. Generally, on the north side of the house, the heap of seeds remains under the cover of banana leaves and stones. After three consecutive days of watering, the seeds of the paddy crop sprout. After twenty to thirty days, the Kodava people transplant the seedlings in rows in the fields (see Richter 87–89).

21 Meat produced from animal farming is called "processed" meat, a product of the Anthropocene (see Westling).

22 Slaughtering, which has a part in the traditional Kodava belief system, is considered sacred.

23 Here I mean worshipping the hunter. The hunter is a Kodava and the hunted is the animal. The Kodava people worship both the hunter and the hunted.

24 In Kodagu, Nari mangala is a ritual where the hunter is male and married to a dead tiger, considered female.

25 Toddy is an indigenous carbohydrate-based alcoholic beverage made of palm wine. In Kodagu, it is locally fermented from the sap of various native species of palm trees such as date palms and coconut palms. In Kodagu, it is also called Kali or Neera (see Law et al.).

26 Here, "cultural determinant" refers to the cultural factors of paddy cultivation. These include the Kodava community's belief system and their sense of bioregional identity that develops from the culturally based practices related to paddy cultivation.

27 Sandalwood, an evergreen tree, is native to India. It has been an important part of Indian culture and heritage for thousands of years and was one of the first items traded with other countries; see Rai.

References

Abbay, R. "Coffee in Ceylon." *Nature: International Weekly Journal of Science*, vol. 14, 1876, pp. 375–8. *Nature*, www.nature.com/nature/journal/v14/n357/abs/014375a0.html.

Accavva, M. S., et al. *Preservation of Devara Kadu in Kodagu District: A Resource Economic Study*. University of Agricultural Sciences, 2002.

Adams, Matthew. *Anthropocene Psychology: Being Human in a More-Than-Human World*. Routledge, 2020.

Anderson, E. N. *Everyone Eats: Understanding Food and Culture*. New York University Press, 2005.

Berg, Peter, and Raymond F. Dasmann. "Reinhabiting California." *Reinhabiting A Separate Country: A Bioregional Anthology of Northern California*, edited by Peter Berg. Planet Drum Foundation, 1978, pp. 217–20.

Biénabe, Estelle. "Towards Biodiverse Agricultural Systems: Reflecting on the Technological, Social, and Institutional Changes at Stake." *Cultivating Biodiversity to Transform Agriculture*, edited by Ėtienne Hainzelin. Springer, 2013, pp. 221–61.

Chisholm, Hugh, editor. "Coorg." *Encyclopædia Britannica*. Cambridge University Press, vol. 7, 1992, pp. 91–2.

Cleveland, David. *Balancing on a Planet: The Future of Food and Agriculture*. University of California Press, 2014.

Counihan, Carole, and Penny Van Esterik. "Why Food? Why Culture? Why Now?: Introduction to the Third Edition." *Food and Culture: A Reader*, edited by Carole Counihan and Penny Van Esterik. Routledge, 2013, pp. 1–15.

De, Subarna. "Ritualizing 'Rust': A Bioregional Reading of Kailpodu." *Gnosis: An International Journal of English Language & Literature*, vol. 4, no. 2, 2018, pp. 125–34. *Gnosis Journal Archive*, http://thegnosisjournal.com/online/book/issue_2_45c48cce2e2d7fbdea1afc51c7c6ad26_9.pdf.

Ehlers, Eckart, et al., editors. *Earth System Science in the Anthropocene: Emerging Issues and Problems*. Springer, 2006.

Estok, Simon C. "An Introduction to 'Ecocritical Approaches to Food and Literature in East Asia': The Special Cluster." *Interdisciplinary Studies in Literature and Environment*, vol. 19, no. 4, 2012, pp. 261–90. ISLE, https://doi.org/10.1093/isle/iss105.

Gadgil, Madhav, and Ramachandra Guha. *This Fissured Land: An Ecological History of India*. Oxford University Press, 1992.

Gangolly, S. R., et al. *The Mango*. Indian Council of Agriculture Research, 1957.

Guiaşu, Radu Cornel. *Non-native Species and Their Role in the Environment: The Need for a Broader Perspective*. Brill, 2016.

Helander-Renvall, Elina. "Animism, Personhood and the Nature of Reality: Sami Perspectives." *Polar Record*, vol. 46, no. 1, 2010, pp. 44–56.

"History." *Kodagu District Police*, https://kodagupolice.in/history/.

Kaplan, David M. "Introduction: The Philosophy of Food." *The Philosophy of Food*, edited by David M. Kaplan. University of California Press, 2012, pp. 1–23.

"Kodagu District Profile." *DSERT*, http://dsert.kar.nic.in/dietwebsite/kodagu/DistrictProfile.htm.

Krishnakumar, V., and S. N. Potty. "Nutrition of Cardamom." *Cardamom: The Genus Eletteria*, edited by P. N. Ravindran and K. J. Madhusoodanan. CRC Press, 2002.

Law, S. V., et al. "Popular Fermented Foods and Beverages in Southeast Asia." *International Food Research Journal*, vol. 18, no. 2, 2011, pp. 475–84. *EBSCO*, www.ifrj.upm.edu.my/18%20(02)%202011/(2)%20IFRJ-2010-122.pdf.

Lynch, Tom, et al. "Introduction." *The Bioregional Imagination: Literature, Ecology, and Place*, edited by Tom Lynch et al. University of Georgia Press, 2012, pp. 1–29.

Mandanna, Sarita. *Tiger Hills: A Novel*. Penguin Group, 2010.

McCook, Stuart. "Global Rust Belt: *Hemileia vastatrix* and the Ecological Integration of World Coffee Production since 1850." *Journal of Global History*, vol. 1, 1996, pp. 177–95. *Google Scholar*, https://atrium.lib.uoguelph.ca/xmlui/bitstream/handle/10214/3163/McCook_2006_Global_Rust_Belt.pdf?sequence=4&isAllowed=y.

Mendis, G. C. *Ceylon Under the British*. Asian Educational Services, 2005.

Mills, Stephanie. *In Service of the Wild: Restoring and Reinhabiting Damaged Land*. Beacon Press, 1995.

Modood, Tariq. "Multiculturalism." *Blackwell Encyclopedia of Sociology*, 2007, pp. 1–4. *Wiley Online Library*, https://doi.org/10.1002/9781405165518.wbeosm129.pub2.

Montanari, Massimo. *Food is Culture*. Translated by Albert Sonnenfeld. Columbia University Press, 2006.

Morse, Larry E., et al. "Defining What is Native?" *Roadside Use of Native Plants*, edited by Bonnie-Harper Lore and Maggie Wilson. Island Press, 2000, pp. 12–14.

Morton, Julia Frances, and Curtis F. Dowling. *Fruits of Warm Climates*. J. F. Morton, 1987.

Nabhan, Gary Paul. *Food, Genes, and Culture: Eating Right for your Origins*. Island Press, 2013.

Nair, K. P. Prabhakaran. *Agronomy and Economy of Black Pepper and Cardamom: The "King" and "Queen" of Spices*. Elsevier, 2011.

Nambisan, Kavery. *The Scent of Pepper*. 1996. Penguin Group India, 2010.

Neilson, Jeffrey. "Environmental Governance in the Coffee Forests of Kodagu, South India." *Transforming Cultures*, vol. 3, no. 1, 2008. *eJournal*, https://doi.org/10.5130/tfc.v3i1.680.

Popenoe, Wilson. *Manual of Tropical and Subtropical Fruits*. Hafner Press, 1974.

Pradeep, M. D., and M. L. Kalicharan. "A Study about Life Style of Jenu Kuruba Tribes Working as Unorganised Labourers." *Adelaide Journal of Social Work*, vol. 3, no. 1, 2016, pp. 79–91. *SSRN*, https://papers.ssrn.com/sol3/papers.cfm?abstract_id=2995351.

Praet, Istvan. *Animism and the Question of Life*. Routledge, 2013.

Pretty, Jules. *Agri-Culture: Reconnecting People, Land and Nature*. Earthscan, 2002.

Proctor, J. "Notes on Evergreen Rainforests of Karnataka State, South-West India." *The Commonwealth Forestry Review*, vol. 65, no. 3, 1986, pp. 227–32. *JSTOR*, www.jstor.org/stable/42608089.

Rai, Shobha N. "Status and Cultivation of Sandalwood in India." *Proceedings of the Symposium on Sandalwood in the Pacific*. US Department of Agriculture, Forest Service, 1990, pp. 66–71.

Richter, Rev. Gundert. *Gazetteer of Coorg: Natural Features of the Country and the Social and Political Condition of its Inhabitants*. 1870. Low Price Publications, 2010.

Robbins, Richard H. *Global Problems and the Culture of Capitalism*. Allyn & Bacon, 1999.

Rooney, Caroline. *African Literature, Animism and Politics*. Routledge, 2000.

Sale, Kirkpatrick. *Dwellers in the Land: The Bioregional Vision*. University of Georgia Press, 2000.

Samson, J. A. *Tropical Fruits*. 2nd ed. Wiley-Blackwell, 1986.

Shiva, Vandana. "Globalisation and the War against Farmers and the Land." *The Essential Agrarian Reader*, edited by Norman Wirbza. Counterpoint, 2003, pp. 121–39.

Snyder, Gary. *The Practice of the Wild*. North Point Press, 1990.

Thayer, Robert L. Jr. *LifePlace: Bioregional Thought and Practice*. University of California Press, 2003.

Venkatesh, B., et al. "Analysis of Observed Soil Moisture Patterns under Different Land Covers in Western Ghats, India." *Journal of Hydrology*, vol. 397, nos. 3–4, 2011, pp. 281–94. *ScienceDirect*, www.sciencedirect.com/science/article/pii/S0022169410007481?via%3Dihub.

Wenzlhuemer, Roland. *From Coffee to Tea Cultivation in Ceylon, 1880-1900: An Economic and Social History*. Brill, 2008.

Westling, Louise. "Dangerous Intersubjectivities from Dionysos to Kanzi." *Thinking about Animals in the Age of the Anthropocene*, edited by Morten Tønnessen et al. Lexington Books, 2016, pp. 19–36.

Willerslev, Rane. *Soul Hunters: Hunting, Animism, and Personhood among the Siberian Yukaghirs*. University of California Press, 2007.

Wirzba, Norman, editor. *The Essential Agrarian Reader*. Counterpoint, 2003.

3 This Compost! India and the History of Global Organic Farming

Mart A. Stewart

For many consumers everywhere in the modern world, who sleepwalk into the acquisition of what they eat, food is something that arrives in attractive pyramids or in shrink-wrap packages in modern supermarkets, separated entirely from the seed and soil from which most of it originally came. Only a moment of reflection can correct this; even those who have accomplished a hermetic bubble of climate-controlled abode, office, and transport, are now and then invaded by a few weeds growing in the rain gutters or the doorstep, or dust and summer seeds floating down on windshields, and through an act of imagination are made aware of the garden or field or orchard behind the chef's virtuosity or the colorful vibrancy of produce departments. And along the imagined path to this garden, as well as in a steaming heap in the middle of it, is compost, as feat of imagination, recipe, and material reality, the stuff from which both mind and soil are renewed. "It renews with such unwitting looks, its prodigal, annual, sumptuous crops/It gives such divine materials to men, and accepts such leavings from them at last," exclaimed Walt Whitman in 1856 in "This Compost!," a paean to the inevitability of returning to the soil.

This chapter will review something much more mundane and will also position one of the origin stories of modern compost—Sir Albert Howard's development of the Indore method—within the global history of compost, organic farming and gardening, and food. Farmers, even in settler societies where soil skimming was common, have always had recipes for creating fertilizers or for agricultural regimes that would renew soils and produce better crops. This chapter will focus on the emergence of methods for making compost in the twentieth century that became connected to agricultural experiments and systems of reform, which by the end of the century had circled the globe, and which in the twenty-first century are the bedrock of regenerative agriculture systems and the foodways that have grown out of them. It will concentrate, in particular, on the Indore method developed by Sir Albert Howard and Indian agricultural laborers in the early nineteenth century at a British agricultural research station, the Institute of Plant Industry, at Indore, which he founded in the 1920s. The methods used by most American

DOI: 10.4324/9781003282976-5

organic gardeners and farmers, as modulated through the research and teachings of the Rodale Institute in Pennsylvania, derive from Howard's development of the Indore method, as have those by organic gardeners in many other places around the globe. Howard's approach, unadorned by the spiritual and sometimes inexplicably occult trappings of the followers of the method that Rudolf Steiner developed in Austria at about the same time, has provided a no-nonsense cornerstone to the modern organic agricultural and gardening sector of the food economy. It is an approach that improves both the quality and terroir of food production environments.

As Whitman explained, everything is eventually compost; everything breaks down, decomposes, and in due course returns to the earth, in one form or another—even us.[1] Whitman, in the nineteenth century, lived in a world much more shaped by the practice of agriculture and one that was also much more organic. The tsunami of plastics that has inundated the environment during the second half of the twentieth century and the beginning of the twenty-first century was not yet upon him. But even these, as Alan Weisman speculates, in his brilliantly imaginative thought experiment about what would happen to the earth if we disappeared (*The World Without Us*), will be reduced eventually to something their creators did not intend. Polymers are relatively "forever," he explains; even when they degrade into microscopic pieces and are ingested by organisms, they remain intact. Nothing that we know about can digest them. No plastic has yet to die a natural death. But on a geological rather than human time scale, they too will eventually become something else: "change is the hallmark of nature" (128). They will break down, will return, and become part of something else entirely different—compost. Just as gardens have been regarded as metaphors for productive visions of human activity, "compost" has been a metaphor for natural change, as well as a metaphor for the imagining of this change. As poet Gary Snyder explained, "Compost is stuff, junk, garbage, anything, that's turned to dirt by sitting around a while. It involves silence, darkness, time, and patience. From compost, whole gardens grow."[2] Everything, in other words, is eventually compost, and everything can come from compost. Whitman opines that "compost" is something fundamental to life, as well as a signifier for a process that has a rich material, as well as metaphorical, meaning.[3]

Agriculturists who have sought to identify ways in which to recycle materials to enrich soils have focused on a narrower meaning of compost. Their understanding is also more material than metaphoric. Simply, compost is "organic matter that has been decomposed and recycled as a fertilizer and soil amendment," explains the generic *Wikipedia* entry.[4] The 2017 edition of *Rodale's Ultimate Encyclopedia to Organic Gardening* provides a fuller but still specific definition:

> Inside a compost pile, billions of bacteria, fungi, and other organisms feed, grow, reproduce, and die, recycling kitchen and garden wastes into an excellent organic fertilizer and soil conditioner. This process

> of decomposition occurs constantly and gradually in nature. When you build a compost pile, you're simply taking advantage of—and accelerating—nature's process to create an invaluable soil amendment for your garden.[5]

Although modern organic agriculture and the use of compost as an engine for it have a discernible and relatively modern history, farmers have long used a variety of methods—used unevenly in most places because of the materials available and the labor demands—for adding organic material to soils and improving fertility. Barnyard refuse, animal manure, marsh mud, wool scraps, marl and seaweed, farm-made brews and concoctions, crop rotations, and animal–crop regimes of all kinds were used in different places at different times to replenish exhausted soils and improve yields. "Compost" as a material reality has been around for as long as farmers and gardeners have piled up or layered dung, green manure of all kinds (including harvested meadow grass and seaweed), crushed oyster shells, kitchen waste, and other materials, to create a fertilizer that both transforms and enriches the lands they wish to cultivate.

While compost making in the last seventy-five years has become the province of gardeners and a small but flourishing sector of farmers who are growing designated "organic" crops, Sir Albert Howard and others who created influential modern models for making compost saw it as something that would be more important to farmers than to gardeners. The ascendance and then domination in the nineteenth and twentieth centuries of the model for explaining soil fertility, developed by German chemist Justus Liebig in the early nineteenth century, focused the efforts of research agriculturists and modern farmers on the addition of key fertility chemicals to soils in order to replenish them, and at the same time marginalized understandings of the interaction of soils and plants that were biological and that emphasized soil ecosystems and the activities of microorganisms in facilitating or replenishing fertility. For the Liebig school of soil science, humus was merely a formula of chemicals, which could be understood and modified through the application of modern soil chemistry.[6] Sir Albert Howard's system meant to restore biological understandings to a central place in agricultural practices. As his research into organic methods developed, he also came to believe that much of what was wrong with contemporary conventional agriculture could be corrected through using such methods. By the end of his life, he and his wife, Louise, had begun to make important connections between the Indore method and the emerging organic farming movement. Making lots of compost and applying it in the right way could restore health to soils, agriculture, and people.

Raised on a farm in England, and educated at Cambridge, Howard began his career as a mycologist for the Imperial Department of Agriculture in the West Indies, before becoming a teaching agronomist back in England for two years. He then moved to India, where for twenty-six years he directed several agricultural research centers, most prominently at Indore, before returning permanently to England in 1931. Howard's research from the outset identified goals that would be beneficial to large-scale agriculture, and also to imperial agendas in India: how to improve key crops—at first, wheat and cotton—important to British agriculture in India. He developed new varieties of tobacco and wheat, most notably wheats that were rust-resistant and more productive than those currently being grown in India. His book *Wheat in India: Its Production, Varieties and Improvement* (Calcutta, 1909)—authored with his wife, Gabrielle, and his first important publication—established his reputation as an imperial agronomist. It also created a medium for the broader circulation of his agricultural research.

Howard developed his lasting contribution to modern organic agriculture while serving as the director of the Institute of Plant Industry in the state of Indore from 1924 to 1931. By this time, he had become convinced that the success of healthy agriculture depended not so much on plants and animals, but on the soils that were the foundation of agriculture. The health of the soil and of plants and animals were linked to each other, he believed, and complex and fertile soils were essential to the productivity and health of the plants that grew from them, as well as to the cattle and humans who fed on those plants. Ironically, the plant most important to his early research was cotton, inedible but absolutely necessary to the imperial agenda in India. However, this research focused on improving soil health using manures and compost and led to the development of what he called the "Indore process" of composting. In *The Waste Products of Agriculture – Their Utilization as Humus* (1931), co-authored with Yeshwant D. Wad, Howard first laid out a complete description of the Indore method. Nearly all of his subsequent publications included at least one section on this composting method. Here, Howard fully explained the methods by which he developed this process and just what it entailed in terms of materials, processing, and outcomes.[7]

The Indore process, which emphasized the use of common waste materials to build humus and soil ecosystems, became a cornerstone of the modern organic method. Created by Howard to strengthen agriculture in British India, it was exported to other parts of the Empire and used by tea growers in Kenya and Ceylon, on sugar plantations in Natal, by British agriculturists in general in Rhodesia, on coconut and rubber estates in Malaysia ("one of the most active composting centres in the Empire"), by followers of the Humic Compost Club in New Zealand, and elsewhere where the "campaign of humus" took root.[8] But it was also soon taken up by practitioners of a different sort, most prominently by agronomist and pioneering organic farmer Lady Eve Balfour in England, and Jerome Irving Rodale, founder of the Rodale Institute in Emmaus, Pennsylvania. Balfour and Rodale transformed the Indore method into a form of small-scale soil improvement that had more applicability to small-scale mixed farming and horticulture than to large-scale plantation agriculture. They and others spread the compost gospel and applied versions of the Indore method into something useful outside the imperial framework. Howard initially developed the method to produce more cotton and healthier cattle in the interests of an imperial agenda in India. But in the US, by the 1980s, it had become a method more often subversive to imperializing industrial agriculture, and was deployed by farmers to grow carrots, sweet peppers, heirloom tomatoes, kale, and other kitchen garden produce.[9]

Though rooted in a long history of farmers processing various types of manure to fertilize their fields, and though Howard sought to spread the gospel of composting through references to this history, he defined the Indore process in a way that made its provenance and originator clear. In *An Agricultural Testament*, first published in 1940, he explained as follows:

> The Indore Process for the manufacture of humus from vegetable and animal wastes was devised at the Institute of Plant Industry, Indore, Central India, between the years 1924 and 1931. It was named after the Indian State in which it originated, in grateful remembrance of all the Indore Darbar did to make my task in Central India easier and more pleasant.[10]

The term "compost" is an old English one for "decayed organic wastes" used by farmers, and Howard acknowledged that any pile of such waste will eventually turn into compost, whatever the farmer does or does not do. But what he meant by "compost" made at his Institute was slightly more refined and required the human touch:

> For those who are not familiar with these accounts it may be briefly stated that the process amounts to the collection and admixture of vegetable and animal wastes off the area farmed into heaps or pits, kept at a degree of moisture resembling that of a squeezed-out sponge, turned, and emerging finally at the end of a period of three months as a rich, crumbling compost, containing a wealth of plant nutrients and organisms essential for growth.[11]

And most importantly, in quantities useful for commercial agriculture. Though it took only seven years to refine the process, Howard had developed its foundation through two lines of agricultural research over the previous twenty-five years. One of these focused on plant parasites and diseases and yielded a set of practices and a larger argument—explained by Howard in *An Agricultural Testament* and other publications—about the relationship between the vulnerability of plants and animals to diseases and problems with the soil in which they grew. Parasites, he explained, "resulted from the breakdown of a complex biological system—the soil in relation to the plant and to the animal—due to improper methods of agriculture, an impoverished soil, or to a combination of both." Howard's second line of research, into new plant varieties important to the colonial enterprise in India, came to the same conclusion: soil conditions were crucial to any improvement in yields, and for "plant-breeding to achieve any permanent success [it] would have to include a continuous addition to the humus content of the small fields of Indian cultivators."[12]

Howard decided that attention to improving soil was the key to solving other problems in Indian agriculture, and he founded the Institute of Plant Industry in Indore in 1924 specifically to focus on methods for doing this. He wanted to take plant research in a new direction, one that centered on soil research and improvement, but also to develop a practical method for manufacturing "humus," or compost. His research there yielded an elaborate but fundamentally simple recipe for compost. The first step involved the selection of vegetable waste: in temperate countries, "straw, chaff, damaged hay and clover, hedge and bank trimmings, weeds including sea- and water-weeds, prunings, hop-bine and hop-string, potato haulm, market-garden residues including those of the greenhouse, bracken, fallen leaves, sawdust, and wood shavings"; in the tropics and sub-tropics,

> the vegetation of waste areas, grass, plants grown for shade and green-manure, sugar-cane leaves and stumps, all crop residues not consumed by livestock, cotton stalks, weeds, sawdust and wood shavings, and plants grown for providing compostable material on the borders of fields, roadsides, and any vacant corners available.[13]

Adding these to a compost heap in a carbon–nitrogen ration of 13:1 was ideal, but just about anything vegetable could provide the base for compost. In order to achieve nitrogen levels high enough to make the compost a satisfactory substitute for chemical fertilizers, animal waste was also required. "No permanent or effective system of agriculture has ever been devised without the animal," Howard observed, and animal dung, urine, and other waste was likewise necessary. "In the tropics," Howard explained, where labor was plentiful and cheap, animal and urine-saturated bedding could be added to compost daily. "In countries like Great Britain and North America, where labour is both scarce and dear, objection will be raised at once to the Indore plan." Here, along with indirectly noting the significant contribution of human labor to the composition of compost, Howard explained that constructing animal housing with pitched floors of concrete could be used to collect urine, "though at all costs urine must be used for composting."[14]

The addition of animal waste and the process of fermentation quickly create a mixture that is acidic enough to reduce the speed of the process, so materials that will make the mixture more alkaline also need to be added to the mix. These can include "carbonates of calcium or potassium in the form of powdered chalk or limestone, or wood ashes."[15] These will provide a base for maintaining the pH (7.0 to 8.0) that is needed for microorganisms that will break down the green manure. Where these are not available, "earth can be used by itself."[16] Along with green manure, animal waste and urea, and an alkaline base, water and air complete the necessary ingredients for a working compost heap; however, always in balanced amounts:

> If too much water is used the aeration of the mass is impeded, the fermentation stops and may soon become anaerobic too soon. If too little water is employed the activities of the micro-organisms slow down and then cease. The ideal condition is for the moisture content of the mass to be maintained at about half saturation during the early stages, as near as possible to the condition of a pressed-out sponge.[17]

Maintaining this perfect balance required careful monitoring, especially if the pile was to be aerated adequately to feed the microorganisms that were turning the waste into humus. Aerating the heap was done with a row of stakes down the middle that exposed the interior of the heap to the atmosphere, and by turning the compost. This was essential in the early "fungal stage" of the process, when the vegetable matter was being broken down by microorganisms; after this, "the synthesis of humus proceeds under anaerobic conditions when no special measures for the aeration of the dense mass are either possible or necessary."[18]

Howard experimented with, and devoted considerable attention to, the architecture of compost heaps in an effort to identify a structure that would allow compost makers to create as much as possible in a short time; his compost was not of the pot-and-heap variety adequate for a backyard garden but was meant to be the main soil builder for agricultural operations. In some cases, where adequate drainage was in place and exposed compost heaps would not become waterlogged, pits were the better system. Pits fostered the heat that speeded up the breakdown of organic materials in the pile. But in most cases, heaps were preferable, Howard determined. In places with monsoon rainfall "like Assam or Ceylon," the heaps needed to be covered with thatched roofs, in order to prevent water logging of the mass.[19] These could themselves eventually be replaced and composted. Howard also devoted careful attention to the size of the pit or heap, with an eye to the extent to which air could usually percolate throughout the pile, but at the same time that would maximize the build-up of heat in the heap. He developed careful specifications for the placement of vents to aerate the whole, but also for layering different kinds of materials to provide adequate drainage at the bottom. He was specific about the need and method for providing adequate aeration to the heap as it was being built, in that early and important stage of its breaking down. Howard also determined how much water needed to be added, when, and even whether it was needed, as the heap went to work on itself:

> The total amount of water that should be added at the beginning fermentation depends on the nature of the material, on the climate and on the rainfall. Watering as a rule is unnecessary in Great Britain. If the material contains about a quarter by volume of fresh greenstuff the amount of water needed can be considerably reduced. In rainy weather when everything is on the damp side no water at all is needed. *Correct watering is a matter of local circumstances and of individual judgement.*[20]

No general rule could be established for watering but, Howard asserts, must be carefully determined by "local circumstances" and the makers of the compost.[21]

Finally, the pile or heap needed to be turned with a timing that would not rupture the functioning of the bacteria but that would aerate and speed up the process of decomposition: the first turn two to three weeks "after charging;" the second, after five weeks and in the reverse direction. Careful attention needed to be applied during the turning to determine if water needed to be added. The second turning capped the process. It was in this final "ripening" stage that the crucial nitrogen content of the humus was fixed: "Under favourable circumstances as much as 25 per cent of additional free nitrogen may be secured from the atmosphere." Howard then explained that methods of storing the finished compost, so that valuable nutrients would not be oxidized or leached out before it could be added to the fields, were all more or less unsatisfactory, and that the best method was to bank the finished compost into the soil as soon as possible.[22]

The result of all this was Indore compost, of a quality and in quantities large enough to restore health to the soil, enhance long-term productivity of any crop, and contribute also to animal and human health. Because of the circuits of imperial science in which Howard was active, and the indefatigable efforts of Howard and his main publicist, his second wife, Louise (the sister of his late first wife, Gabrielle), the Indore method acquired broad currency. The method first made the trip to other colonies of the British Empire, and subsequently to other places.

The Indore method was not the only source of organic methods for improving agriculture and gardening. A kindred method was developed by Rudolph Steiner in Austria at about the same time that Sir Albert Howard was working out the Indore method in India. Perhaps in its hybrid form the Steiner method was ultimately not all that different from the Indore one, but it was developed in a setting dissimilar enough that it acquired a different kind of currency among compost makers, especially in continental Europe. Steiner had scant experience with growing anything and believed that the key to restoring the natural health of soils was through attention to philosophical and spiritual forces, by connecting agriculture to the cosmic forces of the universe (and herbal preparations that would pull these forces into the soil), and to the "biodynamic" holistic integrity of the farmstead on which one labored. The following example, from lectures he gave in 1924 to a group of farmers in Koberwitz, Westphalia that have remained the foundation of the Steiner method, captures as no other summary can the essence of his approach:

> So if we want to work with chamomile, as we did with Yarrow, we must pick its beautiful, delicate, white and yellow flower heads and treat them just like we did the yarrow unbels; we must stuff them into cattle intestines rather than in a bladder ... In this case, since we want to be worked on by a vitality that is as closely related to the earthly element as possible, we need to take these precious little sausages ... and again let them spend the entire winter underground. They should be placed not too deeply in the soils that is as rich as possible in humus. We should also try to choose a good spot that will remain covered with snow for a long time, and where this snow will be shone upon by the Sun as much as possible, so that the cosmic-astral influences will work down into the soil where the sausages are buried. Then, when spring comes, dig up the sausages and store them and add their contents to your manure ... you will find that your manure ... has the ability to enliven the soil so that the plant growth is extraordinarily stimulated. Above all, you will get healthier plants—really much healthier plants—if you fertilize this way ... To our modern way of thinking, this all sounds quite insane. I am well aware of that.[23]

The Steiner method found common ground with other kinds of organic soil husbandry, mainly by its close attention, simply, to care of the soil. It also supported the developing art of organic farming with a belief that chemicals of any kind poisoned the soil, and with an emphasis on recycling plant waste—though not by composting but by letting it lie fallow. The Steiner method required too much labor for most farmers to entertain, and it also simply did not work except for low-nutrient crops like grapes. What gave it influence was its mystical content. At a time when organic agriculture was acquiring and perhaps needed a romantic overlay, Steiner's theosophical soil improvement theory was appealing. Biodynamic farming was influential mainly as an idea rather than as a set of practices. It also converged, partly because of Steiner's political beliefs, with an attention to holistic and elitist purity flourishing among European Fascists in the 1930s (although even these blended Steiner's methods with other ones), and was embraced by National Socialists in Germany and Fascists in France. Much of Steiner's influence elsewhere came from his disciple, Ehrenfried Pfeiffer, whose book *Bio-Dynamic Farming and Gardening* (New York, 1938) in many editions publicized Steiner's ideas in the English-speaking world—though this book did as much to advance Howard's methods (without attribution) as it did Steiner's mysticism. The ideas of biodynamic farming cropped up again in the 1970s in hybrid form in the countercultural organic movement in the US. A version of Steiner's approach to farming, underpinned by compost made in the best Howard manner out of seaweed, produced legendary garden produce in the 1970s at the Findhorn community in Scotland. It is important to emphasize that even though Steiner's influence over biodynamic farming was quite out of proportion to its practical veracity, it appeared in most forms as a hybrid that depended greatly on Albert Howard's methods. It was significant mainly because it enhanced the romantic appeal of those methods and made them appealing to agriculturists who sought to reject industrial agriculture. It gave comfort and justification to avatars of agriculture who needed some mysticism with their compost.[24]

As the Steiner method expanded in Europe and the Indore method circled the globe, they acquired different meanings within different cultural contexts. Practitioners developed variations as they applied these methods to particular places. But the core methods remained the same. Some advocates, such as Eve Balfour, Louis Broomfield, Jerome Rodale, and Alan Chadwick, promoted Howard's core methods with so much pragmatism and romantic embellishment and publicity that these epigoni have also acquired historical reputations as compost pioneers. But it is important to note that the core methods of the Indore method were preserved in the compost recipes of all of these advocates and practitioners. At the same time, both practitioners and observers have debated whether Howard deserved more credit for developing foundational methods for organic agriculture, or quite a bit less—a debate that continues unabated, if current scholarship and papers at academic conferences on the subject are any indication.

Most important to this debate was the extent to which Howard depended, as he increasingly implied and sometimes asserted, on the "peasant wisdom" of the Indian farmers whom he also sought to help. In her report on her late husband's accomplishments, *Sir Albert Howard in India*, Louise Howard recounted in several ways how much the Indore method was shaped by Howard's experience in India. First of all, sensitive to the poverty of the "peasant farmers" of India, Howard designed the Indore method using Indian tools and vernacular units of measurement already in wide circulation:

> The spade, *phawra*, was a kind of scraping or hacking hoe as universally found in the East; measurement was by *tagari*, a sheet-iron bowl with capacity of five-sevenths of a cubic foot; material was carried in a *pal* or stretcher made of gunny-sheet nailed to two seven-foot bamboos; there was a simple wooden rake for charging pits, an ordinary wooden tub for slurry, and the well-known kerosene tin to carry water.[25]

Louise Howard also characterized her late husband's relationship with his laborers as one of respect, interaction, and exchange, rather than of colonial condescension and coercion. He was always learning from them and from the "peasant community" he wished to serve, she contended: "does he not call the Indian peasants his 'professors'?" She also described his development of the Indore method as a weaning away from the limitations of modern soil chemistry and agricultural methods and at the same time a deepening appreciation of the "accumulated wisdom inherited from generation to generation" of Indian and other "peasant" farmers. It was her husband's great accomplishment, she argued, that the experiments at Indore "reintroduced to the world of science, in a way both exact and comprehensive, the Chinese master conception of the restoration of all wastes to the soil by continuous process of decay." He applied and modulated these ancient methods with exact scientific description and method, with system and control, and filled a "great gap in Western thought" that had ignored "an age-old Eastern practice," the use of manures and wastes for agriculture and their time-worn efficacy in the fields.[26] Louise Howard, who published her husband's biography after his death and at the height of the hegemony of Green Revolution chemical agriculture in the 1950s, and whose advocacy of the Indore method became by itself an important contribution to the development of modern organic agriculture, created a kind of agriculturist out of him that was part scientist, part guru, part colonial patriarch, and part visionary. But this depiction of Howard may have played loosely with the truth.

How much of the Indore method was a hybrid of British colonial science and Indian traditional knowledge? Was the Indore method an expression of deep respect for traditional knowledge and a medium for teaching modern Europeans and Americans about the "age-old wisdom" of the East, as Louise Howard contended? Or was it simply another appropriation of traditional knowledge by an imperial scientist, modified to maximize consistent and efficient production for large-scale agricultural enterprises, explained in the purported "universal" language of science, and disseminated through an imperial medium of science that always paired it with Sir Albert Howard as chief author? Or did he create something new, and something structured almost entirely by recent developments in agricultural science? This debate has been important not only because the decolonization of imperial science and post-colonial scholarship in general has made it an important one, but also because it speaks to the history of the cultural content of composting that has been important in the evolution of organic agriculture during the twenty-first century.

The most recent and thorough consideration of this question, based on newly released Howard correspondence not previously available to scholars, by Gregory A. Barton in *The Global History of Organic Farming* (2018), argues convincingly that Louise Howard was a little too much the admiring partner and romantic publicist. Howard certainly had a profound appreciation for Frank H. King's influential *Farmers of Forty Centuries* (1911), as he notes prominently in his explanation of the Indore method in several publications.[27] King had brilliantly identified one of the main sources of a historic feature of Chinese civilization that was missing elsewhere—the ability of Chinese agriculture to sustain larger and more dense populations than in other agricultural economies. He had identified the method by which this had been possible: by the application of night soil, or compost made from it, to agricultural fields. Howard's admiration for King's book highlighted this argument:

> In China a nation of observant peasants has worked out for itself simple methods of returning to the soil all the vegetable; animal, and human wastes that are available: a dense population has been maintained without any falling off in fertility.[28]

King's appreciation for the accumulated "wisdom" of the East was not, however, all that different from Howard's. At the time that he conducted his relatively limited travels in China and studied indigenous agricultural methods, he had recently retired as chief of the soil management division of the US Department of Agriculture; his background and his orientation towards methods for improving soil quality were deeply conditioned by his training and then experience as a Western soil scientist. He did not speak Chinese but worked with translators, most of his conversations were with fellow travelers rather than Chinese farmers, he stayed in good hotels and traveled by steamship and railroad, and he remained quite distant from the very muck he exalted. He was critical of what he believed to be the wastefulness and destructiveness of American agriculture and, therefore, went to China with a mind open to alternatives. He remained blind to the poverty and suffering and grueling regimens of labor of Chinese peasants, however, the hierarchy of power that ensured that they were permanently exploited, and the dead end that Chinese rural agriculture had reached around the time of his travels. His focus on agricultural method rather than agricultural culture yielded an appreciative explanation of the addition of human, animal, and agricultural wastes to the soil as a fundamental component of Chinese agriculture, and one that had for centuries (he was right about this) ensured long-term productivity adequate to support substantial populations. This was an important contribution to conversations about soil among Western scientists and was also quite influential. The point being made here is that Howard's connection to the generations of traditional practices of "observant" peasant farmers in China, by way of King's book, was modulated through a framework of understanding that was quite akin to his own, one that ensured he remained detached from the cultural context and the actual workings of those traditions.[29]

The farmers of India with whom Howard had had much closer contact may have been his "professors," but he never explained just what he might have learned from them, and his attention to methods of composting was always structured by questions that came from modern agricultural science. He was interested from the outset not in how to build organic soils, but in how to conduct agriculture without expensive commercial chemicals. He also devoted his attention not to the support of small-scale agriculture but to the development of soil amendment methods that would beef up commercial agriculture and the production of commodities important to global imperial markets.

As Howard himself explained, the core component of the Indore method did not come from working with the farmers of India. It was inspired and informed instead by a project and a paper produced on the creation of "artificial farmyard manure" at the Rothamsted Experimental Station in England by H. B. Hutchinson and E. H. Richards, and published in 1921 in the *Journal of the Ministry of Agriculture*. The work of Hutchinson and Richards quite simply outlined the process by which barnyard waste could be transformed into a manure that crops could actually utilize. They understood that the nitrogen available in manure and urine could not be directly absorbed by plants, but had to be combined with "carbonaceous matter" (plant litter or straw) and then metabolized by fungi and bacteria into nutrients that when spread upon the fields could be absorbed by the roots of plants. This was also the core principle of the Indore process. While acknowledging this article and the work of the Rothamsted Experimental Station, Howard also claimed a different terrain. He deplored this institute of research, which had been a nerve center for the Liebig tradition of soil science since the middle of the previous century; he considered it an obsequiously obedient servant of the larger infrastructure of industrial agriculture. He also argued convincingly that the addition of agricultural chemicals to compost by Hutchinson and Richards retarded and betrayed the natural process that was fundamental to its success: "It introduces into composting the same fundamental mistake that is being made in farming, namely, the use of chemicals instead of natural manure." In addition, he was astutely critical of their patenting of their process, which he believed added a property regime that reduced the flexibility and creativity that were essential to the ongoing progress of the Indore method:

> the patenting of a process (even when, as in this case, the patentees derive no personal profit) always places the investigator in bondage; he becomes the slave to his own scheme; rigidity takes the place of flexibility; progress then becomes difficult, or even impossible.[30]

Staking out fresh ground in any case may have been necessary, in retrospect, in the twentieth-century history of composting and its relationship to the emergence of modern organic farming and gardening. Something in the way of a romantic veneer was developed by the advocates of composting and by Howard himself, partly because he was never able to quantify just how it worked. Field trials over a period of years demonstrated that compost added fertility by improving soil, insofar as it improved soil health and productivity. But the demand of modern science and industrial agriculture for quantifiable indices of success—like those provided by reducing soil to identifiable configurations of chemicals—which could counter or enter into conversation with the clearer definitions of soil chemistry, eluded Howard. Adding a romantic veneer, something done more by Howard's disciples than by Howard himself, worked quite contrary to his original intent and positioned the Indore method against large-scale industrial agriculture, instead of making it a method that could be integrated into a better version of it. Rooting the method in premodern, pre-industrial, and time-tested "peasant" methods made it the perfect alternative to large-scale agriculture, which was increasingly dependent on agricultural chemicals, on an infrastructure hostile to small producers, and which was increasingly shown to be environmentally unsustainable. In this, Howard's champions, and especially Louise Howard, who never visited India, may have been as important to the success of the Indore method as Howard's discoveries through his work at the Institute of Plant Industry in the 1920s.[31]

This debate over the relationship between the Indore method and the Indian farmers, and who should reap credit for what, misses a crucial point about the labor that went into the making of compost—labor that was both arduous and carefully accomplished. This point is contained in full in Howard's remark, "In the tropics, where labour is plentiful and cheap"—the point being that though he was writing the book and describing the method, it was the Indian laborers who were doing the work of making compost. Though Howard does not tell his audience that Indians were providing anything other than their labor, he makes it clear that a great deal of discretionary judgment is necessary when putting together and managing a compost heap with *phawra*, *tagari*, *pal*, *wooden rake*, and *kerosene tin*—especially in keeping it wet but not too wet, in layering materials in a way that will foster adequate drainage and the movement of air, and that will pay attention to variations in the materials collected in any individual compost heap in order to encourage fermentation and keep the heap from becoming an inert mess. His sharp critique of Hutchinson and Richards' patenting of their process, because it stunted the possibilities for flexibility and creativity in the actual making of compost, also pointed to the necessity for quite a bit of discretionary action when cooking compost the Indore way. The Indore method was a method, but one that was open-ended and required constant adjustment, adaptation, and creative attention; this was essential to the "method" itself, as Howard explicitly explains:

> The test of any process for converting the waste products of agriculture into humus is flexibility and adaptability to every possible set of conditions. It should also develop and be capable of absorbing new

> knowledge and fresh points of view as they arise. Finally, it should be suggestive and indicate new and promising lines of research. If the Indore Process can pass these severe tests it will soon become woven into the fabric of agricultural practice. It will then have achieved permanence and will have fulfilled its purpose—the restitution of their manurial rights to the soils of this planet.[32]

While the Indore method provides a general scientific framework and recipe for making compost, the actual making of it was as much art as science, and here the Indian laborers and heap managers were the artists to Howard's scientist.[33]

What does this mean for our understanding of food and culture, and the role of India within this global history? First of all, as consumers all over the world begin to develop justifiable anxieties about food produced by modern industrial agriculture and to turn towards food produced by organic methods, as the support of agricultural research institutions (and the US Department of Agriculture) grows for organic agriculture, and as the industrial agriculture and food production sector itself begins to integrate organic agriculture into its menu of methods, general methods for improving the soil that rely on returning "humus" to the soil and fostering soil ecosystems have become more important. Many of these do not use the Indore method specifically or compost in general, but rely on the key principle that Howard recognized: namely, that composting improves upon and speeds up natural processes for introducing organic material to the soil, and that soil with organic material is the foundation of all vegetable life. The making of compost, using methods partly derived from the Indore method, and on a scale likely unimagined by Howard himself, is also fundamental to some kinds of organic farming. Food grown by organic methods expresses the importance of soil and soil ecosystems, not just as a medium for providing nutrients and water to plants but in the fundamental interaction between the gestation and growth of those plants. Organic methods to produce food for modern consumers put into practice in one form or another the system worked out by Sir Albert Howard and Indian heap managers and workers in the 1920s in Indore. They do so by way of the material prescriptions of the Indore method, but also through the organic imaginary created by the Howards and their humus disciples, of studious composting as a path to a healthier and more productive agriculture.

Finally, there is the matter of taste: many consumers and cooks contend that food produced by organic methods simply tastes better, and they have created food movements—the Slow Food movement in Europe and the US, and the farm-to-table movement in the latter—that balance these contentions about soil terroir and taste with a dependence on healthy organic soil. All of these, in one way or another, even if sometimes attenuated, connect back to the efforts of Howard and his invisible and exploited but surely astute laborers in Indore, and the open-ended method they created. This compost (!), Walt Whitman makes clear, is something that is going to happen with or without us—and to us. (As this author's unschooled grandfather often pointed out, the ultimate fate of all of us is "food for worms.") "Compost" as a metaphor for poets and philosophers also does not need a literal Indore heap. But the food that is produced by organic farming and gardening all relies on one version or another of the Indore method as a cornerstone. When Alice Waters stood in her restaurant yard garden and celebrated the kale, aubergines, and peppers that went into her Chez Panisse cuisine, or Slow Food high priest Carlo Petrini and his disciples tout the taste of local food grown by "traditional" methods, or Michael Pollan celebrated in book-length form the healthy virtues of organic gardening, or Michelle Obama planted a flagship demonstration organic garden to promote good nutrition on the White House lawn, they all celebrated a small piece of India and the compost makers of Indore at the same time. And whether manure or metaphor, whether organic vegetables or poetic fruits, in India or Austria or California, plunging our arms into piles of steaming muck now and then gives us a sense of where we are on the earth, the food we consume from it, as well as the leavings we return—"this compost!"

Notes

1 Whitman's principle was recently unknowingly ratified by a new law in Washington state that allows composting of human remains as an alternative to burial or cremation; see Karimi and Vera.
2 Quoted in LeGuin, "Harvesting Stories."
3 For a book-length examination of the poetics of compost, see Jed Rasula. Serpil Oppermann has provided a summary ecocriticism vantage on compost as metaphor and of "composting landscapes" as potential sites of activism: "Although it is a vexing site punctured with ferocious entanglements, composting landscapes are rich with alternative ecologies, images, and stories that are not yet encumbered by anthropocentric potencies and can propel change by deepening our understanding of environmentalism." This essay is more grounded in the history and fundamentals of composting as a material practice, but connected to a larger "composting landscape" of the kind Oppermann promotes and that Whitman first explained.
4 "Compost" in *Wikipedia*.
5 "Compost," in Bradley et al. (132). The first edition of this repeatedly revised guide, produced by the pioneering organic gardening and farming research center in the US, the Rodale Institute, was published in 1959.
6 See Heckman (145). Liebig's influence was not automatic but part of a larger history of the expansion of a hegemonic scientific model; see Rossiter.
7 See Barton (63–79); Conford (53–59); L. E. Howard; Berry (xiii–xiv).
8 See Chapter 5, "Practical Applications of the Indore Process," in Howard, *An Agricultural Testament* (53–86); and "The Spread of the Indore Method in the Farming and Plantation Worlds," in Howard, *The Soil and Health* (223–233).
9 In general, a great deal more work can be done on the cultural antecedents of organic farming and gardening in every part of the world. But because most

of the farming was British, imperial, European, and/or North American, the scant scholarship so far has concentrated in these areas. As Barton explains, these collectively were the "major field of action in which organic farming first took root, before spreading around the world into a global phenomenon" (48).

10 *Agricultural Testament*, 39.
11 *Soil and Health*, 211.
12 *Agricultural Testament*, 39.
13 *Agricultural Testament*, 41.
14 *Agricultural Testament*, 43–44.
15 *Agricultural Testament*, 44
16 *Agricultural Testament*, 44.
17 *Agricultural Testament*, 44.
18 *Agricultural Testament*, 44.
19 *Agricultural Testament*, 46.
20 *Agricultural Testament*, 47.
21 *Agricultural Testament*, 44–48.
22 *Agricultural Testament*, 48–51.
23 Conford (65).
24 Conford's book includes a discussion on the Steiner method (65–80); Barton includes a brief discussion of Steiner's biodynamic farming but also a reasonable assessment of its influence (especially 39–45). See also Kirchmann's careful critique of the Steiner method (173–187). For the Steiner method among organic farmers who embraced Fascism in France, see Bivar, especially Chapter 2, "Alternative Ideals, 1944–58"; for a discussion on the mystical gardening practices at the Findhorn community, see Hawkin. The Findhorn community was founded by an international group of young and disaffected idealists. This author briefly visited Findhorn in 1976, talked with community members as well as neighboring farmers about the success of the gardens, and also observed first-hand the composting methods carried out there.
25 L. E. Howard, *Sir Albert Howard in India*, 207.
26 *Agricultural Testament*, 222, 217.
27 Barton, Chapter 5, "The Search for Pre-Modern Wisdom" (80–94), provides a critical explanation of the influence of Frank King's Chinese farmers and other pre-modern antecedents to modern organic farming, as well as the political and cultural reasons why modern farmers sought them out and exalted them.
28 *Agricultural Testament*, 51.
29 For a brief but good critical study of King, see Worster (11–14).
30 See Howard, *Agricultural Testament* (51–52); Hutchinson and Richards (398–411); Barton (203).
31 See Barton (62–79, 202–203).
32 *Agricultural Testament*, 52.
33 More work needs to be done on the relationship between Howard and his laborers and the Indian farmers with whom he worked to parse out what was surely more than a romantic overlay, but also something less than what Louise Howard made of it. Amita Baviskar's recovery of the contributions of the labor of Indian gardeners to the creation and tending of the Mughal Gardens in Delhi might be a model for this; see Baviskar.

References

Barton, Gregory A. *The Global History of Organic Farming*. Oxford University Press, 2018.

Baviskar, Amita. *First Garden of the Republic: Nature in the President's Estate*. Ministry of Information and Broadcasting, 2016.

Berry, Wendell. "Introduction." *The Soil and Health: A Study of Organic Agriculture*, by Sir Albert Howard. University of Kentucky Press, 2006.

Bivar, Venus. *Organic Resistance: The Struggle over Industrial Farming in Postwar France*. University of North Carolina Press, 2019.

Bradley, Fern Marshall, et al., editors. *Rodale's Ultimate Encyclopedia of Organic Gardening: An Indispensable Green Resource for Every Gardener*. 2009. Rodale Books, 2017.

Conford, Philip. *The Origins of the Organic Movement*. Floris Books, 2001.

Hawkin, Paul. *The Findhorn Magic*. Bantam, 1976.

Heckman, J. "A History of Organic Farming: Transitions from Sir Albert Howard's War in the Soil to USDA National Organic Program." *Renewable Agriculture and Food Systems*, vol. 21, no. 3, 2006.

Howard, Sir Albert. *The Soil and Health: A Study of Organic Agriculture*. 1947. University of Kentucky Press, 2006.

———. *An Agricultural Testament*. 1940. Oxford University Press, 1943.

Howard, Louise E. *Sir Albert Howard in India*. Faber and Faber, 1953.

Hutchinson, H. B. and E. H. Richards. "Artificial Farmyard Manure." *Journal of the Ministry of Agriculture*, vol. 28, 1921, pp. 398–411.

Karimi, Faith, and Amir Vera. "Washington Becomes the First State to Legalize Composting of Humans." 22 May 2019, https://edition.cnn.com/2019/05/22/us/washington-human-composting-legal-trnd/index.html. Accessed 16 Aug. 2019.

Kirchmann, Holger. "Biological Dynamic Farming – An Occult Form of Alternative Agriculture?" *Journal of Agricultural and Environmental Ethics*, vol. 7, no. 2, 1994, pp. 173–87.

Le Guin, Ursula Kroeber. "Making Up Stories." *Words Are My Matter: Writings About Life & Books*, 2016. *Harvesting Stories*, www.terriwindling.com/blog/2017/09/harvest.html.

Oppermann, Serpil. "Compost." *Veer Ecology: A Companion for Environmental Thinking* edited by Jeffrey Jerome Cohen and Lowell Duckert. University of Minnesota Press, 2017. Kindle Edition.

Rasula, Jed. *This Compost: Ecological Imperatives in American Poetry*. University of Georgia Press, 2002.

Rossiter, Margaret W. *The Emergence of Agricultural Science: Justus Liebig and the Americans, 1840–1880*. Yale University Press, 1975.

Weisman, Alan. *The World Without Us*. St. Martin's Press, 2007.

Wikipedia, "Compost." https://en.wikipedia.org/wiki/Compost. Accessed 15 Feb. 2018.

Worster, Donald. "The Good Muck: Toward an Excremental History of China." *RCC Perspectives*, no. 5, 2017, pp. 1–54.

Part II

Intercultural Food Practices

4 Environmental Food Documentaries

From *Fast Food Nation* to a Popular Selection of Top 20 YouTube Videos

Pat Brereton

The central problem for ethical food production is that it appears most difficult to get across complex environmental and ethical messages around food security, much less articulating that the global economy ought to shrink, in the struggle to become more environmentally sustainable, while using fewer carbon-based energy sources in the process. Most remain addicted to cheap and freely available food at all times of the year, which facilitates a more destructive form of conspicuous consumption that certainly does not stack up to the growing challenge and demand for long-term environmental sustainability (Jamieson 2012). Alternatively, calling for a stoical, resilient, even frugal, form of de-growth, involving a more holistically conceived and balanced production–consumption model, remains difficult to visualize, much less promote in the media (see Brereton 2019).

While one suspects the future will lie somewhere between such polarizing extremes, Western lifestyles in particular will certainly have to change, and this involves a radical transformation of public perceptions and, most importantly, behaviour around food consumption and waste. Some evidence of this transformation can be garnered from the growth of vegetarianism, coupled with various promotional forms of organic farming. Ecofilm strategies around food and nature generally have developed across a range of academic scholarly readers (see Rust et al. 2013; Weik von Mossner 2014; Hansen and Cox 2017). This chapter will draw on such scholarship to present a thematic and narrative analysis of a selection of online documentaries, beginning with the relatively big-budget feature *Fast Food Nation*, coupled with easily available YouTube documentary shorts, like *Forks over Knives*; *Dirt! The Movie*, and *The Future of Food*, which incidentally has recorded over 104,000 viewings (as of September 2021). Strategies used in this analysis draw on recent textual analysis of *Cowspiracy*, *Food Inc.*, and *Our Daily Bread* (Brereton 2019).[1] All examples are chosen because of their growing public attention and potential influence on viewers and by appearing in various selections of top twenty popular food documentaries. Such environmentally charged documentaries can also signal and promote a *tipping point* towards supporting a more sustainable, even organic, global food

DOI: 10.4324/9781003282976-7

production system. At the same time, some aesthetic and narrative strategies are more successful than others in helping to achieve this transformation. The small sample examined in this chapter ranges from the overtly polemical and preachy, to the more subtle and nuanced invocation of behavioural change, alongside recalling more well-established magazine and news interview formats, which can serve as a benchmark for ongoing audience and textual environmental studies.

Literature Overview

Foregrounding the importance of documentary films in speaking to an environmental food agenda, while teasing out how different aesthetic formats of factual filmmaking are co-opted in this process, remains the focus of scholarly analysis (see Hughes 2014; Jekonowski 2015). The food industry, and for that matter the media and film industry, endlessly co-opts food as a main staple of life, while for more affluent consumers and audiences promoting an ever-expanding style choice for a broad range of added value. In essence this helps to create numerous synergies, all the while explicitly foregrounding the pleasures and inherent benefits of food consumption (Baron et al. 2014: 81).

Stepping outside this bubble of a globalized consumer culture, environmental food documentaries can help remind audiences that agriculture is part of nature and culture, which in turn calls attention to a predominant underlying message and attitude embedded within the need for more critical modes of environmental literacy. Incidentally, scientific and literary publications like *Silent Spring* (Rachel Carson 1962), *The Unsettling of America: Culture and Agriculture* (Wendell Berry 1977), *The End of Nature* (Bill McKibben 1989), *Stolen Harvest* (Vandana Shiva 2000), and other seminal texts continue to actively temper and influence this underlying drive of environmental documentaries, towards expressing the hopes and concerns in securing a sustainable agriculture movement.

While, as argued elsewhere (Brereton 2019), more mainstream fictional movies appear to mask out concrete representations of industrial agriculture, with the food industry simply situated as supporting the maximizing of profits by directing attention towards its well-packaged end-products, this chapter seeks to illustrate how several YouTube eco-food documentaries effectively go back to basics, while explicitly exploring and dramatizing ways in which agriculturally produced food remains an intrinsic part of nature and of human consumption.[2]

Food Security and Sovereignty—Rewilding

To enhance profits, food companies tend to obscure, if not actively hide, direct links between the farm gate and the dining table. Nonetheless, it has to be continuously recognized that without a food safety net, 80% of the world's population becomes immediately at risk of hunger, recalling threats of natural disaster, war, and so on (Sheeran 2011, cited in Mann 2014). The concept of food sovereignty challenges the dominance of an open form of agribusiness and the legitimacy of an unjust global trade system, while alternatively seeking to promote a counter-model of small-scale, localized agriculture becomes an ongoing challenge, being a fairer solution to hunger and poverty. As a broad framing device, food sovereignty posits clear ethical positions regarding land redistribution, the rights of women, resistance to genetically modified organisms (GMOs), and the defence of local economies (Mann 2014: 7). It is frequently suggested that structural inequalities are responsible for food price hikes, violations of the rights of agricultural workers, and the decline in the ability of states to protect their citizens' rights to food (De Schutter, 2011 in Mann 2014). Solutions posited include going back to basics and constructing more radical forms of rewilding nature and food production.

Rewilding has emerged as a popular and scientific expression of new directions in ecology and conservation management associated with the restoration of ecosystem function. As Paul Jepson (2017) argues, it introduces a radical new natural archetype that evokes a positive form of environmentalism. Species reintroductions to restore ecosystem functioning and associated interests in landscape connectivity and the creation of large core reserves are all posited as necessary to help get back to a more sustainable model of resource management.[3]

Manbiot (2013) presents the concept of rewilding as an opportunity for environmental-minded citizens to say what they are for rather than against—retreating from the Biblical doctrines of domination over nature, rescinding perverse agricultural subsidies, while reinvigorating nature-based rural economies and embracing the return of more ambitious conservation groups. This approach permeates the ultimate desired goal of several documentaries under discussion but remains held back by the spectre of nature being continuously exploited. For instance, *Dirt! The Movie*, directed by Bill Benenson, which was a winner in the 2009 Sundance festival, is a good exemplar to be examined later. Narrated by the film star Jamie Lee Curtis—see www.dirtthemovie.org—the trailer begins: "We depend on dirt, to purify and heal the system that sustains us. We are dirt." One-third of the earth's topsoil has been dramatically lost in the last 30 years, while in contrast and at another tangential register, a case study of the harvesting of tobacco can also illustrate further growing tensions around how human nature is exploited.

Tobacco as a Food Allegory

The tobacco plant remains a useful example of the historical transformation from a local natural resource, respected for its medicinal properties, into a disembodied export commodity demonized for its transformation into a toxic and addictive product. As highlighted in a study by

Lopez (2012), European colonists converted tobacco into an export crop, which became so important to the foundation of the United States that the tobacco leaf adorns the one-dollar bill. For instance, a telling scene in Terrence Malick's (2005) film *The New World*—a re-visioning of the old Pocahontas/Captain Smith tale—brilliantly illustrates this historical transformation. We see the conversion of the iconic character of Pocahontas into Rebecca through cultural and agricultural domestication. When the colonists' tobacco crop fails, she helps the domesticated plants survive by using her local intelligence to compost the soil by adding dead fish. Meanwhile, the tragic character of Rebecca in her corseted and constricted Western dress is also being co-opted and domesticated in order to be presented at the King of England's court. As she becomes more and more "civilized," she ends up losing her true (unsullied) nature, while her family's society is also destroyed.

Three hundred years later, monoculture tobacco is fertilized not with fish, but with petroleum-based fertilizer, which is destroying the soil's biodiversity and contributing to contaminated run-off into the Gulf of Mexico, now causing large dead zones in the ocean. Furthermore, commercial tobacco is converted into an addictive product that causes five million deaths worldwide every year (growing to ten million annually within the next ten years), with mortality climbing mostly in peripheral territories. Commercial tobacco is often treated with the same chemicals that can be found in Windex—rat poison and gunpowder. Meanwhile, the multinational tobacco companies become engaged in investment capital and deeply embedded in, if not epitomizing, neoliberal assumptions of market fundamentalism (Harvey 2005). This story is analogous—if on a less stark scale—to the exploitation model applied to other natural resources like water, alongside food, with too much emphasis being placed on heavily processed additives, echoing other kinds of commoditized natural resource that have been exploited over the centuries.

In particular the following food documentaries help to illustrate the growth of monoculture farming, which remains a part of a closed food system that favours corporate food monopolies (Pollan 2006); while at the other organic and healthy extreme, small-scale forms of agriculture and permaculture, which are not controlled by pesticides, petroleum-based fertilizer, or laboratory-engineered seeds, appear to provide more useful environmental and sustainable solutions. As a productive model of resource management, this is also open to the changeable conditions of local ecology and interaction with unpredictable elements such as weather, insects, and native plants where local biodiversity and sustainable solutions are sorely tested. Meanwhile, societies that engage exclusively in monoculture put all their faith in scientific and technological solutions, which is very different in outlook to those that have very limited economies and cultures that promote more sustainable forms of farming practices and agriculture generally.

From Hippy Cultures to Veganism

From those not cognizant of such macro food debates, these tensions are illustrated for instance by the growth of the so-called hippy movement from the 1960s, recalling more recently back-to-nature environmental grass roots movements, which have become the shorthand representational caricature of environmental food production–consumption rectitude within popular media. For instance, in a local Irish journalistic piece by Michael Viney in *The Irish Times* (Saturday Jan. 9th 2016) entitled "Another Life: Galway's Hippy Ideas are Just What the Environment needs," Viney suggests that Galway's relationship with landscape and ocean is rare, while analysing their future plan: "A Vision for Galway 2030" (avisionforgalway2030.wordpress.com). Situated on the west coast of Ireland, Galway, like many similar communities, is looking for solutions in trying to face up to the demands of a low-carbon energy future. One chapter in the transition plan is focused on green ideas for food production and local self-sufficiency. Such ideas have, of course, been around a long time, as the journalist affirms, and they remain slow to take effect, recalling today's demands in dealing with our climate crisis.

Meanwhile, promoting permaculture—from its origins in Australia—and even bringing back non-mechanical technology like work-horses for "renewable, low-impact, alternative energy" across small-scale farms might seem somewhat nostalgic and basically not economically viable. Yet, it must be noted that so many hardy notions, once the province of back-to-nature "hippies" and counterculture ecologists, have endured through the slow eco-awakening of our contemporary society, as ways of re-imagining and facing up to growing environmental threats. Such historical and low-tech solutions probably make even more sense now, with so much wasteful energy spent in, for instance, transporting unseasonable food produce to every corner of the globe.

Closely linked to this movement and identified as one of the top Google trends of 2016 is of course veganism, with the first ever vegan week broadcast on *The Great British Bake Off* (UK, 2018). Veganism as a diet and practice has increasingly become part of mainstream media culture, particularly through social media over the last few years (Doyle 2016). This represents a significant and positive shift in media engagement with food as an erstwhile hippie phenomenon—following years of negative representations of vegans as being anti-modern, typified as eating lentils and wearing non-leather sandals (Cole and Morgan 2011). Vegetarian diets which are wholeheartedly embraced by such alternative communities were heretofore considered across popular discourse as more time consuming, requiring a commitment that differs from conventional diets and therefore more trouble than it's worth. But this has all apparently changed as it moves into the mainstream (Spendrup et al. 2017: 9).

However, the problem with such transformation is not a suspected lack of community cohesion but a gap between people's declared sympathies and intentions and what they actually do in their lives.[4] By all accounts this also remains the key dilemma for environmental communication—pushing good intentions towards concrete action. So, we need more powerful narratives and models of media engagement and persuasion to assist in this transformation. Selling resilience remains a challenge, especially with regard to food production and consumption and facing up to its long-term obligations. Local self-reliant food production coupled with more local employment has to be the way forward.

Unfortunately, Ireland, like much of the Western world, remains seduced by (cheap) monocultural food production, especially with regard to meat and dairy, which remain our biggest indigenous exports. Worldwide, livestock production contributes 14.5% of total greenhouse gas emissions (Gerber et al. 2013). All livestock production affects biodiversity, from positive contributions of grazing animals to valuable semi-natural grasslands (Paracchini and Britz. 2008), to devastating tropical deforestation to meet increased demand for pasture and feed protein. In summary, Sara Spendrup et al. (2017) assert how meat production affects many different environmental areas, and these in turn impact animal welfare levels, which vary widely between species and production systems (citing Steinfeld et al. 2006).

To decrease the environmental impact from the dominant food system, production-side measures, including more resource-efficient systems and the implementation of known technology, will likely not suffice; so consumption-side changes in developed countries are likely to be also needed (Aiking 2014).

Farming Development: From Organic to High-Tech Production

The current global factory farming production and marketing system is generating a glut of cheap processed meats that are fuelling climate change while feeding a pandemic of diet-related ill-health that is costing between 600 and 900 billion dollars a year in healthcare and related costs. Several of the documentaries discussed in this chapter, including *Fast Food Nation*, *Forks over Knives*, and others, draw attention to these worrying trajectories in a very direct and emotive manner.

For instance, if people in developed countries simply ate no more than the recommended levels of meat, more than five million premature deaths could be avoided by 2050, according to Oxford researchers. They further calculate that a worldwide switch to a vegetarian diet would potentially save more than seven million lives. Consequently, progressive environmental food documentaries seek to actively promote vegetarianism and related forms of sustainable organic food production at all levels of society.

At the same time, back in 2014 the influential British Chatham House Think Tank found low public awareness of the true cost of such dietary choices, which is directly responded to and actively addressed by a number of documentaries cited below. As one would expect, "consumers with a higher level of awareness were more likely to indicate willingness to reduce their meat and dairy consumption for climate objectives." Closing what such researchers call the "awareness gap" is a vital first step towards broad-based behavioural food change. Researchers however note the "sticking paucity of efforts" to rein in global food consumption and suggest that governments and environmental groups have been "reluctant to pursue policies or campaigns to shift consumer behaviour." The reason seems to be fear of backlash, principally from powerful interest groups, as dramatized for example in *Cowspiracy* (see Brereton 2019). This growing worry is acutely evident in the United States and other Western countries, where food policy is shaped primarily by the agri-industrial lobby.

But can organic farming, alongside sustainable fishing—as explored in *Seaspiracy* (2021)—actually feed the world? This remains a contested debate, while presenting an unhelpful polarizing framing of the overall global production possibilities.[5] There was, of course, a time when all farming was organic, with fertilizer primarily made up of compost and organic material. Fields were periodically left fallow (unfarmed) to recover soil moisture and nutrients, and crops were historically rotated to prevent nutrient exhaustion,[6] and, most importantly, pesticides were non-existent. Farmers remained, however, at the mercy of periodic droughts (despite irrigation) and insect infestations. As populations grew, so did the demand for food, which in turn led to more large-scale farming methods being developed and normalized. More recently, synthetic pesticides (beginning with DDT) came into use during the 1940s and 1950s and sparked our contemporary environmental movement.

Sustainable Food Production: *Fast Food Nation*

The related pillars of food sustainability and environmental security remain a major challenge for all human societies, which is illustrated by a number of successful contemporary documentaries, including most notably *Fast Food Nation*. Richard Linklater's *Fast Food Nation* translates Eric Schlosser's well-known tome *Fast Food Nation: The Dark Side of the All-American Meal* (2000) into a series of interwoven stories. One story focuses on illegal immigrants who find work in a meat-processing plant; another features disgruntled youths interested in animal rights; and a third is about a fast-food executive who has to find out how manure is getting into the chain's best-selling hamburgers. In a comprehensive overview study of food films, Baron et al. note how when the documentary was released it was rated R, which ostensibly categorizes "disturbing images, strong sexuality, language and drug content." This is probably one of the main reasons *Fast Food Nation* made a miserly one million dollars in the box office. Such a return is extremely low when compared to general blockbusters' box office figures. By any measure the documentary's truly shocking depiction of food safety problems at fast-food restaurants and the "dangerous working conditions at food-processing plants made the film an unappealing co-promotion partner" (Baron et al. 2014: 58).

The dominant aesthetic used in the documentary involves dramatic shock tactics and foregrounding structural and ideological tensions. In turn this remains an abiding dilemma for film makers striving to call attention to audience expectations. If narratives constantly point the finger at audiences and at the shocking dangers of food consumption and factory farming, then it would appear such targeted audiences are less likely to positively relate to such dramatic cautionary tales. Simply stated, such messages make them feel uncomfortable in conspiring with the pervasive aims of "cheap food." However, to fully test this hypothesis, a major cross-cultural and longitudinal audience study is required. Trying to get a systemic environmental message across to consumers around what is good for all concerned, while at the same time not alienating the larger public, remains a difficult balancing act. Certainly, some food documentaries are more successful than others at achieving this. The most successful documentaries speak more directly and cogently to the tangible issues of food security and environmentalism than probably more conventional fictional representations (see Brereton 2019).[7] This is further evidenced through a selection of freely available YouTube videos that cogently signal the importance of food narratives for general public consciousness.

Folk over Knives

Forks over Knives (2011), directed by Lee Fulkerson, for instance, appears high up in the top ten of food documentaries online.[8] The documentary explains the healthy way that people need to take responsibility for their diet and consume more plant-based food. It's that simple. The disease of affluence—precipitated by the dominance of meat in our diet—can be controlled or even reversed by rejecting our present menu of animal-based and processed foods. So many food documentaries speak of the need to move to a vegetable-based diet—both for ethical and, most importantly, environmental reasons—if we are to support a sustainable future. This theme is echoed across a broad range of food documentaries which are freely accessed within YouTube.

Essentially, organically grown crops on average use 25% less energy than their chemical cousins.[9] By using more organic grasses and sustainable methods of production, the major danger of intense farming affecting climate change can at least partially be kept in check, most notably offsetting the fact that agriculture remains the most water-intensive industry on the planet, consuming a staggering 72% of all global freshwater, at a time when the United Nations says approximately 80% of our water supplies are being over-exploited.

Animating *The True Cost of Food*

This animated short is focused on an American mother and her two kids driving to a fast-food shopping centre, rather than a farmers' market on the opposite side of the freeway. Because she is in a hurry to get food for an evening meal, her child secures a golden coupon which enables them to check out their shopping in a special aisle (16A, recalling the *Harry Potter* franchise), where she meets an old woman (the ghost of healthy organic food). There the fraught housewife is presented with facts around the true (economic) cost of food, particularly documenting the enormous energy and water needed to feed and maintain cattle for meat, requiring approximately 25,000 gallons of water per cow. Not to mention the mountains of wasted food which still involves the abuse of scarce resources to produce the food in the first place. The documentary animated format facilitates so many disturbing facts being disseminated, including how cattle and cows defecate (or crap) over 60 pounds of waste material per day, resulting in a massive pollution problem, not to mention the ever-growing methane waste produced by livestock. And even for the more benevolent vegetables the housewife purchases in the regular supermarket, this is also not the real price of production, as these plants are artificially forced to grow faster than is natural in more organic habitats and are also transported long distances. So, a huge bill is presented to the housewife, highlighting the true cost of food.

Basically this dominant form of distribution and food consumption is not sustainable because of monocropping and various aspects of large-scale factory farming. There are so many hidden costs not factored into the final bill for the consumer, with the need for chemicals, not to mention losing over 24 billion tons of top soil a year. Taking into account that 7% of American farmers sell over 72% of the food, big farms therefore receive a majority of the farm subsidies, which was not what was intended. Consequently, the whole system is badly skewed in not actively promoting more sustainable small-scale and organic land husbandry. As a general rule, in the current system, over 13 pounds of grain are used to produce just 1 pound of meat. And then because food is so "cheap" for the consumer, lots of this erstwhile precious produce ends up in landfill. This short animation quickly and effectively gets the eco-message across, while probably over-romanticizing the farmer's (hippy) market, where the family appears too friendly and living so close to the land. Furthermore, after the delicious and wholesome meal back at home, the husband somewhat patronizes his wife for finally purchasing good food, having been worried that, heretofore, she was simply being seduced by fast food, although not taking any responsibility himself for promoting such an unhealthy and unbalanced food system.

Another related and very short documentary calls attention to a *Food Recovery Network* (2011) coming into being, helping American university campus dining halls give back and redistribute so much otherwise wasted food to the poor. The network also supports a meatless Monday, pronouncing that together we can make a dent in the food crisis. This is a simple and clear example of a good food initiative designed to prevent food waste.

Dirt! The Movie

This film opens its storyline with the cosmic big-bang explosion that started the ever-evolving life of planet earth. It's because of this we have the living, breathing skin called dirt that originated in the stars across the galaxy. Bill Cogan, author of *Dirt!*, and Indian deep ecologist Vandana Shiva affirm how we are made of molecules the same as dirt, which is further echoed by the great ecological scholar Fritjof Capra. Our wealth comes from the soil. If we don't take care of it, then we are doomed. It is vital to keep our biosphere alive—kids, for instance, go out to play in the dirt, not the soil. Similarly, Andy Lipkis, author of *TreePeople* (www.treepeople.org/author/alipkis/), talks of how, especially in traditional countries, soil is regarded as the mother and thereby necessary for all forms of fertility.

Unlike the endless and uncontested critique of meat and animals cited above, Shiva (2021), citing specific Indian cultural references, talks of the sacred cow and how its dung is necessary to create more dirt to fertilize the soil, while Pierre Rabi speaks of the healing power of dirt and the power of rewilding (quoted in Hayward 2021). God did not give us this amazing dirt to mistreat it. We live, he affirms, in a potential Garden of Eden, and soil gives us so much of its bounteous fruit.

Concurrently, people have been building houses with dirt and earth for over 9000 years. But demand for natural resources has changed our relationship with dirt towards what we think is more precious—specifically, coal and oil have become more economically dominant across the globe. The documentary shows examples of a mountain being cut in half simply to extract precious resources, while ending up not securing cheap electricity in spite of all this destruction. Such radical forms of excavation remain unbelievably expensive for the eco-system in the long term.

Unlike rewilding, discussed above, desertification remains one way of undoing the security of life in any country. Civilizations have risen and fallen, based on how they treat dirt. For example, the American mid-west in the 1930s in a move to a monoculture ended up killing the soil by destroying its root structure. The soil simply blew away as part of the dust bowl disaster across the American mid-west. Pesticides have also served to destroy the structure of soil and its water base. In another part of the world, thousands of farmers in India have been terminally affected by natural resource depletions, exacerbated by pesticides, while they were trying to cope with economic survival.

The Power of Metaphor and Developing a Utopian Imagination

The metaphor of a humming bird remains the most engaging animated insect of *Dirt! The Movie*. The *mise-en-scène* of a forest on fire and all the animated animals seen running away, fearful for their habitat, remains memorable long after the film has finished. In spite of this danger, the little bird keeps flying back to the fire, with just a drop of water in her tiny beak to try to save the forest; it's all she can do. Meanwhile, big animals like elephants with their long trunks, who could do more, simply stand there, impotent in the face of danger. The allegorical message of the animated sequence and overall documentary is clear. We all have to combine efforts to do our best to save our planet.[10]

Alternatively, in an interview with the great Brazilian photographer Sebastião Salgado, who created provocative large-scale photographs of mass human degradation and exploitation around working in cavernous gold mines, we hear of his new life. Together with his wife Lelia, he has moved away from creative photography and documenting human injustice and environmental exploitation. Instead, he has reverted back to creating his own real-life nirvana by setting up his own "Eden" project—which is similar to other eco-activists like Shiva, as developed in India. One further wonders: can audio-visual representations help promote such eco-utopian dreams?

Meanwhile, showing poor black kids planting trees and seeing how they can make a difference to their local community is a good start. What we have destroyed, we can heal! All of these allegorical and practical interventions can help sow the seeds of active audience intervention, as further demonstrated by *The Future of Food*.

The Future of Food

Planet earth affords us a great range of fresh food, yet we continue to have a huge problem with famine across the world. The earth remains humanity's support system, but for how long is the big worry. Our population is rising and continues to double over shorter periods. By 2025 it will be over 8 billion and by 2050 maybe over 10 billion. With over 28 billion cows being farmed, over three-quarters come from the southern hemisphere, although they are mainly consumed in the northern industrial countries. Although Malthus believed population increase would mean that resultant food production would not match what was needed to feed our ever-growing human population (*Encyclopedia Britannica* 1998), such has not been the case. Thankfully he was wrong, as he was not able to predict the great scientific and technological advances and massive changes that would occur in the intervening centuries.

By all accounts, this documentary appears ostensibly pro-technology and constantly insinuates the benefit of techno-fixes for our global food difficulties. At the same time it also acknowledges that the environmental impact of agriculture has got worse, not better. Human health through eating well is essential for the betterment of global society, and humans certainly need lots of natural nutrients to survive.

The documentary foregrounds a celebration of plant scientist Norman Borlaug, who helped save the Mexican diseased wheat by picking the best and most resilient features and genetically re-engineering them across different sites. He was awarded a Nobel prize in 1970 for his work on the Green Revolution. But there are ecological problems with such solutions, especially through environmental contamination via the prolonged use of fertilizers. And, of course, the most dangerous threat remains in dealing with the possible unintended consequences of GMO food being put back into the food chain. Crudely, one can set up GMO in opposition to biological purity, as being an ongoing tension in the food industry. Within food production, basically the dominant tension is around how to avoid dangerous side-effects, while recognizing the benefits of, for example, seedless water melons and other bountiful GMO crops. The most successful GMO crop variety remains rape seed oil, which is used to feed cattle and thereby helps to provide meat for the human food chain. The future of global food production, many experts believe, will most certainly rely on developments in the science of GMO.[11]

Also much innovation will be made in exploiting the rich resources from the sea and taking into account the huge problem of conventional (over)fishing. Talk of a "Blue Revolution" and the need for more sustainable aquaculture pervades the literature. Japan is really pushing the boat out (metaphorically and otherwise) regarding developing its use of algae, which can become a major food source in the future. We still don't know, however, how our ocean systems work. There is talk, for instance, of adding iron chemicals to the sea to make it more fruitful, allowing more plant life and algae to grow. But alternatively, deep ecological worries continue around the dangers of further unintended consequences of the manipulation of our natural habitats and oceans which need to be constantly evaluated.

Audience Reception of Food Documentary: The Turn Towards Environmental Literacy

Investigating the effects of such food documentaries requiring pro-environmental cognition and behavioural change has been carried out by scholars like Arendt and Matthes (2016). But much more specific research is needed to gauge the effectiveness of such online media (see Brereton 2019). Of central interest remains the concept of connectedness that describes an individual's sense of being linked to nature. Within these are several studies of connecting with nature in zoos, for instance (see Clayton et al. 2014); there is also growing research in teasing out how such spaces might increase connectedness to nature and pro-environmental behaviour. It is important to note, however, that such scholarship has frequently found that food/nature documentary exposure increases pro-environmental donation behaviour, primarily in those already having a strong sense of connectedness (Arendt and Matthes 2016: 453).[12] Meanwhile, extending so-called benevolent ecodocumentaries towards more fraught food discourses and developing effective and broad-ranging environmental narratives remains a challenge.

Nonetheless, nature and food documentaries provide for a more mediated environmental experience. The question thus is whether sitting indoors in front of a screen and watching mediated forms of nature is sufficient to help increase implicit and tangible connections with the reality of food production (Arendt and Matthes 2016: 459). Nature and food documentaries can finally only present a mediated yet powerful construction of reality. Yet it can be:

> perceived to be an expansion of human vision, a means of entering into a world that was invisible to the human eye, an extension of the physical body of the subject, allowing for the creation of pleasure by bringing animals in their natural habitat closer to humans through the act of visualization in moving media images.
>
> (Horak 2006: 459)

Several recent studies (such as Newman 2015) conclude that participants who were most likely to make changes after seeing various documentaries, in and of themselves, are not enough to significantly change the general public's beliefs or alternatively serve as potential tipping points with regard to behavioural change regarding factory farming and especially animal food industries. However from more than 20 years of experience of teaching eco-media, I have found that provocative food documentaries can most effectively help create a nudging tipping point towards environmental behaviour change. One could probably have deduced this without much sustained research, but at the same time, audio-visual media remain just one variable among many in contemporary society's arsenal of social and cultural influences. Hopefully, we can reaffirm a potentially powerful need to change, aided by these and other documentaries, recalling this growing online diet of environmental and food narratives which have come into public consciousness of late.[13]

Concluding Remarks

The toxic materiality of the ecodocumentary, according to Helen Hughes in her provocative *Green Documentary* monograph, is a matter of a complex network of social and material effects of the documentary, which also takes into account the design and mass manufacture of technology, travel and transportation, land use, etc. As already suggested, *we* need all types of documentaries, from the shrill polemical varieties, to the nuanced *avant-garde* aesthetic, to help in the struggle towards activating environmental engagement and in supporting food literacy.

Environmental awareness, defined by Kollmuss and Agyeman, includes "knowing of the impact of human behaviour on the environment" (2002: 253), and serves as the goal of many different kinds of activity concerned with education about the human impact on the environment, including food consumption.[14] However, according to such research, one of the earliest findings of environmental behaviour research back in the 1970s was that knowledge and awareness are not sufficient in to lead to radical changes in behaviour. Yet most environmental non-governmental organizations (NGOs)—and one could add food sustainability documentary approaches, alluded to above—"still base their communication campaigns and strategies on the simplistic assumption that more knowledge will lead to more enlightened behaviour" (2002: 241 cited in Hughes 2014: 12).

All the while, threats to the food supply chain represent a cogent and visceral concern for us all; especially as food speaks so vividly to both short-term and long-term human needs and other manifestations of environmental transformation. The search for food amidst a world of scarcity remains a frequent motif, especially within numerous post-apocalyptic science fiction fantasies like the more scientifically accurate *The Martian* (2015). This is also foregrounded as a core theme with several powerful allegorical images exhibited explored in this paper.[15]

Wendell Berry: "Eating is an Environmental Act" and a Political Act

Citizens support the type of system you feel most benefits the world, while of course not everyone has this choice. Ruth Richardson[16] particularly does not like (preaching) with hard and fast dos and don'ts which are expected as a "take-away" message from such magazine media formats. Much conventional communication scholarship would concur. Of course, she certainly supports local farmers, and she cooks everything from scratch, while she speaks of the importance of promoting family life and eating together. And at the end of the conversation, both experts note they have not even mentioned climate change, which will have much more dangerous consequences on the whole future of food production and consumption.

By any measure, food remains one of the most important attributes, triggers, and barometers of environmental ethics and literacy, as consumers are directly implicated in maintaining food prices as low as possible to help maximize competitive productivity and, even some argue, to maintain long-term sustainability. Deep tensions between factory farming, as opposed to more organic forms of (slow) food production, speak directly to a broad range of environmental and ethical tensions and agendas. All of these have huge implications for day-to-day living for humans across the world. With our exponentially growing populations and increasing demands for corrective economical models of food production, there are grave dangers with unregulated systems of food production and distribution. Such *laissez-faire* developments do not take into account the long-term common good, much less recognize concerns around the precautionary principle that mark growing worries concerning genetically modified food and other food-techno solutions. As evident since Rachel Carson's seminal and prototypical literary text *Silent Spring* back in the 1960s, once a direct health concern and clear connection is made between pesticides and the human food chain, this connection has to be urgently addressed. More recently, worries over the safety of food has reached a tipping point and has spiralled upwardly with ongoing risk debates around GM food and what is deemed acceptable. Furthermore, teasing out what is natural or normative with regard to mass-produced factory food production is of growing concern, especially witnessing heightened levels of obesity and over-consumption. GM food, including consuming less meat, is part of the solution, as visualized across a number of these documentaries. Society has a long way to go to integrate such debates and, in particular, environmental food literacies into coherent strategies for the future, which demand that we as globally responsible citizens address the problem of climate change above all else.

Appealing to public interests concerning the quality of food can finally serve as a useful bridge to other related forms of environmental concerns, especially around climate change. While the lack of environmental literacy and clear discursive communication practices around food stands out as pervasive danger and risk (Lindenfeld, 2010: 383), documentaries have an important part to play in the overall communication cycle around these global environmental issues. Nevertheless, in striving to find new ways of addressing audiences, food documentaries need to provoke more interactive engagement, aided by online media affordances. Hopefully these can succeed by cross-connecting with other forms of new media while speaking to growing food security debates and environmental concerns generally.

Notes

1 With the historical advent of "direct cinema," the works of Fredric Wiseman stand as pivotal in the representation of animals and food in documentary history—*Primate* (1974), *Meat* (1976), *Zoo* (1993), and *American Meat* (2013), most specifically, represent agricultural practices in negative ways that centre on animal slaughter and meat, as signifiers of crisis in the industrial food system (Smaill, 2014: 66). Such historical examples feed off the style and aesthetic modalities of *Food Inc.* and *Cowspiracy* in particular.

2 *The Corporation* is one of the most economically successful documentaries to detail problems in the food industry, yet the film made only US$3 million at the box office. *Flow* only raised US$142,569 gross in the US market,

whereas *King Korn* raised US$105,422 (www.BoxOfficeMojo.com). See also top twenty documentaries and box office receipts up to 2012, which include: *March of the Penguins* (2005) at number 2 with 77m; *Earth* (2009) at number 5 with 32m, and *An Inconvenient Truth* number 9 with 24m—down to number 17 with *Super-Size Me* (2004) at 12m (Baron et al. 2014: 185).

3 For instance, Hastag rewilding has a growing social media presence—much like the terms punk or hippy—it is coming to signify an unsettling—a desire to shake up the present and shape futures. Citizens need to have a stake in the future natures that emerge, yet the shifting-baseline syndrome suggests people value the nature of their youth and are inherently conservative. Rewilding theory and practices confront and unsettle and are therefore an important component of a progressive forward-looking conservation policy (Jepson 2017: 10).

4 Coincidentally Rob Hopkins, the charismatic founder of the Transition Town Movement who spent over seven years teaching permaculture at Kinsale Further Education College in the south of Ireland, remains a leading food and energy activist in local "resilience" to peak-oil and climate change.

For instance, high-tech alternatives to meat, such as the approach of "Beyond Meat" by the US food company backed by Bill Gates, are emerging as possible solutions to the problem. This is activated by using plant-based ingredients to closely mimic the taste, texture, and smells that make meat so alluring, while apparently setting out to trim the health effects and global environmental havoc that our ancient carnal predilections are now wreaking.

5 Somewhat counter-intuitively, however, it is insinuated by food experts that organic does not automatically equal "safe." Africa's and India's crisis in food production, for example, described as the global battle with hunger, is largely rooted in a "soil–health crisis" with new technological methods needed to feed growing populations. Proponents of organic farming counter-argue that this strategy is exacerbating the crisis. But, of course, a myriad of variables affect overall production levels. Experts like Ed Hammer and Mark Anslow remain more positive regarding the overall benefits of organic farming, while asserting in *The Ecologist* from January 3, 2008 that *we* all need to cut down on meat consumption in particular to help normalize the average consumption of one and a half pounds per person per week (43–46).

6 See John Bellamy Foster's critique of post-colonial land abuse and the so-called "metabolic rift."

7 Greg Mitman talks of a contemporary "green wave" of film and television, facilitated by a popular penchant for "eco-chic" that is underpinned not only by commercial imperatives, but also by counter-balancing ethical and environmental concerns. Mitman notes that of the US$631 million in gross revenues earned by 275 documentaries released between 2002 and 2006, US$163 million came from eight wildlife and natural documentaries (216). Food documentaries can learn a lot from the pleasures set up and excavated from within more mainstream nature and environmental narratives.

8 See James McLaughlin, "The Ten Health Food Documentaries that will Change Your Life," Jan. 01 2018, https://greenpress.co/blogs/news/health-food-documentaries, where he places it number 6. [Top ten in reverse order include: *Super Size Me* at number 10; *May I be Frank* at number 9; *Hungry*

for Change at number 8; *Fed Up* at number 7; *Forks over Knives* at number 6; *Food Matters* at number 5; *Cowspiracy* at number 4; *Food Inc.* at number 3; *Fat Sick and Nearly Dead* at number 2; *What the Health by Joe Cross* at number 1.

9 And organic farming can even help salvage the poor cow which has been demonized as a major source of methane emissions.

10 Meanwhile, as many recent commentators suggest, the metaphor of war and dealing with major global crisis needs to be activated.

11 Meanwhile, alternative sources of (red) meat, not to mention developments in GMO, include:

Ostrich—good and less fat with more protein.
Crickets—very healthy if we could get over how they look.
Crocodiles—which taste like chicken and have less colleterial which tastes good.
Kangaroo—again, remains a good alternative to conventional cattle.
Whales—will stop them becoming extinct at sea!

12 Previous research has identified connectedness to nature as a central concept in pro-environmentalism (Bruni, Chance, and Schultz 2012). Connectedness to nature describes an individual's sense about the degree to which he or she is part of nature. Most importantly, it has been argued that if people see themselves as part of nature, they will not harm nature (see Mayer and Frantz 2004). In other words, individuals with a strong connection to nature are less likely to engage in behaviours that negatively affect the environment (Verges and Duffy 2010). Furthermore, it has been found that self–nature associations are malleable (Arendt and Matthes 2016: 454).

13 Incidentally, I would have to agree with Bill Nichols and other scholars, who suggests that audiences expect documentaries to be educational or persuasive, but do not have the same expectations of fiction film (cited in Newman 79).

The uncertainty over whether utilizing graphic footage of animal mistreatment will empower audiences to change, or overwhelm and lead to audience apathy, is reflected in the responses of participants in this study. The participants' comments indicate that images have the ability to shift public opinion, and may suggest that the use of graphic footage of animal mistreatment could be a persuasive means of encouraging people to reconsider their ideas about human treatment of animals.

14 A further goal of environmental education is the promotion of pro-environmental behaviour that, as Kollmuss and Agyeman put it in their survey of approaches to the subject, means "behaviour that consciously seeks to minimize the negative impact of one's actions on the natural and built world (e.g. minimize resource and energy consumption, use of non-toxic substances, reduce waste production)" (2002: 240).

15 When hunger takes a literal rather than a metaphorical form, it propels actions that serve to define what it is to be human—or to be inhuman. Food and water scarcity leads both to brutality and kindness in science fiction films such as *The Omega Man* (1971), *Mad Max 2* (1982), and so on.

16 *See* TVO News feature on food from the Canadian broadcasting (Interview with professional guests Ruth Richardson and Alexander Muller: https://ssir.org/bios/ruth_richardson).

"We are producing enough food for everyone, but still we have not dealt with the problem of the poor. By 2030 we will have to feed 9.5 billion, consequently we have to radically change our agricultural model to meet this growing demand."

Richardson talked of the difference between price and the cost of food and the need to include the cost of dealing with greenhouse gases, transport, and medical costs for humans by promoting obesity and all the problems associated with this. We always need to acknowledge the true cost of such so-called cheap food. Throughout many of the documents highlighted in this paper, this remains the abiding mantra.

References

Aiking, Harry. 'Protein Production: Planet, Profit, Plus People?' *American Journal of Clinical Nutrition*, vol. 100, issue 1, 483S–489S, 2014.

Arendt, Florian and Jorg Matthes. 'Nature Documentaries, Connectedness and Nature, and Pro-Environmental Behaviour'. *Environmental Communication*, vol. 10, no. 4, 453–472, 2016.

Baron, Cynthia, Diane Carson and Mark Bernard. *Appetites and Anxieties: Food, Film and the Politics of Representation*. Wayne State University Press, 2014.

Berry, Wendell. *The Unsettling of America: Culture and Agriculture*. Sierra Club Books, 1977.

Brereton, Pat. *Environmental Literacy and New Digital Audiences*. Routledge, 2019.

Brereton, Pat. *Essential Concepts of Environmental Communication: An A-Z Guide*. Routledge, 2022.

Bruni, C. M., Chance, R. C., and Schultz, P. W. 'Measuring Values-Based Environmental Concerns in Children: An Environmental Motives Scale.' *Journal of Environmental Education*, vol. 43, issue 1, 1–15, 2012.

Carson, Rachel. *Silent Spring*. Houghton Mufflin, 1962.

Clayton, Susan, Jerry Ulbke, Carol Saunders, Jennifer Matiasek and Alejandro Grajal. 'Connecting to Nature and the Zoo: Implications for responding to Climate Change'. *Environmental Education and Research*, vol. 20, issue 4, 2014.

Cole, Matthew and Karen Morgan. 'Vegaphobia: Derogatory Discourses of Veganism and the Reproduction of Speciesism in the UK National Newspapers.' *British Journal of Sociology*, vol. 62, issue 1, 2011, 134–153.

Doyle, Julie. Celebrity vegans and the lifestyling of ethical consumption, *Environmental Communication*, vol. 10, issue 6, 777–790, 2016.

Encyclopedia Britannica. 'Thomas Malthus: English Economist and Demographer.' 1998. www.britannica.com/biography/Thomas-Malthus.

Foster, John Bellamy and Brett Clark. 'The Robbery of Natural Capitalism and the Metabolic Rift.' *Monthly Review*, vol. 70, issue 3, 1–20, July 2018.

Gerber, P.J. et al. *Tackling Climate Change Through Livestock: A Global Assessment of Emissions and Mitigation Opportunities*. Food and Agriculture Organization of the United Nations (FAO), 2013. www.fao.org/3/i3437e/i3437e.pdf.

Hansen, Anders and Robert Cox (eds) *The Routledge Handbook of Environment and Communication*. Routledge, 2017.

Harvey, David. *A Brief History of Neoliberalism*. Oxford University Press, 2005.

Hayward, Susan. *Ecology Documentaries: The Effects of Disrupted Ecosystems, the Migratory Flow and the Unsafe, Inhumane Space of the Unheard*. Routledge, 2021.

Horak, Jan-Christopher. 'Wildlife Documentaries: From Classical Forms to Reality TV.' *Film History*, vol. 18, issue 1, 459–475, 2006.

Hughes, Helen. *Green Documentary: Environmental Documentary in the 21st Century*. Intellect Books, 2014.

Jamieson, Dale. *Ethics and the Environment: An Introduction*. Cambridge University Press, 2012.

Jekanowski, Rachel Webb. 'Green Documentaries: Environmental Documentaries in the 21st Century'. *ISLE*, vol. 22, issue 1, pp.187–8, 2015.

Jepson, Paul. 'A Rewilding Agenda for Europe: Creating a Network of Experimental Reserves'. *Ecography: Media Fauna Special Issue*. Oxford University Press, 2017.

Kollmuss, Anja and Julian Agyeman. 'Mind the Gap: Why do People Act Environmentally and What are the Barriers to Pro-environmental Behavior?' *Environment Education Research*, vol. 8, issue 3, 239–260, 2002.

Lindenfeld, Laura. 'Can Documentary Films like *Food Inc.* Achieve their Promise?' *Environmental Communication*, vol. 4, pp. 378–86, 2010.Lockwood, Alex. 'Graphs of Grief and Other Green Feelings: The Uses of Affect in the Study of Environmental Communication'. *Environmental Communication*, August, 2016.

Lopez, A. *The Media Ecosystem: What Ecology Can Teach us About Responsible Media Practice*. North Atlantic Books, 2012.

Mann, Alana. *Global Activism in Food Politics: Power Shift*. Palgrave, 2014.

Mayer, F. Stephan and Cynthia McPherson Frantz. 'The Connectedness of Nature Scale: A Measure of Individuals' Feeling in Community with Nature.' *Journal of Environmental Psychology*, vol. 24, 503–515, 2004.

McKibben, Bill. *The End of Nature*. Random House, 1989.

Manbiot, George. *Feral: Searching for Enchantment on the Frontiers of Rewilding*. Penguin Books, 2013.

Newman, Lara. 'The Effects of The Cold and Bold Native on Audience Attitudes Towards Animals'. *Animal Studies Journal*, vol. 4, issue 1, 2015.

Paracchini M. L. and Wolfgang Britz. 'Quantifying effects of changed farm practices on biodiversity in policy impact assessment – an application of CAPRI-Spat'. OECD, 2008. www.oecd.org/greengrowth/sustainable-agriculture/44802327.pdf.

Pollan, Michael. *The Omnivore's Dilemma: A Natural History of Four Meals*. Penguin Press, 2006.

Rust, Stephen, Slama Monani and Sean Cubitt (eds.) *Econcinema Theory and Practice*. Routledge, 2013.

Shiva, Vandana. *Stolen Harvest: The Hijacking of the Global Food Supply*. Zed Books, 2000.

Shiva, Vandana. 'Vandana Shiva On why the Food we Eat Matters'. 2021. www.bbc.com/travel/article/20210127-vandana-shiva-on-why-the-food-we-eat-matters.

Smaill, Belinda. 'Documentary Film and Animal Modernity: An Analysis of Raw Herring and Sweetgrass'. *Australian Humanities Review*, Issue 57, pp. 56–75, 2014.

Spendrup, Sara et al. 'Evaluating Consumer Understanding of the Swedish Meat Guide—A Multi-layered Environmental Information Tool Communicating Trade-Offs when Choosing Food'. *Environmental Communication*, May, 2017.

Verges, Michelle and Sean Duffy. 'Connected to Birds but Not Bees: Valence Moderates Implicit Associations with Nature.' *Environment and Behavior*, vol. 42, issue 5, 625–642, 2010.

Weik von Mossner, Alexa (ed.) *Moving Environments: Affect, Emotion, Ecology and Film*. Wilfrid Laurier University Press, 2014.

5 *Bacalhau* in England and Goa

A Case Study of Economy, Ecology, and the Assignation of Value in the Global South, *Circa* 1472–2019

William Spates

In postcolonial cultures around the world, the appetite for salt fish, especially Atlantic herring and cod, is a ubiquitous reminder of a colonial past that can be found embedded in cultures not only in Goa and the other former Portuguese colonies in India, but also along the coast of Africa, from Mozambique and Angola to Nigeria, and across the Atlantic in the Caribbean and South America. This chapter will focus on the changing cultural and economic value of salt cod between the sixteenth and twentieth-first centuries with a focus on metabolic rift and climate change as over-exploited cod stocks collapsed in the late medieval Northeast Atlantic, compelling colonial expansion into the Canadian Atlantic and causing a subsequent collapse of cod stocks in the New World. While this phenomenon has been explored by scientists and historians, I will focus in particular on how these changing dynamics affect not only economic but cultural evaluations of cod as a commodity, as well as how they are recorded in cultural artefacts, including prose, poetry, and drama.

Since this chapter was originally conceived and presented in Goa, India, I will primarily use the Portuguese term for salt cod *bacalhau*, which is in common parlance in the region, but will, from time to time, invoke terms for other types of preserved cod, such as Poor John, clipfish, and stockfish, as they pertain to the topic at hand. Preserved cod was a mainstay of colonial diets, and it exists in a number of forms.

Cod has been caught and processed in Scandinavian countries since at least the early medieval period. In this early period, cod was preserved by drying on outdoor racks in Iceland and Norway. This process is recalled etymologically in the English word clipfish, a loanword derived from the Norwegian *klippfisk* or "cliff fish," which describes the racks of drying cod. Archaeologists, armed with DNA evidence, have established that Vikings harvested Arctic cod and transported—and potentially traded—air-dried, unsalted clipfish, alternatively known as stockfish, in Europe for at least a millennium (Star et al.). Codfish, preserved with salt and known as salt cod (English), *morue* (French), *bacalao* (Spanish), and *bacalhau* (Portuguese), can be traced back to the fifteenth century when Basque, Breton, and Norman fishers began bringing French and Iberian salt on fishing journeys to the North Atlantic to preserve cod (LeHuenen

DOI: 10.4324/9781003282976-8

524–525). A final term, “Poor John,” must also be introduced. Poor John was also salted cod and may refer to smaller fish of inferior quality, arguably ones that were cured green (onboard immediately after harvest). In the context of this chapter, I will use the term stockfish to describe dried, unsalted cod; *bacalhau* to describe salt cod; and Poor John to describe the derogatory early modern English references to poor-quality, green-cured cod.

In addition to Goa, both Portugal and England feature prominently in this narrative. The Portuguese first colonized India and were also instrumental in developing the Canadian Atlantic fishery. After Portugal fell under Spanish dominion in 1580, England became the primary power over a triangular trade route between England, Newfoundland, and Spain that relied on the exchange of *bacalhau*, fortified wine, and salt. This chapter will weave together several critical discourses to examine the changing evaluation of commodified codfish through the prism of early modern English and early modern to postmodern Goan approaches to *bacalhau* as a means of engaging with the continuing synthesis of colonial and postcolonial European products in the Global South, foregrounded by changing social and ecological conditions. This study of the tumultuous interaction between ecological change and colonial exploitation will demonstrate how *bacalhau*, an often-maligned staple of the impoverished in the early modern period, becomes a food of the elite in the late twentieth and twenty-first centuries—a development revealed through an analysis of early modern literary artefacts and contemporary historiography.

By the late fifteenth and early sixteenth centuries, the Scandinavian trade in stockfish was already several hundred years old; however, Renaissance advances in navigation, shipbuilding, and shipboard processing of catch were set to transform the trade. During this period, Southern Europeans, who had access to large quantities of salt, became involved in both harvesting and processing of Atlantic cod. Basque, Portuguese, Spanish, and French sailors would harvest cod in the North Atlantic and preserve the fish on board by salting them. It is likely that the salted but undried catch, preserved immediately on board, was later called Poor John by Shakespeare and his contemporaries. Southern Europeans would return to their home countries and sun-dry this salted catch. Poor John, however, seems to have also found its way to English markets, where it was noted for its peculiar scent. As time progressed, Europeans began drying and salting cod in Newfoundland and Nova Scotia as well.

The very same improvements in navigation and shipbuilding which were enabling the Portuguese to discover sea routes around Africa toward the East Indies were also making possible exploration for a Northwest Passage above Canada to the East. Some scholars argue that the Portuguese presence in the North Atlantic may have predated John Cabot’s “so-called discovery of the territory for King Henry VII of England in 1497" (Cole 1). It is also possible that the Portuguese had followed Basque whalers and cod-fishing people to the New World and that they had known about the extraordinarily fecund Grand Banks fishery off the coast of Newfoundland as early as 1472, when the region began to appear on maps described as *Terra dos Bacalhaus*, "Codfish Land" (Pires 117, 124). Mark Kurlansky conjectures that the Basque sailors may have learned the location of the North Sea and Canadian Atlantic fisheries, as well as superior ship-building techniques, particularly the use of overlapping planks, from the Vikings; furthermore, it is Kurlansky's assertion that Basque access to Franco-Iberian salt and their history of salting fishes and whales guided these intrepid people's forays into the North Atlantic and resulted in the creation of *bacalhau* (*Cod* 113). Emerging nation states with imperial ambitions soon followed Basque, Breton, and Norman fishers, and Sally C. Cole notes that "between 1510 and 1525 the Portuguese attempted to found a colony in Atlantic Canada" (1). Later, in 1567–1568, the Portuguese would also attempt to settle Sable Island off the coast of Nova Scotia; however, as the sixteenth century progressed,

> Portuguese interest in finding an Atlantic route to Asia declined in part due to the successes of the annual India fleet that sailed around the African coast and in part due to the losses of men and boats and the apparent desolation of the North American Atlantic coast.
>
> (Cole 1)

By 1580, Portugal had fallen under the control of King Philip II of Spain, and his ensuing conflict with Elizabeth I of England led to a decline in both Spanish and Portuguese fishing in the Northeast Atlantic. These developments opened the door for the growth of English fisheries and colonies in the later sixteenth and early seventeenth centuries:

> In the earlier half of the sixteenth century, England remained isolated on the edge of continental Europe and played a limited role in global commerce, which was dominated by Mediterranean countries such as Italy and Spain. This marginal position shifted in the early seventeenth century with the growth of transatlantic trade routes opened by the English "discovery" of Newfoundland.
>
> (Test 207)

English ascendency on both sides of the Atlantic led to what Edward M. Test describes as "the trade triangle between England, Newfoundland, and Spain," in which English ships would sell *bacalhau* in Iberia, fill their holds with salt and sack (fortified wine), and then sell the wine in England before continuing onward to Newfoundland to catch and preserve cod with the salt (211). Olaf Janzen recounts an example of this triangular trade route aboard a Scottish trading ship, the *Christian*, in 1726. Since the *Christian* was a merchant ship rather than a fishing vessel, the journey begins with the sale of biscuits in Newfoundland rather than the acquisition of salt in Iberia:

> The investors who had chartered the *Christian* had directed the ship to "St Johns, Ferryland, or the Bay of Bulls, or any Harbour thereabouts," where the master and supercargo were instructed to sell the biscuit "to the best advantage, rather to Masters of Ships, than to the fishermen upon the Island." They were then to acquire "where you best can" a cargo of "good Merchantable fish, well dryed & fair to the eye," without "Spots or blemishes," for subsequent delivery to Barcelona, Spain. There the investors' agent would arrange for the sale of the fish and the acquisition of a partial cargo of cork before the *Christian* began the homeward journey. The ship would stop only at Sanlúcar, north of Cadiz, to complete its cargo with sherry and fruit.
>
> (Janzen 1)

As the *Christian*'s journey demonstrates, this transatlantic triangle trade route was present but not completely straightforward.

The investors' directions about fish quality suggest a complex evaluative process. Likewise, while the triangle trade route often suggests *bacalhau* finding its way to Iberian markets, significant quantities of *bacalhau* and/or Poor John made its way to England. Test himself references the significance of salt cod as a food source in England. As early as 1563, the Elizabethan government advocated for the trade in cod by requiring the observance of numerous fish days (based on originally Catholic holy days which forbade consumption of meat) (Fagan, *Fishing* 173–174). Test further supports his argument by remarking on the numerous literary references establishing cultural familiarity and common usage of salt cod amongst English people (209–210).

Somewhat paradoxically, the exploitation of cod and the creation of *bacalhau* were both an impetus for colonial expansion and a means of continuing that expansion. Brian Fagan posits that the relationship between *bacalhau* and colonialism is particularly close: above all other fish, "cod's great historical importance lies in its easy preservation, its resulting suitability as transported stores for mariners and soldiers, and its sheer abundance" (*Fish on Friday* 49). In light of the twentieth-century collapse of Canada's Atlantic cod fishery, it is ironic that the first European exploitation of this fishery was the result of the degradation of North Sea fisheries.

According to "Historical Overfishing and the Recent Collapse of Coastal Ecosystems," human expansion results in altered aquatic ecosystems via five factors: fishing, pollution, mechanical habitat destruction, introductions of non-native species, and climate change (Jackson et al. 635). In the chapter "Depleted European Seas and the Discovery of

America," W. Jeffrey Bolster provides evidence for all five of these factors in the medieval and early modern period, concluding that

> while it is impossible to state with any certainty whether or not most European fish stocks were being affected, it is clear that the system as a whole had been significantly degraded by 1500 as measured by the depletion of whales, seals, seabirds, and anadromous fish. Five hundred years of fishing had changed the nature of coastal European ecosystems and effected the baselines for what contemporaries assumed to be normal.
>
> (34)

This degradation of European fisheries may have been fairly rapid. James H. Barrett's research on evolving Northern European fishing practices and the technologies required for increasing catches resulted in his identification of a historical "fish event horizon" (850–1050), wherein sea fish—herring and cod in particular—gained an increasing importance in North European diets in the late medieval period.[1]

Barrett's "fish event horizon" most notably hinges upon deterioration of the North Sea fisheries wrought by over-exploitation and climate change during the Medieval Warm Period, *circa* 900–1300 (265–266). Fagan believes that degradation of Northern European fisheries was further exacerbated by climate change during the Little Ice Age, 1300–1870:

> It may be no coincidence that herring schools and fish landings at Yarmouth suffered a major decline in the 1390s and that catches varied dramatically thereafter from year to year. A highly competitive marketplace, overfishing to satisfy insatiable demand, and better salting methods had an impact that varied from port to port. But in the final analysis, it may have been climate change that tipped the northern European fish economy for [sic] sustainable to unsustainable.
>
> (*Fish on Friday* 127)

Fagan's argument gains significance in light of the research of Dull et al. suggesting that one of the causes of the Little Ice Age was reforestation in Central and South America occasioned by the massive demographic changes resulting from Iberian conquest and the concomitant introduction of European diseases to the region beginning in the late fifteenth century (Bergeron).

One may then surmise that late medieval environmental degradation pushed Europeans to seek new fisheries. The necessity of these journeys led to advances in marine technologies, which in turn allowed for longer voyages that culminated in the discovery and conquest of new lands. The Spanish conquest of South America, in particular, proved to be an event that had a profound effect on human geographies—a wave of destruction that caused the reforestation of South America and contributed to the Little Ice Age, which, in turn, seems to have exacerbated the further degradation of European fisheries, thus leading to more Europeans traveling to the New World. A synthesis of Nevle and Bird, Barrett, and Fagan's arguments reveals that cyclical over-exploitation of North Sea and Northeast Atlantic fish stocks, as well as other human impacts upon micro- and macrocosmic ecological and environmental conditions, resulted in a profound incident of metabolic rift. According to John Bellamy Foster, Marx's use of "the concept of metabolism (*Stoffwechsel*) [...] directly sets out in its elements the notion of 'material exchange' that underlies the notion of structured processes of biological growth and decay captured in the term metabolism" (157). Scholars such as Kenneth M. Stokes have romantically imagined that preindustrial societies lived in a state of environmental balance, where the "energy and materials they processed, in the rhythms of their work, and in the archaic technologies, [...] minimally impacted the ecosystems" (10). The evidence provided by Nevle, Bird, Fagan, and Barrett, however, challenges this assumption, suggesting that environmental degradation was the impetus behind globalizing exploitive colonial practices long before the Industrial Revolution.

In the case of Barrett's findings, European population demographics and changes in fishing practices demonstrate the complexity of this self-replicating process: "Sometimes urbanization, state formation, and fish trade went hand in hand. [...] In other cases [...] incipient urbanization and its appetite for sea-fish could precede state formation" (265). In any case, Bolster, like Fagan, contends that by the sixteenth century,

> the European ecosystems seemed unable to produce enough fish and whales to satisfy demand. In the summer of 1578 alone, [...] the Englishman Anthony Parkhurst tallied about 350 vessels in Newfoundland and the Gulf of St. Lawrence, including French, Spanish, Basque, Portuguese, and English ones.
>
> (44)

By the last quarter of the sixteenth century, Europeans had become dependent upon the Canadian Atlantic fishery to meet needs that could no longer be met by fishing European waters. Degradation of European marine environments is a primary theme in Bolster's *The Mortal Sea*, which argues that "time after time [sixteenth- and seventeenth-century] observers compared the compromised European boreal ecosystem that they knew with the fresh one in the Western Atlantic" (41). In *Cod: A Biography of the Fish that Changed the World*, Kurlansky links the collapse of early modern North Atlantic fishing stocks with the destruction of the Canadian Atlantic cod fishery in the late twentieth century, neatly summarizing the broad arc of over-exploitation and deterioration of fishing stocks first in Europe and then in America: "they [late twentieth-century fishers and their consumers] are on the wrong end of a 1,000-year fishing spree" (14). The exact role late medieval and early modern fishing had on the degradation of fisheries in the European North Atlantic is still open to debate; however, overfishing in the Canadian Atlantic undeniably destroyed the fishery, just as the current moratorium on commercial cod fishing in the region offers a still-uncertain promise for the recovery of cod stocks in the region.

This discussion of depleted European marine environments and the parallel growth of colonialism and the North American fisheries can be situated in the larger discourse on early modern ecocriticism. As Jonathan Gil Harris noted, early modern ecocriticism remains a new and still largely unexplored phenomenon (466). In the last several years, ecocritics such as Bruce Boehrer, Joan Fitzpatrick, and Erica Fudge have begun examining the role of non-human characters, including both plants and animals, in early modern literature. Nevertheless, Simon C. Estok's (2007) pronouncement that "ecocritical readings of Shakespeare's animals are certainly new territory," remains valid (61). The exploratory nature of such work is clear in Laurie Shannon's opening lines in "The Eight Animals in Shakespeare; or Before the Human," when she states "the poverty of the single-digit sum" in her title "raises a brow," and she acknowledges that the "ubiquity of those we conventionally shepherd into the enclosure of the term *animals* stands out as a feature of both Shakespearean material and early modern texts generally" (472).

While much work still needs doing, there have been significant scholarly developments addressing the sea and its creatures. In 2009, Steven Mentz identified the field of "blue cultural studies," which he subsequently described as "blue humanities," as a specific subset of early modern ecocriticism ("Blue Cultural Studies" 997; *Shipwreck Modernity*). Mentz distinguishes blue humanities from traditional New Historicist and Atlantic scholarship, particularly in reference to a reconsidering of objectivity and subjectivity: "This new maritime perspective does not view the oceans simply as bodies to be crossed, but as subjects in themselves"—an exercise that he believes "can open up new analytical frames for scholars of early modern English literature, including a newly dynamic (and disorderly) sense of ecological relationships and a different way of articulating multicultural connections in the early modern global world" ("Blue Cultural Studies" 997). Like Shannon's identification of the anthropocentric approach to non-human subjects in Shakespeare, Mentz's approach to oceans as subjects foreshadows Katherine Behar's conception of subjectivities predicated upon complex othering processes. Thus, Behar observes that "object-oriented feminism approaches all objects from the inside-out position of being an object too."[2] Daniel Brayton responds to the challenge presented by blue humanities in *Shakespeare's Ocean: An Ecocritical Exploration* with a study of Shakespeare's sea creatures and their importance not only as objects in his world but as epistemological subjects shaping that world:

> Social structure is as much a product of the organization of the interspecies interaction as it is a matter of policing the boundaries of licit and illicit species. This is especially true of marine animals, as evidenced by the pervasiveness of fish as a vehicle for mediating gender, desire, and matter in Shakespearean drama.
>
> (152–153)

Brayton's grappling with blue humanities and Behar's inside-out approach to object-oriented feminism may fruitfully be applied to the concepts of metabolic rift and commodity fetishism when reviewing the culinary history of codfish, particularly in reference to the species' life as a cultural commodity and the accrued meaning and values assigned to it. In this complex articulation, cod—as subject and object and as cultural artifact and commodity—has taken on a life of its own based upon a complex constellation of events. These events, in particular, involve metabolic rift through the cyclical over-exploitation of cod stocks and commodity fetishism of postcolonial material culture, which up-end Marxist concepts of use and exchange value, not only on the basis of production but upon ecologically mitigated supply and demand.

While collapsing cod stocks may have driven Europeans to North America in the late fifteenth century, the embarrassment of riches they discovered there set a complex chain of events into play. Brayton comments on the resulting changes in this market as "the ubiquity of salt fish—cod, hake, and herring" becoming "utterly quotidian staples" (137). This resulted, perhaps, in a case where familiarity bred contempt, since Shakespeare and his contemporaries deploy salt fish—stockfish and Poor John in particular—as an object of sexual derision and a signifier of poverty. These constructs expand beyond the ancient associations between salt and sex: Kurlansky, for example, notes that the word "Salacious is from the Latin *salax*, meaning a man in love—literally, 'in the salted state' " (*Salt* 3). Finally, Test obliquely references the developing culinary traditions associated with salt cod: "Clearly, the meager diet of Poor John (at least as it was prepared in England) was hardly palatable without some kind of condiment)" (Test 210). As a result, it is no surprise that *bacalhau* would elicit images of sexuality; however, the linkage between fish and poverty was a new one created by the excessive exploitation of early modern fisheries. From the classical period through the medieval period, fish was often viewed as a delicacy and, at times, even a privilege of the wealthy. However, the notable wealth of the codfish trade and its glut of production drove prices down and created cultural constructs equating preserved cod with extremely derogatory images of sexuality and poverty. Thus, in *Measure for Measure*, Lucio—a Charles Chester sort of oral satirist—slanderously describes the circumstances of Angelo's birth:

> Some report a sea-maid spawned him, some that he was begot between two stockfishes. But it is certain that when he makes water his urine is congealed ice; that I know to be true.
>
> (3.2, 16–18)[3]

Gordon Williams[4] suggests that Lucio's fanciful description of Angelo's fishy parentage is meant to serve as a humoral explanation for the "coldness" of his temperament; furthermore, "the dried fish suggest someone in whom the natural juices are dried up" (284). In *Shakespeare's Ocean*, Brayton delves deeper into the importance of stockfish in the following passage:

> Angelo's coldness, literal and sexual, associates him with a "sea-maid," a supernatural being, half woman, half fish, long thought to lure seamen to their deaths. The joke about his frozen urine reinforces the association of the sea and Angelo's "unnatural" (asexual) generation. Angelo is a cold fish below the belt; he was not born but "spawned." His sexual prudishness makes him not only cold but also dry; thus, it is symbolically appropriate to imagine him, alternatively, as the offspring of "Two stock-fishes," emblematic of aridity.
>
> (155)

Brayton finds additional references to stockfish by Shakespeare in *Henry IV, Part I* and *The Tempest*, in both of which he associates the physical qualities, such as the "hardness and dryness" of stockfish, with global/human qualities and conditions in a process that relates the commodified object (salt cod) with objectified human subjects: Angelo, Prince Hal, and Caliban (155). These images are often sexualized: the dryness of stockfish is "figuratively associated with sexual aridity" through Angelo's prudishness and Prince Hal's "abstemious physique" (155). While Brayton's argument that Falstaff's deployment of stockfish imagery is intended to create "sexual insults linking phallic objects with malnourishment," he underplays the other dominant image set apparent in representations of stockfish: those which elicit metaphors of poverty (155). Maria José Pires suggests that

> since the Middle Ages *bacalhau* was a food resource of great importance in Europe, especially for the poor. Because it was not fresh, it was cheaper; it lasted longer without spoiling, and, at the same time, it was very nutritious [...]. Consequently, *bacalhau* won the simplest tables and helped European populations endure periods of hunger and misery through the ages.
>
> (126)

Pires's argument suggests an evolving relationship between the common people and *bacalhau*. Rather than a product fit only for derision, *bacalhau* was winning adherents. Pires, however, is basing her reading on José Quitério's twentieth-century encomium to cod, "Um '*Adeus Português*' ao Bacalhau," and, therefore, both Pires and Quitério have the benefit of hindsight. A remarkable transformation was taking place at this time: *bacalhau* was evolving from a hardy but unpopular staple in early modern kitchens around the world through interaction with new cultures, ingredients, and experiences.

Remarkable transformations aside, Shakespeare and his contemporaries do not laud cod. *The Oxford Companion to Ships and the Sea* reinforces the essentially derogatory nature of early modern salt cod inherent in terms such as "Poor John":

> the name given by seamen to salted and dried fish of the cheaper varieties, when supplied as part of the victualling allowance on board sailing warships of the British Navy. Issues of fish occasionally replaced issues of salt beef or pork and were never popular on the lower deck.
>
> (Dear and Kemp 438)

When Brayton recognizes Poor John as "cheap," he focuses more on its smell and appearance, "limp" and "shriveled" (157). Poor John's role as an early modern cultural commodity is, however, not definitive. Fagan, for example, attributes the creation of this product to "English fisherfolk" who "had invented the light salting and drying cure while fishing Icelandic waters," and he argues that

> these "dry" fish were tastier than the simple dried stockfish of earlier times and fetched a higher price. This type of salting was especially good for moderate- and smaller-size cod, which were not too fat when gutted and thus easier to salt and dry.
>
> Lightly salted cod appealed to the English palate and also found a ready market in Spain. In warmer climates, it had the priceless advantage of a longer shelf life than Icelandic stockfish. From the merchants' and fishers' perspective, this type of dry cod, known to the English as "Poor John" or "Newland fish", required less salt and was cheaper to process.
>
> (*Fish on Friday*, 230)

In contrast, Brayton calls "Poor-john [...] the lowest grade of dried salted cod available in the European market; many months and miles away from its origins in the cold waters of the Norwest Atlantic, it inevitably stunk" (157). The early modern consensus probably lies somewhere between Fagan's laudatory description of Poor John, drawing throngs of eager buyers in England and Spain, and Brayton's semi-putrid fish drawn forth from ships' holds after a long journey.

While both Brayton and Fagan see the vast commercial, social, and political importance of cod, it is perhaps best summed up by Test's argument that "the lowly codfish contributed to the highest concerns of the nation state as an essential staple: domestic stability, national security, and foreign trade" (202). In any case, the commonplaces in Shakespeare and generally across early modern texts clearly suggest that while cod was a valuable commodity that benefited early modern economies and fueled colonial enterprises, culturally cod was viewed with disdain, and images of stockfish, Poor John, and other commodified cod products were metaphorically yoked to poverty and puerile olfactory and/or sexual constructs.

This constellation of derogatory metaphors regarding *bacalhau* carries over into early modern texts written in and/or about Goa. After his return to Europe, Jan Huyghen van Linschoten (1563–1611)—a Dutch merchant who served as the Portuguese Viceroy's secretary in Goa between 1583 and 1588—published *Itinerario* in 1596, revealing the author's stunning theft of Portuguese knowledge. The text was published only two years later in England as *Discours of Voyages into Y East & West Indies.* Huyghen's theft had a notable result: it effectively undermined Portugal's monopoly over East Indian trade. Huyghen had taken advantage of his elevated position in Goa and copied the Portuguese navigation charts that had been kept secret for over a century. This publication would allow the Dutch and British East India Companies to quickly challenge Portuguese commercial ascendancy in the region. Huygen's *Discours* was intended to not only reveal the means of reaching the East Indies but also how Portuguese colonies operated. As a result, he discusses the lives of Goa's Portuguese, *Mestico*, and Indian residents. In speaking of the Portuguese soldiers, he tells his readers their diet consists of "Rice sodden in water, with some salt fish, or some other thing of small value (without bread)" (Huygen reprinted in Shetty, 26). Likewise, in the seventeenth century, the German traveler Jean Albert de Mandelslo remarks of Portuguese and *Mestico* women in Goa as follows:

> They eat no bread, as liking the rice better. Now that they are accustomed to it; nor do they fare over-deliciously as to other things, their ordinary sustenance being salt fish, mangas, or only rice soaked in a little flesh or fish-broth.
>
> (Mandelslo, reprinted in Shetty 113)

Mandelslo, like Huyghen, links salt fish—and the lack of bread—to dearth, poverty, and debasement. Likewise, Charles Gabriel Dellon, a seventeenth-century French physician who was imprisoned by the Inquisition in Daman, Goa, and Brazil and then forced to serve as a Portuguese galley slave, records "rations were a pound and a half of ship's biscuit a day, and six pounds of salt fish a month with vegetables" (Dellon, reprinted in Shetty 219). Thus, the derisive tone regarding stockfish seen in Shakespeare is repeated in early modern continental texts featuring Goa. Huyghen's description of the Portuguese soldiers' diet is indicative of the meanness of their existence in the colony in the late sixteenth century. Huyghen recognizes the great wealth generated in the colony, so his attack is focused more on the faults of the Portuguese, such as vanity, quarrelsomeness, and the hardships of their existence. Mandelslo's derogatory description of the Portuguese and *Mestico* women's diets reflects a seventeenth-century perspective where Portuguese Goa's monopoly on Eastern trade has been undermined. Here, the women's debased diets are synonymous with his argument that the morality and economic vigor of the colony have been undermined. Finally, Dellon's description of the prisoners' diet on the galleys again presents salt cod as a food fit only for the downtrodden.

In subsequent centuries, however, salt cod, a seemingly inauspicious commodity, was transformed into a highly regarded product, both in continental Europe and in postcolonial cultures in Central America, the Caribbean, Africa, India, and beyond. According to Pires, Quitério illustrates the transformation of *bacalhau* in the context of class struggle. Quitério's "narrator plainly emphasizes the preference of the proletariat for consuming *bacalhau* pointing out how they honoured it" (Pires 126). Likewise, Pires argues that "the narrator recognizes that the undervaluing and ignoring of *bacalhau* by the upper classes was just part of the class struggle and these ended up approving and appreciating the patrician worth of cod" (127). Pires's reading depends on a sort of grudging upper-class recognition of working-class inventiveness, which demonstrates an important aspect of bacalhau's ascension to *haute cuisine* in many cultures of the Global South. However, this is only one aspect of a larger narrative. The transformation of salt cod is the result of evolving cultures, technologies, economies, and ecologies, which have, in turn, created a complex web of signification. At some point *bacalhau*'s culinary ascendency, both in Goa and in cuisines around the world, is intrinsically tied to three factors: production and means of production, class and ideology, and ecology.

In Goa, salt cod—as in many other former colonies in Portugal's once far-flung empire—retains its Portuguese name, *bacalhau*, where it has become a valued and valuable cultural commodity retailing, along with Portuguese olive oil and wine, for example, at Loja Costas, Shop Numbers 4, 5, and 6, Jesuit House, Travessa da Revolucão Street in Panaji. A similar evolution may also be seen in nearby former Portuguese colonies in East Africa. Thus, there may be found a Wednesday night *Buffet de Bacalhau* at the Forno do Indy in the Montebelo Girassol Hotel, Maputo, Mozambique. Both *bacalhau* and dried and salted saithe (otherwise known as pollack)—a cheaper alternative to cod—are still sold to, and eagerly purchased by, the thirteen million Bakongo people of Angola, albeit as *makaybu* instead of *bacalhau* (Pleym). Likewise, Portuguese *bacalhau* or Spanish-introduced *bacalao* may be found in many forms throughout the West Indies and Central and South America, peddled, for example, from Caribbean beach-front shacks and prepared in typically South American style (as fritters) by "the Portuguese guy" at *Bacalhau do Tuga* in Arraial do Cabo, Brazil ("Bacalhau do Tuga"). As a Portuguese import in Goa, *bacalhau* is invariably fraught with meaning: a food of faith, class, and nostalgia. Maria Teresa Menezes's *The Essential Goan Cookbook*, for example, describes *bacalhau* as "a luxury" that makes people "misty-eyed" with nostalgia (160). These twenty-first-century incarnations reflect the transformation of *bacalhau*: once common, now rare; once reviled, now treasured. This change in evaluation is a result of the continuing societal effects of colonial history on Goan culture in conjunction with ecological collapse, which this chapter has argued, was also occasioned and expedited by the forces of colonialism.

In the context of *bacalhau* in Goa, individuals and/or group relationships within Portuguese colonial history are further complicated by the Christian fish/flesh dichotomy demanded by a cultural import far more pervasive than Portuguese colonialism—namely, Roman Catholicism. This articulation is simultaneously divisive and syncretic: *bacalhau* dishes, which are in most demand during Christmas and Lent, reflect elements of both culture and class. Both the practice and culture of Catholicism remain pervasive influences upon Konkan and Luso-Indian societies in Goa. Thus, cod has suffered the vicissitudes of history. Salt cod, a once ubiquitous protein staple, became obsolete as a result of technological innovation: in this instance, refrigeration. Declining Atlantic cod stocks have also put pressure on the production of *bacalhau*. This, in turn, has made *bacalhau* a costly luxury item and, in parts of the world such as Goa, a signifier of faith, economic status, and class. Ironically, this too is quite the opposite of *bacalhau*'s medieval and early modern constructs where it was a lowly, but indispensable, necessity.

Notes

1 Barrett situates this change in England between 950 and 1050 AD; "Medieval Sea Fishing, AD 500–1550: Chronology, Causes, and Consequences," in Barrett and Orton (253–254).
2 Behar, "Introduction," 8.
3 All Shakespeare references follow William Shakespeare, *The New Oxford Shakespeare*.
4 Williams 492–498 (fish) and 1193–1194 (salt).

References

Barrett, James H. and David C. Orton, editors. *Cod and Herring: The Archaeology and History of Medieval Sea Fishing*. Oxbow Books, 2016.

Behar, Katherine, editor. *Object-Oriented Feminism*. University of Minnesota Press, 2016.

Bergeron, Louis. "Reforestation Helped Trigger Little Ice Age, Researchers Say." *Stanford News*, Stanford University, 17 Dec. 2008, https://news.stanford.edu/news/2009/january7/manvleaf-010709.html. Accessed 1 Mar. 2019.

Bolster, W. Jeffrey. *The Mortal Sea: Fishing the Atlantic in the Age of Sail*. Harvard University Press, 2012.

Brayton, Dan. *Shakespeare's Ocean: An Ecocritical Exploration*. Kindle edition. University of Virginia Press, 2012.

Bushnell, William D. "New Maine Times Book Review: The Mortal Sea." *New Maine Times*, 28 Aug. 2013, www.newmainetimes.org/articles/2013/08/28/new-maine-times-book-review-mortal-sea/. Accessed 3 July 2019.

Cole, Sally C. "Cod, God, Country, and Family: The Portuguese Newfoundland Cod Fishery." *Maritime Anthropological Studies*, vol. 3, no. 1, 1990, pp. 1–19.

Dear, I. C. B., and Peter Kemp, editors. *The Oxford Companion to Ships and the Sea*. 2nd ed. Oxford University Press, 2007.

Duckert, Lowell, editor. *Shipwreck Modernity: Ecologies of Globalization, 1550–1719*. University of Minnesota Press, 2015.

Dull, Robert A., et al. "The Columbian Encounter and the Little Ice Age: Abrupt Land Use Change, Fire, and Greenhouse Forcing." *Annals of the Association of American Geographers*, vol. 100, no. 4, 2010, pp. 755–771.

Estok, Simon C. "Theory from the Fringes: Animals, Ecocriticism, Shakespeare." *Mosaic*, vol. 40, no. 1, 2007, pp. 61–78.

Fagan, Brian. *Fishing: How the Sea Fed Civilization*. Yale University Press, 2017.

Fagan, Brian. *Fish on Friday: Fasting, Feasting, and the Discovery of the New World*. Basic Books, 2006.

Foster, John Bellamy. *Marx's Ecology: Materialism and Nature*. New York University Press, 2000.

Graeber, David. "Turning Modes of Production Inside Out: Or Why Capitalism is a Transformation of Slavery." *Critique of Anthropology*, vol. 26, no. 61, 2006, pp. 61–85.

Harris, Jonathan Gil. "Recent Studies in Tudor and Stuart Drama." *SEL Studies in English Literature 1500–1900*, vol. 51, no. 2, 2011, pp. 465–513.

Henn, Alexander. *Hindu–Catholic Engagements in Goa: Religion, Colonialism, and Modernity*. Orient BlackSwan, 2014.

Jackson, Jeremy B. C. et al. "Historical Overfishing and the Recent Collapse of Coastal Ecosystems." *Science*, vol. 293 (July 27, 2001), pp. 629–38.

Janzen, Olaf. "A Scottish Ship in the Newfoundland Trade, 1726–1727." *Scottish Economic and Social History*, 18, part 1, 1998, pp. 1–18.

Kamat, Melinda Pereira. "In Search of the Perfect Fofos." *The Times of India*, 19 Jul. 2009, https://timesofindia.indiatimes.com/city/goa/In-search-of-the-perfect-Fofos/articleshow/4794057.cms. Accessed 24 Feb. 2016.

Kittinger, John N., Loren McClenachan, Keryn B. Gedan, and Louise K. Blight. *Marine Ecology in Conservation: Applying the Past to Manage for the Future*. University of California Press, 2015.

Kurlansky, Mark. *Salt: A World History*. Kindle edition. Penguin Books, 2003.

———. *Cod: A Biography of the Fish that Changed the World*. Penguin Books, 1998.

LeHuenen, Joseph. "The Role of the Basque, Breton, and Norman Cod Fisherman in the Discovery of North America from the XVIth to the End of the XVIIIth Century." *Arctic*, vol. 37, no. 4, 1964, pp. 520–7.

Menezes, Maria Teresa. *The Essential Goan Cookbook*. Penguin, 2000.

Mentz, Steven. *Shipwreck Modernity: Ecologies of Globalization, 1550–1719*, edited by Lowell Duckert. University of Minnesota Press, 2015.

———. "Towards a Blue Cultural Studies: The Sea, Maritime Culture, and Early Modern English Literature." *Literature Compass*, vol. 6, no. 5, 2009, pp. 997–1013.

Namaste, Nina B. and Marta Nadales Ruiz, editors. *Who Decides? Competing Narratives in Constructing Tastes, Consumption, and Choice*. Brill, 2017.

Pires, Maria José. "An Encomium of *Bacalhau*: The Portuguese Emblem of a Gastronomic Symphony" *Who Decides?* Edited by Nina B. Namaste and Marta Nadales Ruiz. Brill, 2017.

Pleym, Ingelinn Eskildsen. "Angola – Market of Opportunity for Dried and Salted Fish." *Nofima*, Norwegian Ministry of Trade, Industry, and Fisheries, Jun. 2015, https://nofima.no/en/nyhet/2015/06/angola-market-of-opportunity-for-dried-and-salted-fish/. Accessed 24 Feb. 2016.*

Sebek, Barbara, and Stephen Deng, editors. *Global Traffic: Discourses and Practices of Trade in English Literature and Culture from 1550 to 1700*. Palgrave, 2008.

Shakespeare, William. *The New Oxford Shakespeare: The Complete Works, Modern Critical Edition*, edited by Gary Taylor, John Jowett, Terri Bourus, and Gabriel Egan. Oxford University Press, 2016.

Shannon, Laurie. "The Eight Animals in Shakespeare; or, Before the Human." *PMLA*, vol. 124, no. 2, 2009, pp. 472–479.

Shetty, Manohar, editor. *Goa Travels: Being the Accounts of Travellers from the 16th to the 21st Century*. Rupa, 2014.

Star, Baastion, et al. "Ancient DNA Reveals the Arctic Origin of Viking Age Cod from Haithabu, Germany." *PNAS*, vol. 114, no. 34, 2017, pp. 9152–7.

Stokes, Kenneth M. *Man and the Biosphere: Toward a Coevolutionary Political Economy*. Routledge, 1992.

Test, Edward M. "*The Tempest* and the Newfoundland Fishery." *Global Traffic: Discourses and Practices of Trade in English Literature and Culture from 1550 to 1700*, edited by Barbara Sebek and Stephen Deng. Palgrave, 2008.

Williams, Gordon. *Shakespeare's Sexual Language: A Glossary*. 1997. Continuum, 2006.

6 The Future of Food

Trajectories in Paolo Bacigalupi's *The Windup Girl*[1]

Young-hyun Lee

Paolo Bacigalupi's *The Windup Girl*, named one of the best novels of 2009 by *TIME* magazine,[2] deals with technology and the challenges it poses for human food sources. The human pursuit of comfort and convenience finds a zenith of expression in Bacigalupi. In this novel, set in twenty-third century Thailand, we witness the results of our own anthropocentric civilization and of the view of nature as mere resource: the effect of our ecophobia[3] is destruction of the environment and resource depletion. In this critical situation, such multinational companies as AgriGen and PurCal in *The Windup Girl* ship their seeds at exorbitant rates, and the Thai Kingdom is persuaded of the "merits" of food transformation technology in ways that mirror what is happening with today's small farmers. The patriotic implications of the "generippers" and their use of technology in the novel are also deeply relevant, as I will discuss below, to contemporary multinational agri-politics. Tragic incidents ensue in *The Windup Girl* from the use of genetically engineered crops, and factory workers die from epidemics, a situation that looks startlingly similar to suicide patterns of contemporary Indian farmers following failures of genetically engineered crops. More problematic are unknown dangers of food transformation technology by these profit-driven companies, fictional and real. The epilogue of the novel, a dialogue of two genetically engineered people and a "generipper" left in an already inundated city, implies the demise of human civilization that will result from the avarice of food transformation industries and their technologies. Although technology has, in many ways, helped humanity, we have come to a stage when advanced technology, especially that of genetically engineered foods and animals, is quickening our downfall, as Bacigalupi represents in *The Windup Girl*, which looks with great focus at the transformation of food and animals in the twenty-third century.

The genetic engineering technologies in *The Windup Girl* are ethically problematic. We see this most of all in the scenes with Emiko, a cyborg initially made to gratify men's carnal appetites but who ends up being sold to a club owner after having been forsaken for economic reasons by her Japanese owner. The ethics of food transformation technology today require attention, since these technologies will exert more

DOI: 10.4324/9781003282976-9

enormous influence over all living beings in the future. *The Windup Girl* is a warning. The ethical issues of the fictional future are also ethical issues of the nonfictional present.

In our nonfictional present, the Genetically Modified Organism Exploratory Committee in the US raised ethical issues in the "Executive Summary from the Genetically Modified Organism Exploratory Committee." It explained that we should consider ethical aspects because "[the] use of genetically modified organisms is a practice still in its infancy. The long-term effects of this technology are yet to be seen."[4] The committee especially emphasized the probable effects of genetically modified organisms (GMO) on "herbicide use and resistance" and "untargeted species," environmentally and on human health. Bacigalupi taps into these ethical issues by representing the plight of Emiko. The novel focuses on ethically problematic aspects of transformation technologies by representing Emiko as a genetically engineered woman with problems—she gets hot very quickly, is weak, and so on.

Emiko is engineered not as food, of course, but as a kind of a sex slave, and she no doubt reminds the readers of one of the sex slaves called "comfort women"[5] in the Japanese imperialist era. "Men cheer at Emiko's degradation" (Bacigalupi 241), the narrator explains: "To the men: 'She likes it. All these dirty windups like it.' More laughter" (241). She is constantly subjected to humiliating treatment and regarded as an object of trade.

Technology makes the characters blind to the enslavement and abuse of genetically engineered animals: this is another ethical issue that Bacigalupi raises in this novel. Transformed animals, such as "megodonts" (genetically engineered elephantine animals) in the kink-spring factory[6] run by Anderson Lake, are forced to work in almost unbearable heat. Emiko, similarly, has to sexually entertain men customers under Kanika's supervision every night in a club and must endure the humiliation. Emiko, simply put, is to be consumed by men as animals are to be consumed by human beings.[7] The animals and laborers working for the factory are habitually abused and are forced to endure extremely harsh working conditions:

> The roar of manufacturing envelops Anderson as he enters the factory, drowning out the last despairing howl of Yates' optimism.
>
> Megodonts groan against spindle cranks, their enormous heads hanging low, prehensile trunks scraping the ground as they tread slow circles around power spindles. The genehacked animals comprise the living heart of the factory's drive system, providing energy for conveyor lines and venting fans and manufacturing machinery. Their harnesses clank rhythmically as they strain forward. Union handlers in red and gold walk beside their charges, calling out to the beasts, switching them occasionally, encouraging the elephant-derived animals to greater labor.
>
> (Bacigalupi 9)

Yates[8] is optimistic about the possibility that technology could lead humanity to "A new Expansion! Dirigibles, next-gen kink-springs, fair trade winds" (Bacigalupi 62). "[Those] subjections, the ecophobia, the speciesism, the racism," as he indicates, are "the ethical *sine qua non* of the world food economy" in one of the chapters of *The Ecophobia Hypothesis,* where he explores "the ways in which contemporary western food production mechanisms rely on very socially and environmentally dangerous ethics" (94). Thus, few would deny that enslavement of genetically engineered women and animals represented by Bacigalupi is one of the most urgent issues to attend to in the near future.

As the kink-spring factory run by Anderson abuses and kills the workers and the megodonts, hi-tech industries such as food transformation production companies show little interest in human or animal welfare and care more about their profit margins. In the situations where the factory workers are dying because of epidemics, Hock Sung, a middle manager for the factory, tries to come up with ways of how he can sneak the bodies out and throw them away secretly. Self-interest is rampant in this novel, and it is such an inability to see the importance of compassion for others that is so potent a warning in this novel. Mai,[9] for example, also is worried only about herself because she has no other way to support herself with the factory being closed. Mai and Hock Sung know well that Anderson should shut down the factory because the workers are dying. Mai, worried about losing her job, begs Hock Sung: "I don't want to lose the job. . . . Please don't tell the farang. Everyone knows the farang might close the factory. Please. My family needs. . ." (Bacigalupi 153). Profits and compassion seem incompatible.

Contemporary agribusiness pursuits of unfettered GMO production are clearly a problem today, and the current trajectory of this problem could easily lead to the nightmares pictured in *The Windup Girl*. The novel offers dire warnings for contemporary society. Richard Caplan, an environmental advocate for a US Public Interest Research Group (PIRG), argues why genetically engineered food ingredients or crops should be banned. In "Antibiotic Resistance and Genetically Engineered Plants," he explains how dangerous the methods and unpredictable the results are: "The process of inserting a gene of interest into a plant is," Caplan notes, "crude, haphazard, and random."[10] Among the two methods[11] of gene insertion which are usually used, "neither [one] is precise, as both methods provide no guarantee where the gene will land in the host organism, or even whether the gene of interest has been inserted into the host organism at all." Such a tendency of disregard for potential dangers worsens when it comes to GMO companies.

Food transformation technologies regard living entities as property or as commodities, and this can bring about catastrophic (even fatal) consequences. While it is true that we have a long history of selective breeding, genetic modification is a very different matter. The motive for making genetically engineered animals might sound innocent and benevolent, but the results are irrevocable, as Bacigalupi shows:

> Hock Seng has heard that cheshires were supposedly created by a calorie executive—some PurCal or AgriGen man, most likely. . . when the little princess turned as old as Lewis Carroll's Alice. The child guests took their new pets home where they mated with natural felines, and within twenty years, the devil cats were on every continent and *Felis domesticus* was gone from the face of the world, replaced by a genetic string that bred true ninety-eight percent of the time.
>
> (Bacigalupi 27)

Genetic engineering, however, is far from innocent, and the possibilities of violent effects are very real. Indian environmental activist and anti-globalization author Vandana Shiva points out in *Biopiracy: The Plunder of Nature and Knowledge* some of the possible violence which genetically engineering technologies could have: "first, life-forms are treated as if they are mere machines, thus denying their self-organizing capacity. Second, by allowing the patenting of future generations of plants and animals, the self-reproducing capacity of living organisms is denied" (55). The intellectual properties and patents the GMO companies claim, whether businesses call them "biotechnological inventions," "gene constructs," or "products of the mind," are a flat denial of the self-organizing capacity of living organisms. Carsten T. Charlesworth, in a scientific article entitled "Identification of Pre-Existing Adaptive Immunity to Cas9 Proteins in Humans,"[12] confirms the danger of GMO technologies, using data demonstrating that the immune systems of genetically modified animals (including clones) are severely compromised. Shiva, who is not a scientist, understands how violent and unpredictable genetic modification can be. *Jurassic Park* technology is dangerous. Bringing back species is uncharted territory. Films make it look appealing. Even respected authors such as Diane Ackerman explains joyfully that extinct species may "haunt the earth again" (162) because of our genetic manipulations. The Svalbard Global Seed Vault is all about using such technologies to bring back extinct sources of food.

The restoration of extinct plants and animals advertised as a prodigious achievement in *The Windup Girl* is a dangerous transformation of life. The ideas trumpeted by GMO companies are totally opposite to their actual practices in the novel. There are generippers hacking into designs for TotalNutrient Wheat and SoyPRO, and it is all about money and profit. It resembles Monsanto today and their Roundup Ready Soybean advertisements. One of the representative justifications most GM companies set forth for introducing genetically engineered crops in agriculture is "increasing yields." The reality, however, is that:

> genetic engineering is actually leading to a "yield drag." On the basis of 8,200 university-based soybean trials in 1998, it was found that

> the top Roundup Ready soybean varieties had 4.6 bushels per acre, or yields 6.7 percent lower than the top conventional varieties.
>
> (Stolen Harvest 113)

There are countless examples of farmers who ended up ruining their farming after investing in the genetically engineered seeds, believing the false promises of increased agricultural production. We have good cause to distrust food transformation technologies.

This distrust is well represented in *The Windup Girl*. When Anderson, indicating fruit in a market, asks the merchant whether or not it is safe, the woman shows Environment Ministry certificates to him to prove that the genetically engineered fruit is the latest variation and is first-rate. Far from trusting the science, Anderson views the new fruit with skepticism and thinks that the merchant must have bribed officials for certificates:

> rather than going through the full inspection process that would have guaranteed immunity to eighth generation blister rust . . . The cynical part of him supposes that it hardly matters. The intricate stamps that glitter in the sun are more talismanic than functional, something to make people feel secure in a dangerous world.
>
> (Bacigalupi 5)

Anderson knows that these certificates would do nothing if an epidemic broke out again because "it will be a new variation, and all the old tests will be useless, and then people will pray to their Phra Seub amulets and King Rama XII images and make offerings at the City Pillar Shrine" (5). We see here a desperate situation in which people rely on superstition once an epidemic occurs. Shiva warns against the kinds of risks the novel represents:

> Converting . . . "weeds" into "superweeds" that carry the gene for herbicide-resistance would provoke high crop losses and increasing use of herbicides . . . . In many cases, the weeds that plague cultivated crops are relatives of the crops themselves. Wild beets have been a major problem in European sugar-beet cultivation since the 1970s. Given the gene exchange between weedy beets and cultivated beets, herbicide-resistant sugar beets could only be a temporary solution.
>
> Superweeds could lead to "bioinvasions," displacing local diversity and taking over entire ecosystems.
>
> (*Stolen Harvest* 105)

As more and more damage from invasive species occurs around the world, the threat to biodiversity from GM tampering is increasingly clear.

In a society full of distrust in technologies, such as the one represented in *The Windup Girl*, people come to realize that advanced technologies cannot protect them from either evil or injury. The merchants' behavior and remarks reveal this in the novel, and this should serve as a warning to us today. GMO corporations are more concerned these days about shutting off fears over their products than producing safe food, according to the following news report on how much biotech companies spend on:

> ads ... keyed to show that biotech foods cut the use of chemical pesticides, provide more nutritious food and can help end world hunger by lowering costs. The campaign includes slick educational materials that are being distributed to dietitians, nutritionists, cooperative extension agents and key opinion leaders.[13]

In *The Windup Girl*, faith in this kind of sponsored data has clearly run out, and the fruit merchants have more faith in amulets or prayer rather than in what purports to be scientific data. Measures for prevention of infectious diseases often simply do not work, and distrust quickly becomes endemic in the novel.

As Anderson's transactions show, GMO companies in the novel maintain and expand their power and positions through secret connections and closed-door arrangements with politicians and government ministers, which is nothing short of corruption. This is not far from what happens in real life. William Engdahl makes it clear in *Seeds of Destruction: The Hidden Agenda of Genetic Manipulation* how multinational GMO companies pursue their goals in collusion with government officials: "[the] complicity of essential US Government agencies, legally and nominally responsible for ensuring public health and safety of the general population, was a decisive part of the GMO revolution" (Engdahl 226). *The New York Times* ran an article on January 25, 2001 about how Monsanto took control over its own regulatory industry, through the Environmental Protection Agency (EPA), the Department of Agriculture, and the Food and Drug Administration (FDA). The article quoted Dr. Henry Miller, who had a leading role in biotechnology issues at the FDA from 1979 to 1994: "In this area, the U.S. government agencies have done exactly what big agribusiness has asked them to do and told them to do."[14] In *The Windup Girl*, while foreign companies "[speak] so casually about changing pollution credit systems, of removing quarantine inspections, of streamlining everything that has kept the Kingdom alive as other countries have collapsed" (Bacigalupi 49), the incorruptible Environment Minister Jaidee alone tries to break the chain of corruption in the city.

The Windup Girl offers disturbing examples of how politicians and multinational GMO industries collude and ignore underprivileged species and classes when they enact regulations and laws in support of intellectual property rights. The international laws and measures supporting globalization are both speciesist and classist, benefiting a handful of multinational corporations, classes, and nations. For this reason, environmental justice and food justice are more crucial than ever. Shiva, as an active advocate of food sovereignty and anti-globalization, has argued about the unjustness of intellectual propriety rights and patents over living organisms. These laws and regulations have reorganized relationships, not only between the human species and other species, but within the human community. Arguing that "[instead] of the culture of the seed's reciprocity, mutuality, permanence, and exhaustless fertility, corporations are redefining the culture of the seed to be about piracy, predation, the termination of fertility, and the engineering of sterility" (*Stolen Harvest* 90), Shiva makes it plain how dangerous the laws and measures are that protect the powerful corporations.

Food transformation technologies are increasingly based on intellectual propriety rights and patents and show a collusion between the multinational GMO companies and high governmental officials. These technologies allow for the plundering of resources from small-scale farmers and the Global South. *The Windup Girl* is set in an era when human civilization has depleted natural resources, and most people suffer from fuel shortages. The powerful and the wealthy still do not care about people's hardships. Bacigalupi describes Dog Fucker's[15] response to Hock Seng's astonishment at a gas-guzzling car that has come to pick him up:

> "What's the matter? You've never seen a car before?" Hock Seng stifles an urge to slap the man for his arrogance and stupidity . . . . "Is it coal diesel?" Hock Seng asks. He can't help whispering. Dog Fucker grins. "The boss does so much for the carbon load. . ." He shrugs. "This is a small extravagance." "But the cost. . ."
>
> (126)

Hock Seng finds it "an extraordinary waste," and he interprets it as "a testament to the Dung Lord's monopolies" (126).

Unlike the extravagant lifestyle of the upper class, the laborers at AgriGen have a hard time enduring harsh conditions. Though the factory is a subsidiary of a lucrative multinational GMO company, it is a site of sheer adversity. The novel represents the worsening working conditions caused by global warming:

> [the worker] wipes sweat off his face. The factory is hotter than a rice pot. With all the megodonts led back to their stables, there is nothing to drive the factory's lines or charge the fans that circulate air through the building. Wet heat and death stench swaddle them like a blanket.
>
> (Bacigalupi 23)

Unlike the civilized and comfortable lifestyle of the privileged class, the factory workers have to continuously go through various hardships to overcome hot weather. The multinational GMO companies in the novel claim that whenever they launch a new genetically modified product, it will address hunger or that human beings will be liberated from hard labor, or that the product will contribute to the creation of a more affluent and leisurely human society.[16] Contemporary agribusinesses claim that the gap between the privileged and the underprivileged will lessen and that society will become more democratic and egalitarian.

Such a technologically advanced society as the one in *The Windup Girl*, which tends to resolve problems and issues solely through scientific technologies, does not care for what looks small and trivial—including lower classes and other species. In the spatial background of *The Windup Girl*, nature is merely a source of raw material for human civilization. Algae are used as ingredients for producing batteries in Anderson's kink-spring factory. When some of the workers are ill, Hock Seng is concerned because it could be the precursor of an epidemic, which would mean the closure of the factory. He does not want to believe that an epidemic could happen: " 'It couldn't be cibiscosis? Blister rust? No.' [Hock Seng] shakes his head . . . [He] flinches away, fighting an urge to wipe his hands on his shirt . . . Hock Seng's skin crawls. Two bodies. . . " (Bacigalupi 154). Even though Hock Seng does not seem to care about the lives of the workers at all, no one can live without the other beings. Life is defined by interdependence. As implied in American novelist Jonathan Safran Foer's aphoristic remark, "stories about food are stories about us—our history and our values" (9). Greed for short-term profits causes industry to overlook long-term problems.

An ecological point of view is more beneficial in the long run than an industrial point of view. In *The Windup Girl*, "blister rust and genehack weevil [sweep] the globe" (142) in the vulnerable farming conditions produced by over-use and exploitation. Monocropping produces vulnerabilities; diversity produces strength. Shiva explains that:

> [when] multidimensional, diverse systems are perceived in their entirety, they are found to have high productivity. Their low productivity is a product of an approach that evaluates and assesses within in a one-dimensional framework, which is, in turn, related to an instrumental worldview.
>
> (Biopiracy 124)

In *The Windup Girl*, Bangkok, having tried to survive climate change using advanced technologies of food transformation, is destined to be inundated. In the epilogue, Bacigalupi represents the last days of the capital city of the kingdom:

> [Then] the monsoons came and the last attempts at holding back the ocean were abandoned. Rain gushed down, a vast deluge sweeping out dust and debris, sending every bit of the city swirling and rising. People swarmed from their homes with their belongings on their heads. The city slowly filled with water, becoming a vast lake lapping

> around second-story windows. On the sixth day, her Royal Majesty the Child Queen announces the abandonment of the divine city.
> (336)

As the fall of the city implies, the abuse of any one member of an ecological community may well lead to a domino effect. Seemingly disparate things could turn out to be closely connected. The ecological thought, as Timothy Morton puts it distinctively using his own concept of "strange strangers," "is interconnectedness in the fullest and deepest sense" (7):

> The ecological thought imagines interconnectedness, which I call *the mesh*. Who or what is interconnected with what or with whom? The mesh of interconnected things is vast, perhaps immeasurably so.
> (15)

Bacigalupi represents what happens when this mesh is jiggled. Human civilization will succumb to the power of nature.

After all the worsening problems caused by GMO technologies, people find themselves stuck in a vicious cycle in the novel. Trade Minister Akkarat (who rose to power after Environment Minister Jaidee Rojjanasukchai's fall from grace), explains to his replacement, Kanya, "[the foreigners] are the ones who will be going to the seedbank . . . They only want samples. Genetic diversity for their generipping. The Kingdom will benefit as well" (Bacigalupi 329). Thus, the independent city led by Akkarat collapses. He has been in covert transactions with foreign agents for food transformation companies. These agents speak casually about "changing pollution credit systems, of removing quarantine inspections, of streamlining everything that has kept the [Thai] Kingdom alive as other countries have collapsed" (49). The new normal is absolutely unprecedented.

Climate change is an unprecedented reality, today and in *The Windup Girl*. As American professor of Atmospheric Science David Battisti diagnosed in "Historical Warnings of Future Food Insecurity with Unprecedented Seasonal Heat," the difficulties that the human species would have to undergo in the future will exponentially increase. These include food security threats due to reduced crop yields, closure of densely populated cities owing to rising sea levels, and suffering and abuse (of underprivileged classes, the Global South, and genetically modified animals). Such a situation has quite a few elements in common with the situation in *The Windup Girl*, which represents various and tremendous environmental problems people face. In *Empire of Food*, Evan Fraser discusses the "three warning signs for imminent, catastrophic ecological collapse—a sort of diagnostic kit for environmental death" (Fraser 217).[17] In neglect of these three causes for alarm, humanity derogates its ecosystem.

As the relation between global warming and food transformation industries implies in this novel, it is time to reconsider the common belief that a scientific and technological solution is the best option to solve current environmental crises—global warming, rapid increase of endangered species, and deforestation, to name a few. Wendell Berry's "Two Economies" reminds us of what we have lost due to too much dependence on industrial technologies:

> [Industrial economy] makes itself thus exclusive by the simple expedient of valuing only what it can use—that is, only what it can regard as "raw material" to be transformed mechanically into something else. What it cannot use, it characteristically describes as "useless," "worthless," "random," or "wild," and gives it some such name as "chaos," "disorder," or "waste"—and thus ruins it or cheapens it in preparation for eventual use.
>
> (193)

Genetically modified crops are an example of what Berry describes. The companies value only what they can use for their own profit, but what they cannot use they treat as if it were a weed.

Despite the vital role that weeds and insects play in ecosystems, the GMO industry is committed to eliminating them. Yet, the importance of weeds and insects is not to be underestimated. Their biomass alone is compelling, as the website of the Smithsonian Institute shows: "Insects probably have the largest biomass of the terrestrial animals. At any time, it is estimated that there are some 10 quintillion (10,000,000,000,000,000,000) individual insects alive."[18] Furthermore, it is not easy or wise to replace their role with GMO products. Bees, for instance,

> are critical pollinators: they pollinate 70 of the around 100 crop species that feed 90% of the world. Honey bees are responsible for $30 billion a year in crops. That's only the start. We may lose all the plants that bees pollinate, all of the animals that eat those plants and so on up the food chain. Which means a world without bees could struggle to sustain the global human population of 7 billion.[19]

Bees cannot be replaced, although scientists are currently investigating ways that drones might be developed to solve the disappearing bee problem. In *The Windup Girl*, cats have long since disappeared, and they have been replaced with genetically modified animals called "cheshires."

GM technologies could have an irrevocably serious impact on a society, a country, or the whole human species, and this dangerous technology could drive the destiny of the human species in a way that is irreversible. *The Windup Girl* shows, through its fictional representations of twenty-third-century Thai society, where our current trajectory might lead.

Today "designer babies" have become a topic of considerable debate. In the article "When Baby Genes Are for Sale, the Rich Will Pay," Alex Salkever and Vivek Wadhwa explain that:

> Designer babies are coming in 20 to 30 years. Your children will be able to select, to some degree, their own children's hair color, eye color, and, possibly their intelligence. How can we make sure that everyone benefits from these capabilities, rather than reserving them for those with more cash?[20]

The problem is that such a question sounds highly probable in our own capitalistic society. According to "Rodriguez E," a faculty member at the Interdisciplinary Center for Studies on Bioethics at the University of Chile,

> In December 2015, the International Summit on Human Gene Editing, which gather members of national scientific academies of America, Britain and China, discussed the ethics of germline modification. They agreed to proceed further with basic and clinical research under appropriate legal and ethical guidelines, but altering of gametocytes and embryos to generate inheritable changes in humans was claimed irresponsible . . . [In] February 2016, British scientists were given permission by regulators to genetically modify human embryos by using CRISPR/Cas9 and related techniques only for research.
>
> (3)

The main concern is that it is difficult to predict how this technology will be used. The late Stephen Hawking is also one of those who warned of such concerns. He told the BBC that "The development of full artificial intelligence could spell the end of the human race."[21] His concern is that humanity might not deal well with the consequences of technologies that produce things that make humans obsolete.

The technologies of genetically engineered food and animals in *The Windup Girl* are on a trajectory that our own world is currently following, and although this technology has helped and is helping humanity, the ways in which technologies transform our food may also be hastening our demise. We see in *The Windup Girl* a nonchalance toward living beings, a trend that does not bode well for life or this planet. GMO technology has long been a profitable multinational business, and it is the greed of the GMO company AgriGen in *The Windup Girl* that produces a genetic and food monopoly. Anderson's behaviors in the novel mirror our realities, in which GMO companies maintain and expand their power and positions through secret connections and closed-door arrangements with politicians and government ministers. Such collusive links between the powerful governmental officials and multinational companies went on in the Trump administration no less than in previous administrations that have fostered the growth of companies such as Monsanto.[22] Shiva makes it clear that food is the most essential element of our lives. Our techno-centered-civilization—in its effort to exploit the seeds of our food for more short-term profit—is doomed to a sad demise, unless there is a radical shift or stop, and the world of *The Windup Girl* is the logical trajectory of the food and technology transformations that we see in our world today.

Notes

1 This chapter appeared in an earlier form as "Food Transformation Technology in Paolo Bacigalupi's *The Windup Girl* and What It Means for Us" in *Kritika Kultura*, vol. 33/34, May 2019, pp. 584–599 is used with permission here.
2 See Grossman.
3 In *The Ecophobia Hypothesis*, Simon C. Estok explains that:

> The ecophobic condition exists on a spectrum and can embody fear, contempt, indifference, or lack of mindfulness (or some combination of these) towards the natural environment. While its genetic origins have functioned, in part, to preserve our species, the ecophobic condition has also greatly serviced growth economies and ideological interests. Often a product of behaviors serviceable in the past but destructive in the present, it is also sometimes a product of the perceived requirements of our seemingly exponential growth. Ecophobia exists globally on both macro and micro levels, and its manifestation is at times directly apparent and obvious but is also often deeply obscured by the clutter of habit and ignorance (Introduction 1).

4 See Bates et al.
5 "Comfort women" were women who were forced into sexual slavery by the Imperial Japanese Army before and during World War II.
6 The kink-spring factory is a fictional energy source.
7 American writer and animal rights advocate Carol J. Adams looks into the meaning of meat eating in a patriarchal society by "interweaving of the oppression of women and animals" in *The Sexual Politics of Meat* (13).
8 Yates, as one of AgriGen's personnel, had spent years building the kink-spring factory.
9 Mai is a young girl who depends on Hock Sung for getting a living for her family.
10 See Caplan.
11 According to Caplan's explanation on how to insert genes into organisms, "The first involves a 'gene gun' that literally shoots microscopic particles covered with DNA at a high velocity into the target organism. The second method uses a type of bacteria, with the gene of interest attached, to infect a plant and thus insert the gene." See Caplan.
12 See Charlesworth et al.
13 See journalist Amy Goodman's interview with Vandana Shiva (www.democracynow.org/2000/5/16/stolen_harvest_the_hijacking_of_the).
14 See Eichenwald.
15 Dog Fucker's character is thuggish enough to be called such a term of abuse, though he is a businessman who "works for money [and acts] for money. He

and Hock Seng are different parts of the economic organism, but underneath everything, they are brothers. Hock Seng smiles slightly as confidence builds" (Bacigalupi 73).

16 Simon C. Estok argues that "the reality is that the very system that requires such global distributions—when such distributions in fact, do happen—is the root of deficits in other parts of the world" (95) against the argument of Jennifer Clapp that "[global] food supply chains have also redistributed surpluses of crops from one part of the world to other parts in food deficit, and food safety standards have largely improved" (159).

17 The group of ecologists studied "why ecosystems sometimes collapse under the weight of a pestilence, while at other times the same ecological disturbance doesn't cause lasting harm" (Fraser & Rimas 217). The list of three warning signs, which they published, is as follows:

> The first danger sign is when an ecosystem has too much biomass. A place stuffed to the rafters with leafy greens and wood is likely to catch either fire or the interest of a vicious beetle. Less productive land lacks fuel and bores bugs. So lush ground is more vulnerable than rocks.
>
> The second cause for alarm is connectivity. If the plants jumble together in a promiscuous thicket, flames and beetles can spread quicker.
>
> The third danger is exclusivity. If the thicket is made up of a single breed of fern, a fern-eating bug will gobble the entire growth, not just nibble at a few unlucky individuals. So as biodiversity goes down, vulnerability goes up.

18 See the website of the Smithsonian Institute (www.si.edu/spotlight/buginfo/bugnos): "Most authorities agree that there are more insect species that have not been described (named by science) than there are insect species that have been previously named. Conservative estimates suggest that this figure is 2 million, but estimates extend to 30 million."

19 See Moate.

20 See Salkever and Wadhwa.

21 See Cellan-Jones.

22 See Fraser and Rimas.

References

Ackerman, Diane. *The Human Age: The World Shaped by Us*. Harper Collins, 2014.

Adams, Carol J. *The Sexual Politics of Meat: A Feminist-Vegetarian Critical Theory*. The Continuum, 2010.

Bacigalupi, Paolo. *The Windup Girl*. Night Shade, 2009.

Bates, Timothy W, et al. "Executive Summary from the Genetically Modified Organism Exploratory Committee." *Ethical Issues*, 2 Oct. 2014, www.macalester.edu/~montgomery/GMOs2.htm.

Battisti, David S., and Rosamond L. Naylor. "Historical Warnings of Future Food Insecurity with Unprecedented Seasonal Heat." *Science*, vol. 323, no. 5911, January 2009, pp. 240–4.

Berry, Wendell. "Two Economies." *Review & Expositor*, vol. 81, no. 2 (1984), pp. 209–23.

Caplan, Richard. "Antibiotic Resistance and Genetically Engineered Plants." June 2002, www.iatp.org/files/Antibiotic_Resistance_and_Genetically_Engin_2.pdf.

Cellan-Jones, Rori. "Stephen Hawking Warns Artificial Intelligence Could End Mankind." *BBC News*, 2 December 2014, www.bbc.com/news/technology-30290540.

Charlesworth, Carsten T., et al. "Identification of Pre-Existing Adaptive Immunity to Cas9 Proteins in Humans." *Nature Medicine*, vol. 25 (2019), pp. 249–254. doi: 10.1101/243345.

Clapp. Jennifer. *Food*. Polity Press, 2012.

Eichenwald, Kurt. "Redesigning Nature: Hard Lessons Learned; Biotechnology Food: From the Lab to a Debacle." *The New York Times*, 25 January 2001, www.nytimes.com/2001/01/25/business/redesigning-nature-hard-lessons-learned-biotechnology-food-lab-debacle.html.

Engdahl, William. *Seeds of Destruction: The Hidden Agenda of Genetic Manipulation*. Global Research, 2007.

Estok, Simon. *The Ecophobia Hypothesis*. Routledge, 2018.

Foer, Jonathan Safran. *Eating Animals*. Little, Brown, 2009.

Fraser, Evan; Andrew Rimas. *Empires of Food: Feast, Famine and the Rise and Fall of Civilizations*. Arrow Books, 2011.

Goodman, Amy. "Stolen Harvest: The Hijacking of the Global Food Supply – A Speech By Vandana Shiva." *Democracy Now*, 16 May 2000, www.democracynow.org/2000/5/16/stolen_harvest_the_hijacking_of_the.

Grossman, Lev. "The Top 10 Everything of 2009." *TIME*, 8 December 2009. content.time.com/time/specials/packages/article/0,28804,1945379_1943868_1943887,00.html.

Moate, Maddie. "What Would Happen If Bees Went Extinct?" *The Earth Unplugged. BBC*, 4 May 2014, www.bbc.com/future/story/20140502-what-if-bees-went-extinct.

Morton, Timothy. *The Ecological Thought*. Harvard University Press, 2010.

Rodriguez E., et al. "Ethical Issues in Genome Editing using Crispr/Cas9 System." *Clinical Research & Bioethics*. vol. 7, no. 2, 2016, doi: 10.4172/2155-9627.1000266.

Salkever, Alex and Vivek Wadhwa. "When Baby Genes Are for Sale, the Rich Will Pay." *Fortune*, October 23, 2017, fortune.com/2017/10/23/designer-babies-inequality-crispr-gene-editing/.

Shiva, Vandana. *Stolen Harvest: The Hijacking of the Global Food Supply*. University Press of Kentucky, 2016.

———. *Biopiracy: The Plunder of Nature and Knowledge*. North Atlantic Books, 2016.

7 Metaphors and Metonymies of Food in Four Asian Texts

Chitra Sankaran

Food is an urgent and topical subject to examine in the present day. The *Lancet* Commission Report categorically states that "[f]ood in the Anthropocene era represents one of the greatest health and environmental challenges of the 21st century" (Willett et al.). It highlights how, though global food production has kept pace with population growth, more than 820 million people have insufficient food and many more consume low-quality diets that cause micronutrient deficiencies and contribute to a range of health problems. The Report asserts that "current dietary trends, combined with projected population growth to about 10 billion by 2050, will exacerbate risks to people and planet" (Willett et al.). However, the risks associated with uneven food distribution in the future world and even its non-availability are only some aspects of the several problems associated with food. Its more abstract dimensions and ways in which these may adversely impact cultures need greater scrutiny.

The present essay explores the multivalence of food that is echoed in Terry Eagleton's "Edible Écriture": "[i]f there is one sure thing about food, it is that it is never just food. Like the post-structuralist text, food is endlessly interpretable, as gift, threat, poison, recompense, barter, seduction, solidarity, suffocation" (25). In the four Asian texts—Anita Desai's *Fasting, Feasting*; Vida Cruz's "Song of the Mango;" Michele Cruz Skinner's "Mango Season;" and Wayne Ree's "Satay"—I examine the focus on food and their significance to the people's identity and their communities. Indeed, food has long been used as metaphor and metonymy in literary fictions. The four contemporary texts from the Global South (India, Singapore and the Philippines) discuss the making and eating of food and exemplify the diverse cultural connotations surrounding the idea of nourishment and demonstrate how these varied cultures contribute to or challenge ideas surrounding the eating and wasting of food. The four texts, subtly or overtly, predict or mirror the varied problems that one associates with or can foresee in the Anthropocene.

The Indian writer Anita Desai's novel, *Fasting, Feasting* (2000), not only leads to an interesting comparison between the dietary habits of Indians and Americans but also explores the larger connotations relating to food in two diverse cultures. The Filipino writers Vida Cruz and Michele Cruz

DOI: 10.4324/9781003282976-10

Skinner sketch their narratives around "the mango," which becomes a metonymy for food in their short stories. In the "Song of the Mango" (2018), Cruz weaves a mythical tale about warring clans who fight over a mango tree, while Skinner narrates a family drama in "Mango Season" (2000), thus signalling how this native fruit and its varied significations are not only an intrinsic part of their culture and imaginings but are also entrenched in their ancient and contemporary histories. Finally, the short story "Satay" (2018) by Wayne Ree, a Singaporean, is set in a post-apocalyptic world where local food becomes a tool symbolizing power that can bond or break communities. In these fictional narratives from diverse cultures and distinct genres—science fiction, fantasy, family drama and a social-realist novel—food becomes more than a source of nourishment and sustenance. Here, food reflects and symbolizes deep-rooted cultural beliefs, mediating lives and negotiating destinies. But most of all, it becomes an active political tool that the characters consistently desire and use in order to consolidate and/or augment their power.

Wayne Ree's "Satay" is set in post-apocalyptic Singapore, which has been deluged by the sea and where the sky scrapers are under water. All the lowest floors are already submerged. In the Three Towers settlement live the privileged upper-level and the poverty-stricken lower-level families. Rafi and his father, Reza the "satay seller," are among the few residents from the lower levels who have access to the upper levels. Their access is based on the fact that they cook and sell chicken, beef and mutton satay. Satay is shown to be a class leveller since "people from every level would climb up or come down to the old man and give him a reverent salaam" (79). Ironically, the description elevates the satay seller, who grills this popular street food like a "high priest" officiating at an important state ceremony. Reza explains with majestic certitude that "[t]he satay is for everyone" (79) and thus imbues him with a certain moral authority. To his son, Rafi, his father's intrepidity in defying the "upper levels" and upholding the rights of the subalterns to eat satay makes him a heroic figure. Reza's egalitarian impulses are undergirded by his communitarian ethic, whose constant mantra is "community is what matters" (79). But the mystery that overshadows Rafi's hero worship is about where his father procures his meat from for the satay. Since there are no known sources for beef, lamb or chicken in the deluged building, this is a legitimate worry. As Rafi gradually unearths well-hidden secrets, he realizes that his father gets the meat from the Spriggan, a powerful elite, in exchange for information about potential rebels and radicals from the lower floors. Therefore, the convivial, inclusive atmosphere that is generated around Reza comes at the cost of the betrayal of the trouble makers at both the literal and metaphorical "lower levels" of the community. In this context, the connection between food and survival is reinforced through the politics generated by the time-worn conflict of the entitled Self and the underprivileged Other. The satay that Reza proclaims as the leveller of class differences actually becomes the device that enables the decimation of the lower-class dissidents. Reza's guilt is off-set by his satisfaction that, in his own unique way, he is serving the community by supplying it with an indispensable commodity. This is why, when he is with the Spriggan at the dead of night, he intuits his son's hidden presence there, and as if to assuage his guilt, remarks loudly to the Spriggan Sergeant, "community is what matters" (89), in all probability to remind Rafi of the reason for his actions. This is a lesson that Rafi appears to absorb, for, after his father's death, Rafi moves into the trade, continuing the use of satay as a unit of barter.

The text thus complicates Reza's upholding of communitarian ideology, for he is shown as simultaneously both enabler and disabler, the guardian and the betrayer of communitarianism. Satay becomes a metonymy for power and is a metaphor for not only biological but also political survival. The meat for the satay as a unit of barter in exchange for the information that Reza supplies to the Spriggan is the ultimate commodity. The complexity that surrounds the procuring and eating of food mirrors the complex politics that surrounds the production and distribution of food in today's world. It serves to remind us that for the longest time, colonialism and globalization have thrived precisely on the commodification of food, with powerful nations sanctioning it or withholding it from countries and peoples for political ends. Vivero-Pol reinstates this power link when he classifies the concept of food into two contrasting modes: as "commons or commodity" (442). The latter view licenses the use of food to punish nations that do not align with "approved" codes of conduct. As the sole suppliers of satay to lower-floor residents with no money or means, Reza and Rafi accrue power that arises out of the commodification of food. In the process, they become arbiters of life, making decisions on who should live and who is dispensable. Thus, Terry Eagleton's observation that "[i]t is significant that our word for the use of a commodity—consumption—is drawn from the guts and the gullet" (25) is particularly appropriate.

In spite of the text subtly exposing the power games deployed around food, it appears comfortably unconscious of the irony involved in the emphasis on meat eating, which is one of the prominent factors causing climate change in the Anthropocene. "Satay," which centrally concerns the procurement of meat and the ethics of "food power," tells the story about the central ethics around meat eating. Thus, Reza's and later Rafi's communitarian ideals only include the "brotherhood of 'man'" where women and live animals are rendered voiceless and invisible in this male-centred narrative.

Wayne Ree's post-apocalyptic Singapore uses food as a means to explore the emerging class differences in "meritocratic" Singapore. It offers a thoughtful thesis on the growing class differences that appear to create huge chasms in even this small, tightly governed nation state. Finally, we deduce that its "Machereyan silences" on the consequences of the predatory acts of "hegemonic masculinity" on women and animals are as evocative by their absence as are its prominent themes by their presence.

Food as the great divider is also the central theme of Skinner's "Mango Season." Here again, it is undoubtedly presented as a tool of power. Mrs. Clara Salcedo relives her secret, romantic yearnings that are linked to her memories of eating mangoes from her garden with her childhood sweetheart, Danny. Though eating mangoes is traditionally a family activity, when Clara and her three children sit around the table stained with sticky mango juice, it becomes a trigger for reliving memories from her teenage years. Clara's sensual memories of Danny are closely linked to the sensory sweetness of mangoes: "We used to eat mangoes together, Danny, his sister and I. That is one of my secrets, us sitting in the heat of the summer, on the dry grass by the fountain, juice around our mouths (301)." Clara's secret yearnings for the "lower-class," poor Danny associates with the mango they share such that this innocent activity gets "tainted" and overshadowed by adulterous yearnings, especially since they intrude on Clara's marital intimacies with her husband. This line of thought aligns with Rüdiger Kunow's views when he affirms the representative value of food registering the fact that "ethnographers and cultural studies specialists have long been demonstrating how food not only feeds but also organizes us, how the making, taking, and disposing of edible ingredients are socially and culturally inflected" (151). Mangoes represent the social cement for Clara that makes her relationship with the "lower-class" Danny possible. She believes that the mangoes ensure that "our tongues were sweet and spoke easy placating words to my mother and grandmother who tolerated the friendship because we were children" (Skinner 301). Clara's rich family, descendants of the landed gentry, would otherwise prohibit her interactions with the impoverished Danny and his sister. Thus, the sharing and eating of mangoes become communal acts, erasing social barriers of class and affluence. The fruit is also symbolic of the secret yearnings and forbidden desires carrying an emotional baggage in the life of Clara.

For Nick, Clara's husband, and Marissa, her ten-year old daughter, food, eating and class are closely allied. Marissa is put off by her mother's aunt, Tita Lucy, who "slurps, coughs, chews noisily, and spits fish bones onto her plate" (303) and has grown too old to care about table manners. Marissa is affronted by this lack of finesse and refuses to have anything to do with Tita Lucy. Nick, who believes in ownership and property, views the mangoes as *their property* which should not be shared. Therefore, Clara's confessions about sharing the mangoes with her neighbours, granting permission when the "trees grow heavier with mangoes and a few of the neighbours ask if they can pick some" (310) is a secret that she can only share with the readers, never with her family, who view it as a radical and subversive act. Later, when the "yard man" brings workers to repair their fountain, once again, Clara's sharing of her mangoes with the workers becomes a forbidden act that she needs to hide from her husband. Clara's views are clearly opposed to Nick's. She confesses that her "husband has already told me I shouldn't let them … But he isn't around" (310). True to Loveleen's view, food (here, the mango) represents power, social status, family relationships, sexuality, wealth, and group identity (2018: 1593). Sharing food is seen as a betrayal of an elitist group identity.

Besides this betrayal, the sharing and eating of mangoes unearth hidden memories of secret relationships invoking sensual images. Clara's sexual yearnings for Danny that get reinforced by the smell and sight of the mangoes also connotes loss, a grieving—"[n]o one is waiting for me under the mango tree by the river" (303)—rendering the mango a symbol for a lack in her marriage. This underscores Kunow's idea about the semiotic quality of representation as "a stand-in, a sign of something that is absent" (154). Similarly, Brad Kessler's idea that food sometimes becomes a memory trigger, reminding characters of the past, transporting them to another time through the memory of a similar previous sensory experience (157) is made patent in this story. "Mango Season" ends on a note of sadness and nostalgia: "I hold my hands to my face and smell on them the mango flowers that I sliced" (316). The prescriptions and proscriptions surrounding the sharing of mangoes become political codes that include the hegemonic and exclude the subdominant. Once again, food becomes a metonymy for power and status.

These authors' presentation of the wide use of food as a "power tool" resonates with Pope Francis's sorrow, when he bemoans the fact that "the struggle against hunger and malnutrition is hindered by market priorities, the primacy of profit, which have reduced foodstuffs to a commodity like any other, subject to speculation, also of a financial nature." He rages against predatory capitalism which has "made the fruits of the Earth—a gift to humanity—commodities for a few, thus engendering exclusion" (reported by Pullella, 2014). This theme, clearly present in both "Satay" and "Mango Season," is also strongly fielded in the ensuing text, "Song of the Mango," a fantasy, by Vida Cruz, where food becomes a source of power so great that wars are fought to gain access to it.

This short story, "Song of the Mango," set in Salayan mountains, narrates a mythical tale about how Maragat, a *duragma* (an honourable soldier) of the Ayuran tribe, in service to Tila, the young, beautiful but frivolous *awitana* (priestess), is killed by a wild boar he goes hunting to bestow as dowry to marry her. Maragat's sister, Saha, the narrator of the tale, a songstress, also in service to Tila, goes in search of her brother and when she finds the dying Maragat, holds his head on her lap and sings her distress. Her beautiful song lures Salayan, first among the *Diwata* or spirits, to Saha's side. Moved by Saha's song, Salayan bestows a boon that the dead Maragat will transmogrify into a mango tree. Saha then leaves Tila and resides under Maragat, the mango tree. The delicious golden mangoes from the tree provide magical treatment for all ailments. When the gentle Maragat urges Saha to cure all kinds of ailments of the villagers using the mango, word spreads about the witch, Saha, and the magical mangoes. True to Brad Kessler's words about food being a magnet, the mangoes draw people from near and far. The fruits are at the centre of the dramatic action (153). Sadly, the infamous southern *rahan*, Sumanlul and his friends, hear of this and arrive to uproot the tree and abduct Saha along with the tree to their palace to replant it there. The tree and Saha are then forced to serve only their wives and progeny. Thus, the medicinal mango, which should have been the right of the common people, gets commodified and becomes the property of the rich *rahan*. Finally, years later, Tila, the *awitana* arrives, widowed, captured and impregnated by the barbarian *rahan*. Saha, with the help of Maragat's mangoes, aborts the baby and together they escape with a few hidden mangoes, reluctantly and at his behest, leaving Maragat behind. Finally, years later, after having served Tila faithfully, Saha, ageless, retires to a remote island with a mango seedling, which once again grows into a healing tree. Thus, Maragat's legacy is perpetuated. Saha's narration is to ensure that the story of Maragat is never forgotten. It ends with an invitation: "And now that I have told this story, are you certain you still want to stay and take part in this thankless but important work? If so, here is a mango—I invite you to take a bite" (173).

The narrative that begins and ends with a pointed reference to a mango prioritizes the power of food. It reiterates what Wong-Chung Kim means when he states that "eating is above all things, an exchange of energy and one of the most intimate and direct forms of communion with others" (685–686). The mango that caused the southern barbarian lords to abduct Maragat and Saha also becomes the tool by which Saha is able to befriend the other wives of the southern lord and their children. It is the same fruit that helps Tila abort her unwanted child. The mango with "a single black spot the size of my smallest fingernail," as Saha describes it (167) becomes a potent tool that ejects the unwanted foetus and reinscribes Saha's identity as *awitana* of her clan. Thus, the mango is not only a curative and a medicine but also a weapon that forcefully reinscribes and re-establishes communal identity.

The noble and valorous Maragat, when he becomes a tree, bestows on its fruits his finer qualities underlining the belief in the unitary basis of all life forms, pervasive in indigenous Filipino myths. He wants it to serve the community. Like Reza in "Satay," Maragat's motto too is "community is everything." He prompts his reclusive sister to cure the people who come their way of their injuries and ailments. Thus, mango becomes the medicine that serves the community. It is when this curative food is coveted by the barbarian lords that the perennial battle of food that rightfully belongs to the commons gets commodified. Saha's battle is to reinstate the basic right of the people to the medicinal mango, and her final invitation to the readers restores this right to the common people, nominally to us, the readers.

The *Encyclopedia of Food and Culture* defines the term "foodways" as first used by folklorists to refer to "the connection between food-related behavior and patterns of membership in cultural community, group, and society." Food and eating have deep ideological overtones. The interdictions surrounding food often inscribe and circumscribe a specific (individual or) communal identity. Many religions have strict rules surrounding food and eating. Desai's novel, *Fasting, Feasting*, in fact, revolves around precisely the theme of the importance of food in constituting identity, both familial and communal. Once again, its themes emphasize the power games linked to the making and eating of food.

A Booker Prize finalist in 1999, Anita Desai's *Fasting, Feasting* has two parts. The first is about a family in India: Papa, Mama, their two daughters, Uma and Aruna, and their son, Arun, while the second part, set in America, focuses on the Patton family. Arun, who travels to Massachusetts for study and spends a summer with the Pattons, is the link between these two families who live on opposite sides of the globe. Although culturally worlds apart, both families have similarities such as a high-handed patriarch at the helm, whose power is unchallenged; besides which, the fathers in both families are great believers in the benefit of meat eating.

Uma, the focalizer for the first part, is the underperforming oldest daughter, whose life is spent in servitude to her parents—dubbed "mamapapa" to underscore their inseparability—whose endless demands keep Uma tied to the home. Uma's father subscribes to the view that "progressive" Indians need to eat meat in order to perform optimally in their chosen pursuits. Therefore, Arun's, the cherished son's, refusal to consume meat comes as a shock and a disappointment to "papa." The Patton family in America viewed through Arun's eyes seem curiously to re-enact certain patterns visible within his own family. Mr. Patton asserts his masculinity through his enthusiastic consumption of meat. Mrs. Patton's futile attempts to assert her individuality, and her wish to be inclusive of Arun by turning vegetarian during his residence there, are derided and ignored by her husband. Their daughter, Melanie, is bulimic. Her torturous attempts to imbibe large quantities of unappetizing food, only to vomit them out immediately afterwards—her binging and purging reflected in the title of the novel—go unnoticed by the parents for a long time. Hence, aside from the patriarchal power structure, what links both families is a preoccupation with food and eating, and an indifference to the lives of their daughters.

Food and related imagery are used to symbolize power and status, oppression of women, rejection or endorsement of entrenched cultural and/or religious values and also to signify relationships and their breakdown. One scene encapsulating the play of power through descriptions of eating occurs when Mama carefully peels an orange, removes the pips and hands it to Papa. After Papa has finished eating all of it, a finger bowl is placed in front of him and he is handed a napkin to wipe his fingers dry, while Uma looks on or waits for orders (24). Everything revolves around Papa's comfort and desires, and food becomes a central component of this display of power. Indeed, the book opens with one such conversation between Mama and Papa. "'We are having fritters for tea today. Will that be enough? Or do you want sweets as well?' 'Yes, yes, yes—there must be sweets—must be sweets, too. Tell cook. Tell cook at once' " (3–4). The frenetic command not only establishes Papa's power but also the centrality of food in reinforcing the power structure within the family.

Concepts of fasting and feasting, however, go beyond the literal to absorb every aspect of life in the novel. Uma, for instance, can be seen as having metaphorically fasted on education since she is forced to abandon her schooling at the convent to look after her younger brother, Arun. Her isolation within her home depletes her of cultural exposure and travel. Her two near-marriages involve a lot of feasting but sexually she is "fasting," for her unions remain unconsummated. She is also starved of personal attention and care. Her periodic epileptic fitting and her severe myopia are dismissed as unimportant by "mamapapa." Thus, metaphorically, she is starved for love, care and indeed any kind of joy in life. In contrast to her situation, the beloved son, Arun, is lavished with attention and care. He is nourished on a strict diet that Papa has prescribed to encourage his growth and development, both mental and physical, into a strong high achiever. His education is carefully overseen in order to prepare him for studying overseas.

The title, which juxtaposes a pair of opposites, alerts us to the idea that parallelism is favoured in the narrative. Uma's predicament of fasting in life is paralleled by her accomplished cousin, Anamika's. Despite her many talents and brilliance, which procure her a place at Oxford University, Anamika is married off to a dour, grim, much older man in a sadistic family. Anamika's radiance is dimmed gradually through the cruelties she suffers on a daily basis. She is literally and metaphorically starved by the family on a regular basis and finally murdered, though they pretend it was an accident. Throughout, her parents keep silent, more intent upon putting up appearances that all is fine with their daughter than fighting for her rights and life. On the other side of the globe, Melanie Patton binges and purges, quite literally feasting and fasting, until her condition is finally noticed by her parents, leading to her admission to a rehabilitation centre for bulimics. For Melanie, her condition is a means of drawing the attention that she craves from her parents. For all the three young women in the novel—Uma, Melanie and Anamika—"fasting and feasting" become central metaphors describing their lives and living.

The person who, above all others, epitomizes fasting in the novel is Mira Masi, Uma's widowed aunt, who stops by their house en route to her various pilgrimage destinations. The frugal and deeply religious Mira Masi, who does her own cooking while at Uma's house, is more than a fringe character. She brings in her person a debate critical to the ethic of the text and one which is still fairly important to Hindu India: the idea of the "purity and healthiness of a vegetarian diet" versus "the importance of animal proteins in human diet for health." This is a debate that has troubled Hindu India since colonial times. "Adhyathe Ithi Annam"—that which is consumed by all living creatures for survival is food, says the *Rig Veda Āranyam*. *Rig Veda* (1700–1100 BCE), and the *Purānās* (800–300 BCE) are only two of the many texts in Hindu Classical literature that focus on food. There are many stories in the *Purānic* literature illustrating the influence of food on the mind and actions of a person. The *Vedas* categorize food into three, namely *Achanam, Paanam* and *Kaadhaha*.[1] Food is perceived as contributing critically to our longevity, health and happiness. How it is produced, distributed, cooked and served and the environment in which it is eaten are thought to contribute to physical health and spiritual nourishment. *Taittreya Upanishad* insists that "Man consists of the essence of food" ["Adhyetha cha bhoothani thasmaath annam thadyuthacha ithi"]. *The Bhagavad Gita* in its verses (17:8, 17:9 and 17:10) discusses *Sattvic*, *Rajasic* and *Tamasic* foods and ways in which these affect a person's behaviour and disposition, making them temperate, prone to passions or slothful, respectively. Claude Fischler's convincing argument in "Food, Self and Identity" which states "that food constitutes the self" is one that is embraced by Hindu thought. Fischler states: "'[y]ou are what you eat,' bespeaks not only the biochemical relationship between us and our food but also the extent to which food practices determine our systems of beliefs and representations" (277). In many religions, including Hinduism, identity is closely linked to dietary habits. Vegetarianism and the consumption of meat often divide people, even within the religion, into opposite camps.

The ancient ideas and conflicts get subtly foregrounded during Mira Masi's visits to Uma's house. On the insistence of Uma's westernized, progressive father, their family not only cook spicy food but also eat meat, which becomes an affront to the orthodox Hindu widow, who is deeply scornful of the "meat-eating, polluted outcasts" (63) and therefore:

> cooks her own meals at a safe distance from the cook who laughed contemptuously in the kitchen where he fried up onions and garlic and stirred the mutton curries and grilled the kebabs that made Mira Masi cover her mouth and nose...
>
> (40–41)

This categoric self/other divide is a pattern that Mark Stein accentuates when he observes that food "does more than satisfy one's biological need for calories, nutrients, water. Food choice divides communities and has the power to delineate the boundaries between them. Food taboos can serve to mark outsiders as unclean, unhealthy, unholy" (134).

Arun is placed at the centre of this controversy when he is shown, even as a child, to prefer vegetarian food. Mama is upset when he wolfs down Mira Masi's vegetarian preparations while abhorring the choicest of meats carefully prepared for his nourishment by the cook under the watchful eyes of Mama, following Papa's explicit instructions. As Simon C. Estok points out, "[o]ur food choices grow out of a great variety of concerns, including but not limited to concerns about health, religion, ethics, money, convenience and so on" (682). For Papa, vegetarianism is a sign of cultural stagnation and signals an insistence on traditions at odds with modernity. He equates meat eating with progress. On the other hand, Mira Masi's vegetarianism, however, reflects an adherence to religious beliefs that to her cannot and should not be contravened. Her eating habits become more frugal and austere as she grows old and fasting becomes a central feature of her dietary habits. Both Papa and Mira Masi are portrayed as being irrational, hidebound by beliefs in their own distinctive ways.

Mira Masi's austerity, however, stands in stark contrast to the excesses of the American family. Mrs. Patton takes to "vegetarianism" with Arun's entry into her home and she goes on endless shopping sprees with no eye on what is needed, as if it is impossible to satisfy or satiate a consumerist demon that resides within her, one that Desai gently hints has taken over not only American society but the entire world. Mrs. Patton's orgy of shopping is mirrored and mocked in her bulimic daughter's orgy of eating and purging. Despite Terry Eagleton's rather caustic observation that "[t]here has been much critical interest in the famished body of the western anorexic, but rather little attention to the malnutrition of the Third World" (26), it has to be admitted that Melanie's condition is presented as a direct consequence of parental neglect. Like Arun, who despite Mrs. Patton's attempts at dishing up unappetizing vegetarian meals, often ends up starving, Melanie too is starving not only for healthy food and nourishment that cater to her palette but also indeed for love and care from her family. Thus, starving takes on both literal and metaphoric overtones. This makes her comparable to Uma. Similarly to Clara in "Mango Season," for Arun too, food becomes a "memory trigger" and makes him liken Melanie, though culturally distant, to his sister, Uma.

In deliberate contrast to vegetarianism and to the dietary discordances of his daughter, Mr. Patton and his athletic son, Rod, emanate the masculine ideal that scorns any alternative diets that are different to what they consider "the norm." Playing on a strange concordance, Mr. Patton's scorn of "untraditional attitudes" to food can appear similar to Mira Masi's, who mirrors the masculinity of Mr. Patton's. Thus, eating and food are central markers of personalities and identity, echoing Fischler's words that "[f]ood is central to our identity" (275). At the end of the summer, Arun is happy to move out of the Pattons' residence back to his college dorm to pursue his own erratic, highly personalized eating habits around the time that Melanie's illness is finally recognized by her mother.

To conclude, all the four texts that were analysed emerge from the Global South focusing on the subject of food, underscoring the view that the availability of food or its lack thereof are not only pervasive subjects but very divisive topics in Asia. Food as the central theme is treated in both literal and metaphorical terms. It is shown to cement and build communities, to cure and care, to tease hidden memories and to rule relationships. Like the kernel of the mango fruit, food is shown to contain the seed for the secret of survival, both as individuals and as communities. Food nourishes and an absence of care in nourishment is shown to end in rebellion of both body and mind. In all four texts, food and eating become metaphors and metonymies of something larger that breaks or bonds families and communities. Above all, food is shown to have become a political tool in all four texts. These narratives inevitably open the door to relevant speculations about the future of food in the Global South in the Anthropocene era.

Note

1 *Achanam* is food that is chewed and tasted, *Paanam* is fluid while food that needs to be bitten by the teeth and chewed well is *Kaadhaha*.

References

Barthes, Roland. *Mythologies*. Hill, 1972.

Cruz, Vida. "Song of the Mango." *Lontar: The Journal of Southeast Asian Speculative Fiction*, 2018, pp. 146–73.

Davis, Delmer. "Food as Literary Theme." *Identities and Issues in Literature*, N. page. eNotes.com. 2011.

Desai, Anita. *Fasting, Feasting*. Vintage, 2000.

Eagleton, Terry. "Edible Écriture," *Times Higher Education*, October 24, 1997. www.timeshighereducation.co.uk/ features/ edible- ecriture/ 104281.article. pp. 25–7.

Estok, Simon C. "An Introduction to 'Ecocritical Approaches to Food and Literature in East Asia': The Special Cluster." *Interdisciplinary Studies in Literature and Environment (ISLE)*, vol. 19, issue 4, Autumn, 2012, pp. 681–90.

Fischler, Claude. "Food, Self and Identity." *Anthropology of Food*, vol. 27, issue 2, June 1, 1988, pp. 275–92.

Foer, Jonathan Safran. *Eating Animals*. Little and Brown, 2009.

"Foodways." *Encyclopedia of Food and Culture. Encyclopedia.com*. 11 Aug. 2020 www.encyclopedia.com.

Jameson, Fredric. "Progress versus Utopia; Or, Can We Imagine the Future?" *Science Fiction Studies*, Special Issue: Utopia and Anti-Utopia, vol. 9, issue 2 (1982), pp. 147–58.

Kessler, Brad. "One Reader's Digest: Toward a Gastronomic Theory of Literature." *The Kenyon Review*, vol. 27, issue 2 (2005), pp. 148–65.

Kim, Wong-Chung. "A World in a Rice Bowl: Chiha Kim and Emerging Korean Food Ethic." *Interdisciplinary Studies in Literature and Environment (ISLE)*, vol. 19, issue 4, Autumn, 2012, pp. 685–6.

Kunow, Rüdiger. "Eating Indian(s): Food, Representation, and the Indian Diaspora in the United States." *Eating Culture: The Poetics and Politics of Food*. Edited by Tobias Döring, Markus Heide and Susanne Mühleisen. Universitätsverlag, Winter, 2003, pp. 151–75.

Loveleen, R. T. K. "Food for Thought: Relevance of Food Narratives in Salman Rushdie's *Midnight's Children* and Arundhati Roy's *God of Small Things*." *International Journal of Academic Research and Development*, vol. 3, issue 2, March 2018, pp. 1591–7.

Macherey, Pierre. *A Theory of Literary Production*. Translated by G. Wall. Routledge & Kegan Paul, 1978.

Pullella, Philip. "Pope Says Food Commodity Speculation Hurts Fight Against Hunger. *Lifestyle*, November 20, 2014. www.reuters.com/article/us-health-hunger-pope/pope-says-food-commodity-speculation-hurts-fight-against-hunger-idUSKCN0J417X20141120.

Ree, Wayne. "Satay." *Lontar: The Journal of Southeast Asian Speculative Fiction*, 2018, pp. 79–92.

Skinner, Michele Cruz. "Mango Season." *Hoard of Thunder: Philippine Short Stories in English 1990–2008*. Vol. 1. Edited by Gemino H. Abad. The University of the Philippines Press, 2000, pp. 297–316.

Stein, Mark. "Curry at Work: Nibbling at the Jewel in the Crown." *Eating Culture: The Poetics and Politics of Food*. Edited by Tobias Döring, Markus Heide and Susanne Mühleisen. Universitätsverlag, Winter, 2003, pp. 133–49.

Vivero-Pol, Jose Luis. "Food as Commons or Commodity? Exploring the Links between Normative Valuations and Agency in Food Transition." *Sustainability*, Basel, vol. 9, issue 3, 2017, pp. 2–23.

Willett, Walter, et al. "Food in the Anthropocene: The EAT-Lancet Commission on Healthy Diets from Sustainable Food Systems." January 16, 2019. http://dx.doi.org/10.1016/S0140-6736(18)31788-4.

Part III

Crises, Disintegration, Food

8 Agrarian Distress and Food Sovereignty in the Anthropocene

A Reading of Namita Waikar's *The Long March*

P. Rajitha Venugopal

This chapter analyzes Namita Waikar's novel, *The Long March* (2018), in the context of the agrarian crisis in the Global South in the Anthropocene epoch. Industrial agribusiness, which is energy-intensive, ecologically unsustainable, and enmeshed in international trade policies, has destabilized agrarian economies of the Global South. One such case of a disrupted rural economy is the Vidarbha region of Maharashtra in western India. The novel discusses the current agrarian crisis and farmer suicides in the region, the efforts of a group of farmers to reclaim their rights and the resistance they put up against the oppression of the nexus of government and agribusiness corporations. It exemplifies one case of the effects of the Anthropocene within a certain regional and class context in the Global South, instead of studying Anthropocene on an abstract and global scale. Therefore, this chapter explores the possibilities of agroecological methods for addressing the agrarian crisis as depicted in the novel.

My analysis is based on the hypothesis that it is problematic to consider the Anthropocene as a concept in the abstract and universal. Dipesh Chakrabarty, in his articles on the Anthropocene, argues that humans have to assume responsibility *collectively as a species* for their contribution to anthropogenic climate change, as well as for working towards mitigating the effects of climate change.[1] Chakrabarty has been widely criticized for taking an abstract universalist approach to the problem of the Anthropocene, although he is known to be a Marxist and postcolonial historian and scholar of Subaltern Studies. Biermann et al. argue that considering the anthropos as a common geological agent "masks the diversity and differences in the actual conditions and impacts of humankind, and does not do justice to the local and regional contexts" (342). In order to have a nuanced understanding of any ecological issue in the Anthropocene, it is important to place the issue in its "context-dependent, localized, and social understanding" (342). Biermann et al. emphasize that in terms of policy research and development for the Global South, we should approach the Anthropocene from a "cross-scalar perspective that takes into account developments at local, regional and global levels, variant connections among these levels and issue domains, as well

DOI: 10.4324/9781003282976-12

as societal inequality and injustice" (342). A large section of the Global South constitutes poor, developing, agrarian economies, whose traditional agriculture has already been interfered in by global hegemonic powers with the introduction of the Green Revolution. The adverse impacts of the Green Revolution have exacerbated since the 1990s with the opening up of a market for free trade based on international trade policies. Food producers across the world broadly consist of two categories—industrial food producers and small farmers. These two groups of food producers do not bear equal responsibility in terms of both contribution to anthropogenic climate change and the impact of climate change. While agribusiness companies enjoy the profits, local farmers disproportionately suffer the eco-social consequences. Besides being stifled by economic constraints, the farmers in the Global South are also affected by anthropogenic climate change. Extreme and erratic weather conditions cause immense crop loss, thereby challenging their very survival. In the complex web of affairs, farmers have lost their food sovereignty and their sense of self-sustenance. While they contribute by producing food for the nation, ironically, they are trapped in deprivation, poverty, hunger, and a bleak future. Against such a background, this chapter will analyze *The Long March*, which depicts farmer suicides and the entrenched state of rural agriculture caught in the nexus between government and international trade policies. I argue that a differential treatment and approach considering the local, regional, and sociopolitical context is required to understand the issues and concerns related to food production in the Global South in the Anthropocene.

The Long March portrays the agrarian crisis in a multi-pronged way and suggests possibilities for confronting the issue. These possibilities include an awakening of consciousness from within the farming community about their rights, and an acknowledgment of their knowledge base about systems of production and their local, regional, social, and ecological conditions. Waikar's novel approaches the agrarian crisis from two perspectives: (1) from that of the urban educated social worker who wants to make a difference to rural lives—through the characters of Mallika Joshi and Sriram Kasbekar; and (2) through the rights-conscious member of a farming family in rural Vidarbha—Vikram Sonare, and his fellow farmers. Sriram and Mallika work for a Mumbai-based non-governmental organization (NGO) and are traditional intellectuals in Gramscian terms.[2] Vikram, a resident of the Sonsawali village of Wardha and a son of a farmer who committed suicide by consuming pesticide, is a person who has lived the agrarian crisis at a personal level and hence is a Gramscian organic intellectual. He is from within the community and symbolizes a political awakening in mobilizing his fellow community members and organizing them in new ways to address their problems. While the contribution of the urban social worker is an external mobilizing force, the efforts of Sonare and his network of people is an intrinsic, rights-conscious approach that asserts their agency and subject position.

In order to portray the agrarian crisis, Waikar explores it from various angles, such as caste, class, regional politics, religion, and education. One of the earliest metaphors she uses is that of a shop named "Farm Essentials," which sells pesticides and ropes, implying that the requisites for dying by suicide are also among the essential commodities a farmer would need by virtue of his situation. Waikar portrays the crisis in detail from the perspective of the class and caste context of rural Maharashtra. This is evident from some of her references, such as to Dr. B. R. Ambedkar, a champion of equal rights for the Dalits, to signify the caste context, and a metaphor of comparison between ants and humans to signify the class context. Early on in the novel, Waikar includes references from Ambedkar's *Annihilation of Caste* (25). The novel begins with the suicide of Vikram's father due to his inability to repay a bank loan of forty-five thousand rupees following crop failure. Vikram recollects his childhood when his parents urged him to study well so that he could have a different future from theirs, and also so that he could read the works of Ambedkar and be conscious of his rights. He remembers the relentless toil of his parents on the fields, their low wages, the social humiliation, and the sense of entitlement prevailing among the upper-caste people of the village. The generation of his parents, even though aware of Ambedkar's ideas, had been too conditioned to their social situation. Although Ambedkar's ideas are only briefly referenced in the beginning of the novel, they shape Vikram's views on equality, rights, and constitutional guarantees.

The novel depicts the class context of rural Maharashtra through the metaphor of the ants and anthill. Vikram observes the movement and activities of ants, "especially the way they carried food *marching* soldier-like in single file" (italics added). Sometimes he would try to break their order and distract them, and noticed that despite their lines being disrupted they would reorganize and march forth (72). Vikram curiously reads up more about ants on the internet, and is surprised to learn about the social division of labor among them. He learns that there are worker ants, queens, and drones and yet "the colonies operate as a unified entity and work together to sustain the colony" (73). Thinking analogically about human society, he notes that unlike "the drones and queens [which] were biologically different from the majority of the worker ants, humans were equal creatures physically and yet, most of human society lived like worker ants, while a privileged few could afford to live like drones and queens" (74). This reference marks the awakening of class consciousness and ideas about inequality and injustice in Vikram. In rural Maharashtra, as also in many other parts of the country, the class issue is enmeshed with the caste issue as rural farmers face oppression from people who are often both upper-caste and upper-class. The farmers also include people from various oppressed communities, including Dalits and Adivasis.[3] The reference to the anthill reappears later in the novel as a source of inspiration for Vikram when he plans to develop a new collective of farmers across the country (197). This metaphor works effectively in reflecting the hierarchy within human society in terms of caste and class, as well as in terms of integrating the scattered farmers into a collective consciousness about their rights.

Waikar critiques the futility of the government's welfare measures and the corruption of the bureaucracy in addressing the farmers' crisis. She discusses various aspects of rural agrarian life, such as unaffordable costs of production, lack of profit in agriculture, burden of loans, threats from banks and local moneylenders, persisting exploitation, stifling trade policies, land grab issues, encroachment and appropriation by real estate mafia, displacement, and the involvement of government officials in these matters. She also discusses ecological challenges such as scarcity of rain, crop failures, loss of forest land, pollution of water sources, and systemic problems such as corruption and crony capitalism affecting farmers in different ways.

In one instance in the novel, a parliamentary committee on agriculture visits the villages of Yavatmal, Kopardi, and Govargaon in the Vidarbha region because "Queen Seeds Inc., the American company, had showcased all three villages as beneficiaries of their Genetically Modified cotton seed that had near total monopoly in India's cotton sector" (64). The state government officials who accompany the committee, which is supposed to meet the farmers and enquire after their situation, mislead and redirect them to a different village where a fake scenario is staged with some traders dressed up as farmers who give false reports to the committee. This spurious group of "farmers" is supposed to give a positive report to the committee about the benefits of using Queen seeds and the "prosperity" that followed (67). This shows that the traders and government officials are hand-in-glove in supporting the American company, as well as the fact that the committee is not really interested in the actual welfare of the farmers. In a turn of events orchestrated by one of the brave farmers, the committee is taken to Hemarja, where a huge crowd of "actual" farmers had gathered, "including the tribal Adivasis and Banjara people and around thirty widows of farmers" (68). They protest when the village head begins to give false reports and voice their concerns regarding insufficient rains, inadequate irrigation facilities, rising input costs, and the inability to repay debts because of poor returns even if they sell their produce to the government. Witnessing the suicide of so many people, the younger generation sees no future in farming (68). Another problem they raise is the scarcity of water and the need for greater irrigation for patented seeds, whereas ordinary seeds do not require such huge quantities of water. Furthermore, they do not have enough electricity to use the pumps, which have rusted away. Waikar uses minute detail to emphasize the hardship of sustaining agriculture in rural areas. She portrays farmers as having a curious mix of hope and hopelessness as they report their situation to the committee.

Another instance of bureaucratic corruption is outlined in the context of the Rural Job Scheme, "a new venture for the officials and their cronies to make money" (186) in the name of the rural poor. The government schemes and welfare measures do not reach the right hands and do not yield the intended outcomes. Instead, the middle men and officials further down the hierarchy, who are employed in the implementation of these schemes, engage in fraudulent activities and take advantage of the schemes. There is a reference to a Job Scheme Colony (186) where government officials, who were involved in implementing the job scheme, have prospered and built large houses for themselves. The minister for Water Resources is accused of being involved in a major land grab scam (61). These instances show some of the failures of the government welfare measures that are thwarted due to corruption. For instance, a farmer's widow hints at the futility of a government scheme that gives a cow as compensation and measure of relief to farmers:

> Do they not know that to keep a cow, one requires fodder and water? Do they not know that there is a shortage of fodder and water in this region? What are we going to do with the cow? It only gives us four litres of milk, which does not add up to much money. And should I starve my family and feed the cow? And the cow was not free. It was only subsidized. I had to pay Rs. 5000 for it and Rs. 500 as commission to the officer who was looking after this whole affair. (102)

Thus, Waikar portrays the failure of the government's centralization method that considers farmers as objects at the receiving end of policies and schemes as opposed to an approach that treats farmers as subjects with whom there can be possibilities of dialogue. The top-down approach of governance alienates farmers and dooms their lives. Critics like P. Sainath argue for more agency and autonomy of farmers so that they have a say in their lives and futures. The farmers' suicides show that they have been cornered by both corporations and government and by climate crisis. Given these circumstances, the assumption of humans "as a homogeneous geological agent" (Chakrabarty) contributing to climate change is inaccurate and unjust. In the Anthropocene, ecological issues must be studied in the context of differentiating factors because disparities do exist between the Global North and South. Although Waikar does not discuss these aspects in her novel, she portrays the causes and consequences to give a larger picture of power dynamics behind global agrarian crisis, food crisis, and climate crisis.

Vandana Shiva discusses two paradigms of food production—industrial and ecological. She notes that the mechanized, industrial mode of production, which is the globally dominant paradigm, has created the farmers' crisis. Governed by the "Law of Exploitation," the proponents of this paradigm see the world as a "machine and dead matter" (1) and does not recognize the human–nature interrelationship other than in terms of mastery and subservience. In contrast, proponents of an ecological paradigm appreciate the interconnectedness of all living beings and understand the human role in nature, which is to "act as co-creators and co-producers" with nature. The industrial paradigm of food production forcibly draws small farmers into the multinational and overwhelming circuit of production, with high input costs and low profits. Ecologically, this production method degrades the soil, water, and air (due to the use of pesticides), and harms the health of all human and non-human lives in the ecosystem. Consequently, and reflected in *The Long March*, farmers have become more dependent and deprived.

The novel portrays an instance of a farmer's family which had cultivated *jowar* and other food crops on their land. Growing their own food crops, they were quite self-sufficient, in that they would keep some of the harvest for their consumption and sell the rest in a nearby shop. However, all of that changed once they switched from food production to growing cotton as it became a trend in the market. Now, they neither grow food for their own consumption nor get much profit from growing the cash crop, since they sell the produce to a trader in town. The payment they receive depends on the fluctuating price of cotton in the global market. They are then forced to borrow money, which they are barely able to repay, and the cycle continues until they pay with their lives.

The novel reflects the Kisan Long March that farmers undertook in Mumbai and Delhi in March 2018 and February 2019, respectively. It also reflects the agrarian crisis and farmer suicides in the Vidarbha region of Maharashtra in western India. P. Sainath notes that "in 20 years, between 1995 and 2015, 310,000 farmers committed suicide according to the NCRB [National Crime Records Bureau]. That is a gross underestimate, but it is a hideous figure" (quoted in Konikkara). The aforementioned years correspond to the era of neo-liberalization when government regulations were revoked. Sainath observes that the reforms have fundamentally altered the base of Indian agriculture, moving it from the hands of the farming community into the realm of the corporations. Prices and regulations are fixed by transnational corporations, which in turn put unprecedented pressure on farmers to grow cash crops (in place of food crops) and to compete with the global market.[3] Loss of food sovereignty is the most severe problem that the peasants of the Global South face. Multinational seed corporations sell patented seeds, pesticides, and fertilizers to grow crops, and small farmers are brought into this network of large-scale production. Consequently, even if small farmers were to grow food crops, they are required to sell them to the company to which they are contracted. In this manner, farmers have no rights over what they produce or how they choose to sell it. While previously they could produce what they wanted to consume, now their terms of production are dictated by the market.

Another problem with centralization and the government's approach that Waikar raises in relation to trade policies concerns the nexus with corporations. She notes that government regulations on trade are one of the major problems because they are paraded as beneficial to the farmers, when actually they are beneficial only to the corporations. One of the farmers in the novel observes that "when we [farmers] get bumper crops and export them, the nation makes money. That adds to the GDP [gross domestic product]. But more importantly, aren't farmers providing food for the nation?" (109). Therefore, the nation should acknowledge their hard work and sacrifice and support them in times of crisis. He states that government always gives better subsidies to the business sector rather than the agricultural sector.

Instead of having a top-down approach of governance agroecological methods are more effective in addressing the farmers' crisis, particularly concerning food security in the Anthropocene. The United Nations Food and Agriculture Organization (FAO) defines agroecology as "an integrated approach that simultaneously applies ecological and social concepts and principles to the design and management of food and agricultural systems" (1). In place of large corporations holding a monopoly over the agricultural sector, smaller, decentralized initiatives—such as farmers' cooperatives that are more inclusive, participatory, and democratic—can help ensure more ecological, social, and economic sustainability.

In contrast to the flawed governmental measures, Waikar highlights the work of an organization called the Institution of Agricultural Technology that is set up in the village and works according to the needs of the farmers and also helps in educating the young in the village. The organization always includes farmers in discussions regarding cropping patterns and work towards a transition back to cultivating food crops as cotton cultivation has done so much harm to the soil and society. Experts in the organization keep a check on the weather and inform farmers about suitable times to work. This kind of cooperation is the best example of agroecology, where scientific experts and researchers work in tandem with the empirical experts—the farmers (105). This proves that technology can be used to benefit the farmers. This also confirms the point raised by Professor M. S. Swaminathan that the present agrarian crisis has not been caused by technology, but by economics. This statement is a critique of trade policies, the monopoly of agribusiness companies, and the government's negligence of the agrarian sector (Jitheesh and Jipson).

The biggest irony concerning the agricultural sector is that farmers who had once been growing food crops now forcefully produce cash crops—which has caused impoverishment instead of prosperity. The Green Revolution has increased productivity, but the profits and prosperity have not reached the farmers.[4] As a result, they end up starving. The novel brings out such portraits of hunger and deprivation. On visiting Yavatmal, Sriram, the urban social worker, meets a sixty-year-old farmer who says:

> I would have offered you something to eat but there is nothing left now ... I was walking near the grain shop yesterday and found some

> red chilies that had fallen on the ground near the entrance. I snatched them up before anyone saw me and brought them home and ate them. I had to drink four glasses of water as the chilies were really hot. But that was good as it quenched my hunger, at least for a while. This is how it is every day.
>
> (114)

While this instance portrays the severity of hunger, another farmer in a different village tells Sriram the transition from food crops to cash crops and from a life of self-sustenance to one of dependency and loss of self-respect. He reminisces about a time when food was sufficiently available because they produced what they wanted. There was a greater sense of liveliness in the village, with many people engaged in farming because it was rewarding. With cotton cultivation, however, things have changed. He says that cotton was like "white gold" as "it brought prosperity" for a while, then there was blight, for which they had to use more pesticides. Every time they had to buy new, patented, hybrid seeds, and pesticides, all of which were expensive, they had to take out loans from the banks, and then from local money lenders. He notes that:

> Money was easy to get. Difficult to return at first, and then, impossible. The interest grew faster than the cotton. Everything else was shrinking: our land ... our self-respect ... and the cotton shrank even further and the debts kept growing ... I am a farmer and I have no food to eat. What can possibly be funnier than this?
>
> (116–117)

Thus, Waikar portrays that these farmers produce to sell because they need money to repay their debts. The crop for the next season is also often sowed on debt. And they do not gain profit when they sell their harvest. Moreover, when they buy food from the market, the prices are exorbitant. The loss of food sovereignty is worsened by extreme weather events that deplete crop productivity. Food sovereignty refers to "the right of peoples to healthy and culturally appropriate food produced through ecologically sound and sustainable methods, and their right to define their own agricultural methods" (Rosset & Martinez-Torres 2). Waikar portrays how the farmers of Vidarbha region have neither access to "healthy and culturally appropriate food" nor the right to define the terms of farming. In order to regain food sovereignty, food activist Eric Holt-Giménez argues for agroecological methods. He notes that "capitalist media [teaches us] that industrial agriculture—the Monsantos, Syngentas, Cargills and Bayers—feeds the world, but that's a myth. It does not. Industrial agriculture only feeds about 25 to 30 percent of the world." He debunks the myth by asserting that farmers are the people who really feed the world. He adds that "about 2 billion of them produce nearly three-quarters of the world's food on about a quarter of the Earth's farmland."[5] Despite the fact that they produce food to keep away the hunger of the world, ironically, "70 percent of the hungry people of the world are poor farmers, and most of these are women and girls." This is the hard reality of farmers in India too, leading to suicides and protest marches in recent years.

Waikar portrays such pitiable conditions of farmers in the first half of the novel. It is hardly surprising that farmers are often forced to take their own lives owing to the dire conditions and lack of help from authorities. However, the novel also presents a survival strategy. After decades of struggle and astounding rates of suicide (or genocide, as Nandan Saxena and Kavita Bahl describe in their documentary *Cotton for my Shroud*), recent times have witnessed a new awakening and consciousness among farmers, as demonstrated in the Kisan Long March and the Kisan Mukti March.[6] From a position of defeat, they are now fighting for their rights in a political sense. Waikar portrays this awakening as the characters working towards an organized movement to address the crisis. A distinctive factor of this movement is the radical participation of the farmers themselves in voicing their concerns.

Using a local myth regarding a local religious pilgrimage called the Vaari of Pandharpur, Waikar illustrates the awakening of hope in the farming community. Pandharpur is a place where the famous temple of the local deity Vithoba is located. Vaari refers to the pilgrimage made by devotees of Vithoba, wherein devotees from different parts of Maharashtra walk to Pandharpur over twenty-one days. Many farmers and their families from rural Maharashtra participate in the Vaari after sowing their crops. The journey supposedly is one of hope and meant for seeking blessings from the deity. The devotees believe that their prayers will be answered. The pilgrimage is also a thanksgiving for prayers that have been answered.

Whilst undertaking the Vaari, Mallika, the social worker, meets Sita, a farm widow whom she had met earlier in Wardha during her field visit. Mallika also notices that at different points of the pilgrimage, local politicians from all the political parties are actively engaged in ensuring facilities for the pilgrims. She later tells Sriram that: "One thing that stood out was the hypocrisy of the political system and the administration that honoured and felicitated farmers as pilgrims on the Vaari. But the same farmers were abused in their role as food producers for the nation" (174). Waikar uses the religious pilgrimage as a metaphor for awakening, and juxtaposes it later with the idea of a political pilgrimage. The long march of hope and thanksgiving to the deity serves as an analogy for the long march "to be heard and seen"—by the public, by the bureaucracy, by the urban population—as a reminder that the farmers exist, and that they are the source of food.

The myth surrounding Vaari is one of hope and thanksgiving on which the farmers often depend for summoning the rains and saving the crops. Mallika's return from the pilgrimage without completing it symbolizes the need for immediate political action rather than blindly relying on hope and rainfall. She arrives at this awakening after meeting Sita and is surprised by her indomitable spirit and resilience. Her interaction with farming families, particularly with women, and her witnessing of their grit and resoluteness make Mallika realize the urgency for action and the need to organize immediately. The Long March she coordinates, with Sriram and other volunteers on the one hand and with Vikram and his companions on the other, turns out to be a political pilgrimage to gather information, support, and solidarity, and leads to a bigger march for self-assertion and reclaiming rights. It demonstrates that farmers and farming families (of men, women, children, and the young and old) are a force that the nation cannot ignore if it is to continue eating.

Mallika and Sriram's team undertake a political journey, a *padayatra* (journey on foot), through different parts of rural India starting from Wardha and Akola (in Maharashtra), traveling through central and north India—through different villages in the states of Madhya Pradesh, Uttar Pradesh, Bihar, and Jharkhand. From north and central India, they travel eastwards to Odisha and southwards to Telengana and Karnataka. From Odisha, Vikram travels separately eastwards to Kolkatta and Shillong to expand this network; on his return, he goes northwards to Delhi, Uttar Pradesh, and Punjab. He also meets urban professionals who are willing to work for the cause of the farmers.[7] Altogether, the team meets farmers in different parts of the country who are engaged in different types of agricultural production and face varied problems related to their ecosystems and regional and local politics. The team record stories of struggle, resistance, resilience, and urban migration for labor due to failure of agriculture. They hear narratives on rural unemployment, inefficacy of government schemes that promise employment, and the corruption and prosperity of middle men who monitor and implement these schemes.

Waikar discretely shows a difference in approach employed by the team of social workers and the farmer-to-farmer interaction Vikram has with his fellows throughout the political journey. The social workers are interested in gathering information, conducting surveys, and documenting details, whereas Vikram works to develop a network of farmers in different parts of the country in order to create a sense of community awakening. This camaraderie is reminiscent of the Campesino a Campesino movement (meaning farmer to farmer) that Eric Holt-Giménez discusses in his experience of working with farmers from different parts of Latin America. The movement follows a decentralized and communitarian approach where farmers from different places come together, discuss their problems, share their knowledge, and debate how to address their concerns. Waikar portrays a similar situation in her novel, where a collective is organized. The work of this collective is different from the experience of an outside group of experts dictating terms and solutions to them. It is also different from the condescending and undiscerning measures offered by the government as welfare. Measures from within the community are ecologically and socially informed, sensitive, and therefore sustainable. This decentralized, ecologically sustainable participation of farmers in agricultural production amounts to agroecological methods of farming, which seeks revival through integration of sociopolitical and ecological aspects of the crisis. Such methods of resistance and revival are evident in Waikar's novel, which discusses farm suicides, agrarian crisis, the futility of government measures, schemes, and projects, and the insufficiency of the efforts of NGOs and social service groups, as well as the relevance of an internal awakening among farmers to take their situation in their own hands. Like the efforts of the Campesino a Campesino movement, the novel also provides a similar awakening and consolidation of a network of farmers and solidarity towards asserting and reclaiming their rights.

This travel to different parts of the country shows the diversity of agriculture owing to different topography, climate, and biodiversity, as well as social, cultural, and regional politics. The challenges of farmers in these areas are also as diverse. The fact of these challenges being diverse further underscores the idea that a uniform national farm policy from top down could never work effectively and homogeneously in all parts of the country, as it would not be equipped to address the particular and diverse problems of farmers from different regions. For example, the social workers meet Adivasis in the Haripur village (in Odisha), who are struggling against a mining company that extracts iron ore. The government wishes to displace the farmers, own the land, and give it to the mining company. The villagers do not want to leave, since they are able to produce and earn a good income already and leaving their land for urban labor would be a risky choice. This is a case of forceful displacement; in other areas, farmers leave their villages due to drought and crop failures.

Another important aspect of the farmers' revival that Waikar refers to is education and employment. The novel begins with the following lines: "It was a day after the education minister in Delhi had declared a policy change in school curricula" (11). The crux of the new policy was that "geography is more important than history." Vikram interprets it as follows: "It is because geography is about land and trees, rivers and dams, whereas history is about wars and killings and records of what happened in the past" (12). Although this interpretation is problematic with respect to history, it is a significant one from an agrarian perspective. The health of natural resources and the ecosystem is vital for the sustenance of agriculture, and for life as a whole. What goes unsaid is the plunder of these natural resources by the powerful, which causes socioeconomic and ecological exploitation of the place and the people who live there.

Madhav Gadgil and Ramachandra Guha, in their studies of the ecological history of India, divide the Indian population into three groups based on the association with natural resources: "The ecosystem people, omnivores and ecological refugees" (4). They define the "ecosystem people" as "those communities which depend very heavily on the natural resources of their own locality." This includes a major part of the rural Indian population, such as farmers, laborers, Adivasis, small-scale workers, and artisans. They define the "omnivores [as] individuals and groups with the social power to capture, transform and use natural resources from a much wider catchment area, sometimes indeed the whole world" (4). This includes big industrialists, government officials, political leaders, urban professionals, rural elites, landlords, and prosperous farmers. The ecological refugees are the "ecosystem people" who have been displaced and deprived of their resources by the intervention and exploitation by the "omnivores." *The Long March* depicts a scenario where farmers have already become ecological refugees by the exploitation and indifference of the "omnivores," which includes the corporations and bureaucracy. Studies on the Anthropocene have to take into account such social and class differences to ensure better food justice and climate justice, particularly to the underprivileged people in the Global South, who are ecologically and economically more vulnerable. An undifferentiated and abstract approach to the anthropos will not help address particular problems in particular ways or with effective, mitigative action. *The Long March* offers differential perspectives in terms of caste, class, region, and the multiple levels of exploitation the farmers face in society. Waikar clearly portrays the conflict between the "ecosystem people and the omnivores" (Gadgil & Guha), where the politically and financially powerful omnivore invariably gains the upper hand. She also obliquely introduces an aspect of environmental justice, writing that the educational system needs to make people, particularly the rural poor, aware of their geography and rich natural resources.

Further, Waikar suggests possibilities for research, innovation, and technology in the area of agriculture. Vikram works at the Institute of Agriculture Technology, which helps farmers make sustainable and productive use of technology for their benefit. When Vikram travels to Shillong, he learns about using social media and other technological innovations which may help him in expanding his network and furthering his cause. When Mallika's team travels to Belgaum, they meet a young farmer, with a degree in agricultural science, pursuing research in organic cultivation at the university. He also teaches techniques of organic cultivation to other farmers in his village and has become a source of information and inspiration for youngsters. He notes that youngsters in his village also wish to study agricultural science because they are skeptical about going to the cities in search of work at a time of rampant unemployment. Through these instances, Waikar shows Gramscian organic intellectuals making use of technology to develop their network and solidarity, and to organize farmers. This parallels Eric Holt-Giménez's Campesino a Campesino movement where, he notes, farmers tend to trust and adopt the practices and experiential knowledge of fellow farmers, rather than receive guidance from any outside agency; In the former case they get first-hand information from one of their own kind which helps them assert their agency (Rosset and Martinez Torres 7). The knowledge from fellow farmers helps them understand their problems and consider addressing them organically, rather than waiting for external help from people who have less grassroot understanding of the problem than themselves.

Thus, Vikram embarks on his metaphorical journey towards a new farmers' cooperative that will eventually lead to the Long March. He exhorts his fellow villagers about the need for a community awakening and call for action. He talks about the young people he met in different places and their commitment to the cause of understanding rural poverty and the farmers' crisis. They include student volunteers from cities, young journalist trainees, and social workers. Comparing the young people and the farmers, he says, "who knows about these things better than you and I? We are born into this world of never-ending hardships" (198). However, he realizes that not everybody accepts their conditions as such; instead, in many places, farmers are putting up a brave fight against the government and industrialists, against land grabbing and the exploitation of natural resources on their lands in order to save their livelihoods. What Vikram found remarkable in these people is their attitude of holding on to their rural way of life, rather than giving it up for urban labor.

Through his journey, he develops a large database of farmers who want to fight against exploitation and reclaim their rights and self-esteem. He suggests forming a political party to ensure democratic participation in the political process, as the existing parties have not proven to be of much help. Although the novel does not discuss the formation or development of such a party, it suggests the need for a political awakening and consciousness of one's rights, and the right to resistance and protest in a democracy. The references to the unattractiveness of urban labor in the novel are substantiated through a lifestyle survey. During this survey, Vikram comes face to face with the shocking disparity between affluent "modern palaces" (205) of Mumbai, and the darkness of the huts in his village. He suggests setting up a new collective of farmers which will be a decentralized network where groups of farmers can help each other in their agricultural and political causes and initiatives. He explains the need for a new "co-operative that ties several villages to one or more towns and cities in a sort of business of exchanging goods and services" (200). This resonates with the argument of Peter M. Rosset and Maria Elena Martinez Torres for the need to revive agriculture through agroecological methods, through a concept called "repeasantization." They note that the small-farmer approach follows "decentralized circuits of production and consumption, with strong links between food production and local and regional ecosystems and societies," whereas industrial agriculture follows a "centralized pattern … of production that is de-contextualized and de-linked from the specificities of local ecosystems and social relations" (1). The resistance to industrial agriculture and bureaucratic exploitation and indifference, in the novel, is shown through a similar process of "repeasantization" that Vikram initiates.

The network of farmers created by Vikram is able to organize farmers and put up a large show of resistance in times of dire need. Crops have failed miserably due to late and inadequate rains. This was followed by a water crisis, a drought, and a rise in price of essential commodities such as rice, wheat, and pulses. The farmers, being alienated from their own food production, await government welfare measures to relieve them of their misery. Many receive nothing because the supply of goods runs out before their turn in the queue. On the other hand, grains rot away in large quantities in government granaries and repositories. A few panel discussions and hour-long news debates ensue while many who wait for supplies starve to death (206). These deaths testify to the farmers' loss of food security and sovereignty, confirming Eric Holt-Giménez's statement that farmers are among the poorest and the most starved, despite contributing to the production of food for the nation.

Vikram's communitarian outreach and the social workers' grass-root work find common ground in organizing an unprecedented kind of protest march that is democratic and peaceful. This protest had "people from rural India [marching] into the cities, claiming their rightful place in the nation's prosperity. They wanted a share—a fair share in the better life that their urban countrymen had been enjoying every day of their lives" (212). They gather to resist and protest with their bodies, barefoot—the bodies that toil on the farm to grow food. Their large numbers shock the mundanity and normalcy of the metropolis and the indifference of the government. In this one spectacular instance, Waikar brings together people divided by class, region (urban/rural), power, wealth, and living conditions. This is a situation where a large section of the population, so far invisible and treated as insignificant, has broken the silence and risen up. The protest march is symbolic of the awareness of farmers of their rights, fighting to reclaim their food sovereignty, and declaring their autonomy by resisting the terms of the corporate–government nexus. This scenario can be seen as resistance to attempts by government and media to ignore agrarian issues, which is precisely what homogenizing the anthropos risks.

This disparity and diversity of issues even within the Global South shows the inadequacy and the fallacy of assuming the anthropos as a collective and homogeneous category. Hence, the importance of reiterating Biermann et al.'s argument about the need to contextualize the Anthropocene in order to address particular issues and concerns, so that such actions may eventually add up to larger positive outcomes concerning the climate and food crisis in the Global South. Thus, Waikar's narrative is a statement that underscores the importance of contextualizing the Anthropocene, rather than considering the anthropos as a homogeneous category contributing to anthropogenic climate change.

The fictional instances in *The Long March* are representative of the agrarian crisis and farmer suicide in Vidarbha, which has been extensively documented by P. Sainath.[8] The novel shows the importance of differentiating between, broadly speaking, the two classes of "human agents" in food production and the consequent impact of each of them in terms of risks and benefits. The large-scale, energy-intensive, industrial agribusiness is profit-oriented and ecologically and socially unsustainable, while the small-scale, agroecological initiatives by farmers are more socially and ecologically sustainable because they are informed by the particularities of the local, regional, and cultural ecosystems. Whether it is the agrarian crisis, food crisis, or climate crisis, it is always the impoverished farmers and, often, women who suffer the most.[9] Like peasant solidarity movements such as La Via Campesina, Waikar portrays a decentralized, communitarian, organic movement of farmers that is more democratic, participatory, and self-assertive. Such a movement shows farmers as capable of addressing their own issues to find solutions, thereby gaining autonomy in their work. Waikar demonstrates that such movements are organic, capitalizing on traditional and experiential knowledge (of soil, resources, region, ecosystems) and ingenuity. Hence, such efforts are effective modes of resistance to combat the hegemony of agribusiness, help farmers regain their food sovereignty, and contribute actively and positively to better food, environmental, and climate justice.

Notes

1 Chakrabarty's articles on the Anthropocene include: "The Climate of History" (2009); "Postcolonial Studies" (2012); "Climate and Capital" (2014); "The Politics of Climate Change" (2017); for some of the responses and criticisms to Chakrabarty's views, see Emmett and Lekan, *Whose Anthropocene?*; Boscov-Ellen, "Whose Universalism?"

2 Antonio Gramsci (1891–1937) was an Italian Marxist intellectual, activist, and politician and is best known for his theory of cultural hegemony and the concepts of traditional and organic intellectuals.

3 "P. Sainath: Significant Win for Farmers," *YouTube*, 12 Mar. 2018; see www.youtube.com/watch?v=8YkMnvWRy54.

4 See the documentary: "Yield: Testimonials on the Suicides of Indian Farmers from Vidarbha," *YouTube*, Tadpole Artists Collection, 27 July 2014.

5 Interview with Eric Holt-Giménez by Tracy Frisch, Part 1, "The Agrarian Transition," *Eco Farming Daily*; www.ecofarmingdaily.com/the-agrarian-transition/.

6 The Kisan Long March refers to a massive protest rally carried out by about 50,000 farmers organized by the All India Kisan Sabha. The farmers walked 180 km from Nashik to Mumbai over six days, from 6 to 12 March 2018, demanding the implementation of schemes the government had announced, such as loan waivers, the Forest Rights Act (2006), compensation for crop damages, and implementation of the Swamination Commission's recommendation for fixing a minimum support price; see "Kisan Long March: All You Need to Know about Maha Farmers' Agitation," *Economic Times Online*, 12 Mar. 2018. The Kisan Mukti March was a large protest rally of farmers from across the country who marched to Delhi on 29 Nov. 2018. The Second Kisan Long March, from Nashik to Mumbai, was carried out on 19 Feb. 2019.

7 Sainath, in an interview with *The Caravan*, talks about the idea of farmers for the nation, regarding the countrywide movement for solidarity with farmers. He mentions that during the course of the Long March, there was increasing support from middle-class urbanites and professionals. People from different walks of life declared their support for the farmers, including doctors, teachers, and even *autoriksha wallahs*. See the news report by Konikkara.
8 P. Sainath's work *Everybody Loves a Good Drought* has case studies and testimonies of the dire situations farmers in rural India suffer. Sainath is an Indian journalist and founder editor of the People's Archive of Rural India.
9 For a feminist analysis of agrarian distress, see Bina Agarwal on feminist environmentalism and Kota Neelima on the widows of Vidarbha.

References

Agarwal, Bina. "Environmental Action, Gender Equity and Women's Participation." *Development and Change*, vol. 28, no. 1, 1997, pp. 1–44.
———. "The Gender and Environment Debate: Lessons from India." *Feminist Studies*, vol. 18, no. 1, 1992, pp. 119–58.
Biermann, Frank, et al. "Down to Earth: Contextualizing the Anthropocene." *Global Environmental Change*, vol. 39, Jul. 2016, pp. 341–50, www.sciencedirect.com/science/article/pii/S0959378015300686.
Boscov-Ellen, Dan. "Whose Universalism? Dipesh Chakrabarty and the Anthropocene." *Capitalism, Nature, Socialism*, 23 Aug. 2018, https://doi.org/10.1080/10455752.2018.1514060.
Chakrabarty, Dipesh. "Climate and Capital: On Conjoined Histories." *Critical Inquiry*, vol. 41, no. 1, 2014, pp. 1–23.
———. "The Climate of History: Four Theses." *Critical Inquiry*, vol. 35, no. 2, 2009, pp. 197–222.
———. "The Politics of Climate Change is More Than the Politics of Capitalism." *Theory, Culture & Society*, vol. 34, nos. 2–3, 2017, pp. 25–37.
———. "Postcolonial Studies and the Challenge of Climate Change." *New Literary History*, vol. 43, no. 1, 2012, pp. 1–18.
Emmett, Robert, and Thomas Lekan, editors. *Whose Anthropocene? Revisiting Dipesh Chakrabarty's* "Four Theses." RCC Perspectives: Transformations in Environment and Society, 2016.
Food and Agriculture Organization of the United Nations. "The 10 Elements of Agroecology: Guiding the Transition to Sustainable Food and Agricultural Systems." www.fao.org/3/i9037en/i9037en.pdf.
Gadgil, Madhav, and Ramachandra Guha. *Ecology and Equity: The Use and Abuse of Nature in Contemporary India*. Penguin, 1995.
Jitheesh, P. M., and John Jipson. "Root Cause of Agrarian Crisis Lies in Economics and Not in Technology: MS Swaminathan." Interview with M. S. Swaminathan, *NewsClick*, 13 Apr. 2019. www.newsclick.in/agrarian-crisis-roots-economy-MS-Swaminathan-interview.
Konikkara, Aathira. "Strike at the Root." Interview with P. Sainath. *The Caravan*, 27 Nov. 2018. https://caravanmagazine.in/agriculture/p-sainath-farmers-march-delhi.
Neelima, Kota. *Widows of Vidarbha: Making of Shadows*. Oxford University Press, 2018.

Rosset, Peter M., and Maria Elena Martinez Torres. "Rural Social Movements and Agroecology: Context, Theory and Practice." *Ecology and Society*, vol. 17, no. 3, Sep. 2012, https://dx.doi.org/10.5751/ES-05000-170317.

Sainath, Palagummi. *Everybody Loves a Good Drought: Stories from India's Poorest Districts*. Penguin, 1996.

Saxena, Nandan, and Kavita Bahl, directors. *Cotton for my Shroud*. Top Quirk Films, 2011.

Shiva, Vandana. *Who Really Feeds the World? The Failures of Agribusiness and the Promise of Agroecology*. North Atlantic Books, 2016.

Waikar, Namita. *The Long March*. Speaking Tiger, 2018.

9 Dalit Food, Ecology, and Resistance

Samuel Moses Srinivas Kuntam

Food and landscape are intricately linked with the caste system in India. The caste system[1] originated from the Vedic assumption that the natural order is hierarchical. The leitmotif of "food" and "eaters" is the principal characteristic of the natural hierarchy in the *Vedas*.[2] Nature is considered to dictate the hierarchical order of the food chain. At the top of the Vedic "natural" world are the supernatural gods feeding on sacrificial oblations, substitutes for human sacrificers, followed by the humans who eat animals, and then animals who eat plants, which, in turn, drink the rain or water from which all food is ultimately generated (Smith 17). Food is not just a physical requirement or economic status; it is the essential characteristic of Vedic society. It is proclaimed in the *Upanishads*:[3]

> O, the wonder of joy!
> I am he who eats the Food of life …
> I am the Food which eats the Eater of Food.
> (Mascaro 111)

This assertion resonates the hierarchical order of things in Vedic society.

The post-Vedic text, the *Manusmriti* (Laws of Manu),[4] stated the continuity between nature and culture, with food being a central tenet, as it proclaimed that those without movement, fangs, and hands become food for those so possessed, and further declared: "cowards are the food of the brave" (Laws of Manu 5.29 in Doniger & Smith 110). The hierarchical order of nature was perceived as a continuum to the social world, which is one of rulers and ruled, consumers and consumed, exploiters and exploited, the strong and the weak: "The eater is superior to his food, in society as well as in nature" (Smith 187). Food, too, is the central tenet of the caste hierarchy.

The social hierarchy in contemporary India is a continuation from Vedic times. This hierarchy is, as Dr. B. R. Ambedkar proclaimed, represented by "those who are vegetarians [at the top], those who eat flesh but do not eat cow's flesh [in the middle] and those who eat flesh including cow's flesh [at the bottom]" (*Annihilation of Caste*, 329).[5] Mukul Sharma,

DOI: 10.4324/9781003282976-13

an Indian environmentalist, opines in his book *Caste and Nature* that the continuation of the caste system from Vedic times to contemporary Indian society is a result of the "rationalization and justification of [the] caste system through nature" (16). The justification and rationalization transpire from the notion that the habitats occupied by each caste are for their natural utilization, which helps to stabilize the community as well as the ecosystem. Contrary to this, land in Indian society is hierarchized.

The Brahmins have always been at the center of the village where the temple is situated and the Dalits pushed to the edges. The landscape of Dalit territory was mostly barren and contributed to their enslaved way of life, itself a result of the lack of resources for cultivating food. Although I agree with Sharma's viewpoint on the reasons behind the continuation of the caste system, I propose that it is also the result of the intersection between food, landscape, and caste that has cemented the caste system in Indian society. In this chapter I will analyze Dalit food narratives through Dalit literature—poetry, fiction, and memoirs—and argue that food, landscape, and caste are inextricably interwoven, and that this has contributed to the continuation of the caste system in India.

Dalit Food and Habitat

Land is essential for any living being. As Shelley Egoz has pointed out, "it is a place that ought to support life (survival), livelihood and well-being, all values that are at the core of universal human rights" (330). The notion of place is also essential to one's identity. Place identifies one's roots, and through memory, one connects to place. Place and memory are crucial elements in terms of identity (Stewart & Strathern 2). The relationship between landscape and identity is fundamental to the understanding of hierarchical social systems in India. In this regard, Anand Teltumbde, a Dalit critic, states as follows:

> Social systems come into being because the material conditions demand them ... these [material] factors can perhaps be located in the uniquely rich natural endowment of the Indian subcontinent for the biotic mode of production extant in ancient times. In terms of plentiful flat, fertile land; rivers and water bodies; abundant sunshine and congenial climate, the Indian subcontinent may scarcely have a parallel on the planet in its richness for agriculture. These factors might be seen to be the key to fathoming the mystery of the unique system of stratification in the form of the caste system.
>
> (23)

In India, the priority of wetlands over drylands is ascribed to "plentiful flat, fertile land" for agriculture. This in turn contributed to the hierarchization of social systems.

Curiously, recent scholarship on caste system states that the persistence of the caste hierarchy is prevalent mostly in the wetlands, such as the Gangetic, Narmada, Krishna, and Godavari plains (all of them being riverine landscape). Human communities viewed wetlands as resource materials. The surplus produce from these wetlands has constructed human civilizations. G. Aloysius, a social activist and writer, in a talk on "Law and Caste: Historical and Sociological Development," stated that such surplus produce has given freedom for some people to supervise and others to do labor. The surplus produce created certain functions for each person in the community. Aloysius remarks that these functions became stagnated, thus creating hierarchy and hegemony. Drylands, on the other hand, Aloysius posits, are much more egalitarian, as everyone is forced to labor for basic needs. The village systems in India are mostly structured around the wetlands.

The villages of India depict caste-graded inequality through the space that each of these castes occupies. Discussing the Indian village, Dr. B. R. Ambedkar states that "in every village, Touchables have a code which the Untouchables are required to follow. This code lays down the acts of omissions and commissions which the Touchables treat as offenses" (*Annihilation of Caste*, 21). Ambedkar lists fifteen omissions and commissions: the first and most important one is that "the Untouchable must live in separate quarters away from the habitation of the Hindus. It is an offense for the Untouchables to break or evade the rule of segregation" (21). They were denied food, water, or any natural resource from the village community by the Touchables.

The space that each member of the village occupies determines one's cultural and political status. Chinese scholars and translators Xuanzang (Hsuan-Tsang) and Faxian (337–442 CE) wrote in great detail on their observations about the caste hierarchy in India. They delineated that the *chandalas*[6] and other lower-caste communities have their dwellings outside the city. It is only *chandalas* who keep and sell "flesh meat" (quoted in Sen 86). The location of the dwellings of the *chandalas* (untouchables or outcastes) is a sign of their food habits. The *chandalas* keep "flesh meat" for two reasons: firstly, they live in a barren landscape where nothing can grow, and, secondly, they are not allowed to possess any wetland for cultivation. There are many examples describing food habits conditioned by their landscape. Kumara Suresh Singh, an anthropologist, claims that Musahars were known as "rat catchers" or "rat killers" (in the Bhojpuri language, *musa* means rat and *har*, catcher or killer). According to him, "Musahars picked up grains from harvested fields as well as out of rat holes. The natural environment made their role as rat eaters or food gatherers important in the past" (quoted in Sharma, *Caste and Nature*, 92). The unavailability of land for cultivating food made the Dalits dependent on the upper castes. It also contributed to a lack of food and livelihood.

Dalits became bonded laborers with food being their only remuneration. But the foods given to them by the upper caste were discarded resources. Some of these were coarse grain, grain gleaned from cow dung, *Jhootan*,[7] cast-off clothes, rats, pig, and snails. Sujatha Gidla has delineated the remuneration of food with graphic imagery in her autobiography, *From Malapalli to Brahmin Town* (2008). She talks about a canal, the Kolivi, which runs across a Dalit colony called Slaughter Peta, and a Brahmin colony, in the town of Gudivada, South India. It was the center of a variety of cultural and daily activities. As Gidla recounts:

> the Brahmins would shit in the sand and the Pakis, a sub-community of untouchables, would come and remove the shit with a broom or their bare hands. They weren't paid for the job since it was the duty of their caste to perform it. If a Brahmin was charitable, he could feed them scraps of foul-smelling leftover food (it had to smell bad to be fit to be offered to untouchables), but they had no right to demand it. You would think this inhuman practice had ended long ago but in the countryside and small towns, Pakis are still not allowed to seek other types of jobs.
>
> (quoted in Purushotham et al. 183)

This dehumanizing act of removing human excrement with bare hands is a duty for Dalits. Their livelihoods depend on Brahminical benevolence. The benevolence has to follow certain traditional and complex rules. It was based on Vedic tradition and should be practiced accordingly: "Shudras who behave properly should shave their heads once a month, follow the rules of purification laid down for Vaisyas, and eat the leftover food of twice-born persons" (*Laws of Manu*, 5.140 in Olivelle 145). The untouchables in the villages were hereditary menials employed by the village administration.

Dalit's ghettoization and the lack of cultivable landscape forced them to do menial jobs for survival. Ambedkar, in his writings on *Untouchables or The Children of India's Ghetto*, states that in ancient India:

> as a part of their remuneration the whole body of Untouchables get a small parcel of land assigned … which is fixed and never increased and which the untouchables prefer to leave uncultivated because of its excess fragmentations. Coupled with this is given to them the right to beg for food.
>
> (*Writings and Speeches* 24)

The remuneration of this small parcel of uncultivable land dissipates untouchables' livelihood. It enables the upper castes to dictate every aspect of Dalit life. Gopal Guru, an Indian sociologist, writes that:

> the upper castes have not only prescribed food for themselves, but they have designated foods for other castes as well. For example, in

> Manu's ritual strictures, *Jhootan* and the meat of dead cattle were prescribed to the untouchables as their staple food.
>
> (11)

The consumption of dead cattle depicts the untouchables as subhuman. Guru states that "consuming this food folded them into what could be called a 'Savage Identity'" (10). Guru further states, "the irony is that the untouchables produced food grain but were denied the legitimate share of it. They got only the inferior part of this product (coarse grain, grain gleaned out of cow dung, *Jhootan*, and cast-off clothes)" (11). The depiction of the untouchable community as subhuman is not just a social norm but also a religious acceptance.

The upper-caste communities retaliated violently if they found out that Dalits were attempting to eat "upper-caste" food. Such a retaliation was to force the Dalits and other lower sections of society to follow their decree. One such incident is cited by Ambedkar in his seminal book on the caste system, *Annihilation of Caste* (1936), which happened in the village of Chakwara in Jaipur, Rajasthan, some time on or about the first day of April 1936. An untouchable of the village hosted a sumptuous dinner for his fellow untouchables on the successful completion of a pilgrimage, and the items served also included ghee (clarified butter). Knowing this, hundreds of armed upper-caste Hindus ransacked the gathering as they believed it to be an impudence for the Dalits to serve and taste ghee, as consumption of this product was a mark of high social status (217). Such incidents were very common in India and continue to be so today. In another case, Dalits were flogged and lynched on suspicion of carrying beef.[8] On 11 July 2016, at the village of Samadhiyala, Una Taluka, in Gujarat, some thirty-five *gau rakshaks* (saviors of the cow)[9] belonging to upper-caste communities beat seven Dalits with iron rods and sticks. They kidnapped four of them and took them to Una, tied them to a car, and flogged them publicly through the town. They accused the Dalits of slaughtering a cow (*Indian Express*). These incidents highlight the indignities the Dalits had to go through to earn their livelihood.

The violence faced by Dalits also raises a pertinent question concerning environmentalism: how much does the modern environmental movement really know about the indignities of the vulnerable? As Ramachandra Guha, the Indian environmental historian, rightly points out, the "poor were, quite simply, too poor to be green. Their waking hours were spent foraging for food, water, housing, energy. How could they be concerned with something as elevated as the environment?" (148). Modern environmental activism somehow overlooks these aspects as there is a tendency to perceive the conflict as "man against nature." It is imperative to comprehend the poor person's relationship with nature, as Guha suggests, through the environmentalism of the poor. It is only through the poor that one has a "greater stake in the responsible management of the environment" (149). For the Dalits, particularly in the Una case, it was their livelihood and the only way they could survive.

Dalit stories and life experiences provide a case in point on the responsible management of the environment for the environmentalists. One such life experience is offered by G. Kalyana Rao, in his novel *Untouchable Spring*, which portrays the lives of untouchables who have overcome their humiliation and suffering through memories and knowledge of their landscape. The novel follows the lives of four characters, Reuben, Ruth, Yellanna, and Naganna. Through Naganna's childhood memories with his parents, the narrator describes the conditions of the untouchables, their food habits, and their relationship with the landscape: "Naganna's childhood was spent among the palm trees on the fields and in the shade of the Tumma groves[10] of Yennala Dinni" (Rao 26). An incident at the beginning of the novel, when Naganna, with his mother, Latchimi, goes to meet his father, Narigadu, to give him his packed lunch, portrays the lives within untouchable communities. Narigadu climbs the palm trees to chop the fronds and collect palm milk. Naganna's father brings down the kernels for him to eat. The narrator explains that "after eating the kernels, he would go towards the ridges in the fields. He would string thin snail shells with palm withes into a necklace" (24). This shows two things: firstly, the relationship the characters of the novel have with their landscape, and, secondly, the author's celebration of food through each of his characters' knowledge about the landscape. The narration, from a child's point of view, portrays a childlike attitude toward their livelihood. Innocence and happiness overlie hardship and humiliation. The narrator continues:

> he would keep the necklace near crab holes and make a sound. The crabs would think water was entering the holes and come up. He would hold the crabs that came out. He would break their large claws and would put them into a palm frond. Sometimes he could not catch them easily. They would run along the bank ... he would light a fire with palm leaves in the field and roast them ... father would eat the roasted crabs with rice ...
>
> (Rao 24)

For the family, the roasted crabs were the food for that day. Rao states that Narigadu "did not have even a tiny parcel of land. All that he had was an axe to fell trees" (24). His occupation was collecting palm milk from the trees, and that was his livelihood. For them, food is not simply a means to "develop a consuming body but more importantly feeding the earning body" (Guru 16). The food that feeds them is no more prejudice. The child's exuberance in catching the crab and, later, the snail portrays their assertion of self-respect and dignity. Through their literary narratives, using food as a symbol, the Dalits tried to restore their sense of self and identity.

Beef, the Symbol of Dalit Resistance

To the Dalits, beef is a symbol of resistance because the cow is regarded as divine by upper-caste Hindus. For the majority of Dalits, however, beef is a traditional food that nourishes them. Some of the traditional dishes made with beef include *Rakti*, prepared with coagulated blood, *Chanya*, cooked with preserved meat, and *Wajadi*, prepared by scrubbing the skin of the animal's intestines (Tak & Aranha). Dalit food is regarded with abhorrence by the upper castes. Thus, the Dalits use the food of aversion in order to assert their identity. Their food and celebration of the same is a political act which has become a conflict zone to reclaim identity and self-respect. N. K. Hanumanthaiah's poem "Eating Cow, Becoming One" (2003) resonates this assertion when he says that he has become a cow:

> Eating cow-meat I have become a cow,
> Dancing, I roam the forests and mountains,
> The hills and valleys, and plains.
> (quoted in Sharma, *Caste and Nature*, 91)

Cow meat gives him freedom. The exuberance of freedom in the poems is in stark contrast to his real life, which is one of enslavement and toil. His freedom to dance and roam the countryside is snatched away, restricting his life. The code of the untouchables is that he:

> must observe the rule of distance pollution or shadow of pollution as the case may be. It is an offence to break the rule. It is an offence for the member of the Untouchable community to acquire wealth, such as land or cattle.
>
> (21)

This code clearly indicates a curtailing of freedom.

For a long time, the Dalits ate meat from dead cattle (*Murdada*).[11] This was followed by a radical shift to eating *Hatfatka*,[12] meat acquired through hunting, and then to *Toliv*,[13] the meat of slaughtered animals. This huge change, due to reformists such as Dr. B. R. Ambdekar, would result in the restoration of dignity and self-respect. When the narrator proclaims that he has become a cow, he seems to be reclaiming his identity. It "resignified what is downgraded or looked down upon as filthy" (Guru 16). Eating cow meat, which was taboo for a long period, has now given him back his freedom. The poet continues:

> Standing firm on the ground,
> Raising my tail, I lash at the rainbow
> Spearing the clouds
> I turn the deserts green.
> (Sharma 91)

The image of him "[s]tanding firm on the ground" is powerful. In real life, the Dalit had to genuflect before any touchable individual. To demonstrate that he is an untouchable, he is not allowed to wear clean clothes, or silver and gold ornaments, or to possess a contemptible name. His life is one of humiliation. For the narrator in the poem, with this newfound dignity and self-respect, he can raise his head high and dream of freedom. This freedom is self-acclaimed, not given but taken. Eating beef for Dalits is an act of resistance to achieve liberation from their lowly status thrust on them. The small act of defiance of eating beef is a political act. He further proclaims:

> I am untouchable.
> Yes, I eat cow-meat
> With udders sprung all over my body
> I feed every hungry mouth.
> (Sharma 92)

There are pride and assertion in his voice. He is not bothered by the labels "untouchable" and "beef-eater." There is dignity in his stature. His food is not filthy but essential, and he too is not filthy. He is the one who produces food by toiling through day and night. The last line denotes his pride in feeding "every hungry mouth" through his hard work and sacrifice.

In a similar vein, Gogu Shyamala, in her poem "My Food, My Wish" (2012), transforms beef into a symbol of Dalit resistance. By giving her poem such a title, she engages directly with the upper caste. The poem expresses anger and agony, questioning Brahminical hegemony:

> Beef is our culture,
> Beef – our living green nature.
> Life's diversity,
> The breath of our soul.
> (quoted in Purushotham et al. 84)

Beef is the food for celebrations and festivals too. By declaring beef as her cultural food, the poet is asserting her cultural right against casteist humiliation. She reclaims her self-respect through this cultural representation. By stating beef as "our living green nature," "life's diversity," and "breath of our soul," she is signifying it is beef that made her life green and gave her breath. Due to the narrator's habitat, which is a barren landscape with hardly any food resources, beef offers a "living green nature" and "life's diversity."

For the Dalits, beef is a source of nutrition. By attaching cultural value to it, the speaker informs the upper-caste listener that they do not have any right to question her about her culture, as the upper castes were never a part of it. So, she asks some pertinent questions:

> "Do not eat beef!" "But how?"
> Who are you to tell me what to eat?
> Where have you come from?
> What is your relationship with me?
> I ask.
>
> (84)

With anger and agony, the speaker confronts and resists the upper-caste people. They sustain her desire to resist and salvage her identity. The upper-caste people have upheld this "othering" of the Dalits for over two thousand years, and this questioning is assuming a political importance. As discussed earlier, beef eating in India was considered taboo because eating the flesh of a dead cow (*Murdada*) was not socially acceptable. The cow could have died from a disease. Dalits used to preserve the flesh of the dead cow. Preserving foods was intrinsic to Dalit food practices. Preserved cow meat is called *Chanya*.[14] It is essentially comprised of long slices of sun-dried beef that can last for a few months.

The taboo, and the divinity attached to the cow, has led Hindu social reformist movements, such as Arya Samaj[15] and Brahmo Samaj,[16] to insist Dalits discontinue eating beef. The famous Gandhian reformer and nationalist from South India, Jala Rangaswamy, wrote against the evils of eating beef and unclean habits in his book *Maalashuddhi* (*Cleansing the Malas*, 1930):

> Oh women, stop these dirty habits and shed ignorance. You hold food in the earthen pot and stand outside. Holding it in the hand you start eating. You ask your neighbor about the food they cook. If they cook meat, you ask for it. You only eat meat and bones ... how long do you want to lead such a dirty life?
>
> (quoted in Jangam 115)

For the Hindu reformist, eating beef was unworthy of respect and a dirty habit; in order to become a respectable Hindu, one should refrain from eating it. Rangaswamy's address specifically to women is a deliberate attempt to appease the Dalit communities. For the upper caste it is the woman who is the custodian of the values of the community. *Manusmriti* imparts detailed description of the duties to be performed by women. Manu states that good people call a woman who controls her mind, speech, and body a "virtuous woman" (Laws of Manu 9:29 in Doniger & Smith 171). If the woman detaches herself from "polluted and dirty" food, for Ramaswamy, the whole community will be purified.

Shyamala, on the other hand, by "othering" the upper caste in her poem, is alienating herself from them. Her writing aligns with that of Kancha Ilaiah, a political theorist, who says the Dalits and Shudras are culturally and socially different from the upper castes. In his book *Why I am not a Hindu* (2019), he writes as follows:

> The question is What do we, the lower Sudras, and Ati-Sudras (whom I also call Dalitbahujans), have to do with Hinduism or with Hindutva itself? I, indeed not only I, but all of us, the Dalitsbahuhans of India, have never heard the word "Hindu"—not as a word, nor as the name of a culture, nor as the name of a religion in our early childhood days. We heard about *Turukollu* (Muslims), we heard about *kirastaanapoollu* (Christians), we heard about *Baapanollu* (Brahmins) and *Koomatoollu* (Baniyas–Vaishyas) spoken of as people who were different from us. Among these four categories, the most different were the Baapanoollu and the Koomatoollu.
>
> (Ilaiah, introduction, 11)

In this context, Shyamala, like Kancha Ilaiah, is reclaiming her unique cultural identity. By questioning the upper caste's presence, she is disconnecting from them completely. Through voicing her unique identity, she is resisting "the dominant forces in the culture" (Cooks 95). She further questions,

> To this day
> Have you reared a pair of bullocks?
> A pair of sheep?
> A buffalo or two?
> Have you driven them to the forest to graze?
> Have you ever reared a pair of fowl?
> Have you once waded into the stream
> To scrub and wash their bulk?
> You've never plumbed a bullock's ear,
> Nor do you know the number of its teeth.
> Don't know [how] to trim its painful hooves?
> Do you know of cattle fuzz?
> What, in the end, do you know,
> My friend, but to say "Don't eat beef"?
>
> (84)

The speaker, by questioning the practices of the upper castes, reveals her ignorance and arrogance. Rearing, herding, scrubbing, washing, and trimming are some of the physical activities carried out by the Dalit communities—as a result of which they are considered menial. Historically, these activities were looked down upon when compared with the pursuits of the intellect. By stating clearly these lowly esteemed physical activities, the speaker asserts her identity. For the Dalits, their body is their livelihood, as it enables them to perform all their physical activities. As such, the narrator claims that eating beef is necessary in order to strengthen the body.

The assertion of Dalit identity is better understood through oral and folk tales describing the cultural historicity of the untouchables. One important oral myth from the Dalit community is *Jambava Puranam*, the origin myth of the Madigas, an untouchable caste from Andhra Pradesh and Karnataka in the southern part of India. The text illustrates the origins of the Madigas and describes how eating cow meat contributed to the emergence of untouchability. The myth is recited by professional singers and performed as a dance, known as *cindata*.[17]

Most of the Dalit castes and subcastes in South India claim this origin myth as their own, although we were unable to trace the origins of the myth. A version of the myth, described by Emma Rauschenbusch-Clough, a British theologian in colonial India, narrates the story of the relationship between a boy and a cow. The Madiga community considers Adijambavu as their great ancestor, and he is also believed to be the "grandfather" of their community. Kamadhenu is a wish-fulfilling cosmic cow, considered to be divine in the Hindu religion; she is seen as the "cow of plenty."[18] A boy, whose name was Vellamanu, tended the cow, and she gave much milk. Adisakti, the primeval energy worshipped by the aborigines, permitted the gods to drink Kamadhenu's milk. Vellamanu had an overwhelming desire to taste the milk, but the gods said, "You shall not by any means partake of it." The boy could not stop thinking about the milk. One day he lay down feigning sickness and, by stealth, drank the milk from the pot from which the gods had drunk.

He thought to himself: "If the milk tastes this good, how must the meat taste?" Kamadhenu became aware of his intentions, and at the mere thought that anyone should desire to eat her flesh, her spirit departed, and she dropped down dead. The gods heard what happened and came to investigate. Finding Kamadhenu dead, they asked themselves, "What should be done?" They went to Adijambavu and said, "You are the greatest among us. You must divide her into four parts." This, he did—one part he retained for himself, another he gave to Brahma, yet another to Vishnu, and the final piece went to Siva. They took their shares and went away. But the gods decided not to eat the meat and declared, "We must have the cow again." They brought their three parts and called for Adijambavu's share. But Vellamanu, in the meantime, had cut off a piece and was boiling it. As it bubbled in the pot, a particle of the meat rose with the bubbles and fell into the fire. He took it up, blew against it, so that the moisture in his breath touched the meat, and put it back into the pot. Adijambavu took his part of the cow, and with the other three parts proceeded to create a new cow. Alas! The flesh that had been boiled and breathed upon could not be replaced, and Kamadhenu was not as she had been before. Loose skin hung down from her chin as the flesh that had formerly filled it was gone. She was reduced physically and mentally. From her proud stature of two heads, four horns, eight feet, and two tails, she dwindled to the size of the present-day cow. The gods said, "Adijambavu has to come down from his height and be beneath us." Thus, the day of his humiliation began. This led to the sinking of the Madigas into untouchability (Rauschenbusch-Clough 13–14).

Adijambavu's fall from being an all-powerful "first man" to an untouchable is celebrated within the Dalit communities, as the myth resonates with their real-life situation. It is said that "when the Aryans first came in contact with the sons of the soil, the day of humiliation came to Adijambava. He fell from his height" (Rauschenbusch-Clough 13). The theory about the caste system being brought to India by the Aryans is well known. Sir Herbert Risley, the British ethnographer, argued in his introduction to the *Handbook of Tribes and Castes of India*, that "the ultimate origin of the caste system lay in the hierarchical distinction between the 'higher,' 'fair-skinned Aryan,' and the 'lower' 'black Dravidian'" (quoted in Fuller 6). Although the Aryan invasion has been archeologically[19] and genetically[20] proven, the question of caste is still in speculation. The above-described myth portrays the Dalits' plight in Indian society; they were humiliated not only for eating beef but also for not obeying the orders of the dominant castes.

The myth also reveals the hegemony of the dominant castes through gods such as Brahma, Vishnu, and Siva. Hegemony is achieved through the hierarchization of the local gods. This is done through co-option and assimilation. M. N. Srinivas, an Indian historian, called this process "Sanskritization." He delineated it as Sanskritizing the "non-Sanskritic deities and non-Sanskritic ritual and belief—for example, the worship of village deities, ancestors, trees, rivers, and mountains, and local cults in general" (quoted in Staal 262). Through Sanskritization, the upper castes have legitimized the hierarchy of the gods in India.

This Sanskritization is evident in the origin myth *Jambava Puranam*. It discloses the hypocrisy of the gods as they do not hesitate to indulge in eating cow meat, but, on the other hand, Adijambavu, even though he does what the gods asked him to do, is "punished" and humiliated. Vellamanu's desire in itself is seen as problematic, as it was this desire that brought about his humiliation. Not only was he not allowed to drink the cow's milk, even though he tended to her needs, but he was even forbidden to possess such a desire. For the gods, on the other hand, cow's milk is their main interest, and they only keep the cow for the sake of their material needs. The gods, by transforming Adijambavu and Vellamanu into untouchables, create a new social hierarchy. These misappropriations were denounced through folk and oral songs by the Dalit communities.

Songs are part of the Dalits' work culture, as the popular Telugu phrase *pani-paata* (work-song) indicates. "The song has been at the core of the Dalit relationship with labour, nature, and Dalit goddesses (the possessed pour themselves out in the form of a song)" (Purushotham et al. 1). *Jambava Puranam* (translated by Velcheru Narayana Rao) is one such song and is in dialogue form, a conversation between a Dalit and a Brahmin:

> You call me Madiga, and keep me at a distance
> But you use my leather for your drums.
> And your whip is leather from me.
> And your shoulder bag as well.
> (quoted in Purushotham et al. 3–4)

The Madigas are leather workers by occupation. The poet categorically states that the leather made from the skin of the cow and the buffalo belongs to the Madigas, but the whip and the shoulder bag are the property of the upper castes. The writer's use of the pronoun "my" is not mere possessiveness of the cow. She is their life and life giver. The untouchables tend the cow by washing and milking her and bringing her to graze; moreover, they belong to communities such as the Chamars, Madigas, or Paraiyars, whose job is to remove the carcass of a dead cow from upper-caste homes, colonies, or neighborhoods. As Gurram Seetharamulu, a Telugu writer, narrates,

> the upper castes allotted turns to Madigas for caste services. We children also used to work in their houses during festivals and other celebrations. We removed carcasses and guarded the funeral pyres, and being Madigas, manually cleaned their dry latrines.
> (quoted in Purushotham et al. 202)

The songs remind Dalits of their shared suffering and along with that a sense of togetherness.

No upper-caste person will ever touch the carcass of a dead cow, which belongs to the Dalits. Their food and livelihood come from this carcass. It is suggested that the Dalits tend the cow while she is alive and the cow tends the Dalits after her death. With the skin of the dead cow, some of the Dalit communities make leather products such as shoes and bags. Only after it has been made into a product can the upper castes use it. The Dalits need to purify the dead cow skin to make it usable for the upper castes. This resonates with the latter regarding the cow simply as a material resource. In this context, Carnatic artist T. M. Krishna's discussion about the making of mrdangam, a classical percussion instrument used by upper-caste musicians, makes sense. The production of mrdangam is a Dalit's duty and its use, a Brahminical art. Krishna says that:

> Mrdangam-making involves skinning, cutting and curing hides, and hence this work was seldom done by the mrdangam artists. In the established caste order, skin-work has always been allotted to the lowest of castes. Even a century ago, when the conversions began,

> the procuring of hide and the making of the mrdangam would have been executed by caste groups that worked with skin and leather, and were considered "untouchables."
>
> (11)

The upper-caste mrdangam artists say that no animal is killed specifically for the instrument. According to Krishna, this is a false claim—either these artists are ignorant or it is a deliberate attempt to avoid blame. Rajamanikkam, a mrdangam maker, in an interview published in the magazine *Outlook* (2003), raises the question and then answers it:

> Have these people ever been to a slaughterhouse to see what we do? We examine cows and choose the healthy ones that have good, lustrous, soft skin ... For the mrdangam, it is always the skin of the female animal that is used. The logic is that the skin of a female that has delivered at least twice is more stretchy. For another instrument, called the suddha maddalam, they use the bull, since that requires a thick, tight membrane.
>
> (quoted in Krishna 160)

The specific use of female cows and, particularly, cows which have given birth at least twice, shows us the resource value attributed to the cow rather than any emotional quality. This aspect shows the Brahminical attitude toward the cow as a physical being—devoid of emotional concern.

The divinity attributed to the cow is only for the benefit and salvation of the upper caste. In light of this, the hypocrisy of the upper castes concerning food habits is clear:

> We make your shoes,
> You put them on your feet,
> When we ask to be paid,
> "Go, stand at a distance," you say
> Your shoes are polluted by my saliva?
> You keep them right there at your door.
> (quoted in Purushotham et al. 3)

Here, the narrator says he makes shoes with a cow's skin. For the upper caste, the feet are the dirtiest part of the human body. The *Purusha Sukta*[21] from the *Rig Veda*[22] state that if Brahmins originated from the mouth of Adi-Purusha,[23] the Shudras came from his feet (Griffith 924). The untouchables are not even part of Adi-Purusha. The same feet, which are considered to be impure, need protection. Protection for the feet is made from the skin of the cow by the untouchables. The poet reminds the upper castes that the making of shoes is an unclean job: "The tanning of animal skin to produce leather transforms a messy, smelly, and rapidly decaying substance into one that can be experienced as sweet and clean and of great utility" (Charsley 270). It is the Dalit, an untouchable, who transforms the foul body, the dead animal, into something pure that the upper castes can use. In this context, Krishna states that:

> the cow is removed from the artist's sight. Since the killing and skinning happen beyond his circle of existence, he can act as if it does not happen. The maker stands at the threshold, keeping the cow and the Brahmin apart, helping the latter maintain his purity.
>
> (187)

The cow, just like the Dalit, has a utility value for the upper castes in spite of its divine reverence. This utilitarian aspect resonates in the poem:

> Blood turns into milk.
> Milk becomes curd.
> You churn the curd to get butter.
> Milk, curd, butter—you eat them all, right?
> Then, why do you say you can't touch us?
>
> (3–4)

Gogu Shyamala's text questioning the upper-caste reader is an important characteristic in Dalit literature. The purpose of this questioning is to examine the ethical and social values of the upper castes. Here, the narrator asks the oppressor to examine his values. There is no hesitation about eating or drinking items produced by the Dalits, but ironically the Dalits are considered untouchables.

For the upper castes, milk, curd, and clarified butter are a fundamental part of their daily diet. Ghee is an important part of Hindu rituals. The *Rig Veda* contains the hymn "Ode to Ghee," which is an exaltation, as it is the favorite food of the god of fire, Agni:

> They pour over the fire, smiling,
> Like beautiful women on their way to a festival,
> The streams of butter caress the logs,
> And Jatavedas [meaning obscure], taking pleasure in them,
> Pays them court.
> I watch them eagerly; they are like girls,
> Painting themselves to go to the wedding
> There where the soma juice is pressed, where sacrifice is made,
> The streams of butter run down to be clarified.
>
> (IV 58; quoted in Sen 37)

The hymn reveals not just the importance of ghee but also of sacrifice, which is a significant aspect of the Hindu religion. During Vedic times, "the sacrifices entailed killing animals and offering the meat to the gods, after which it was eaten by the patrons and their guests and later by the person performing the sacrifice" (Sen 37). The *Vedas* are primarily focused on the theory and practice of the fire sacrifice (*Yagna*). These rituals of sacrifice were monopolized by the priests, which gave them power over society, as the sacrifices were basically made to appease the gods:

> In the Vedic texts, the sacrifice plays a pivotal role in the perpetual redistribution of food. The sacrifice was the dining hall of the gods; humans fed the divinities in the expectation that the sated diners would in turn, feed the universe.
>
> (Smith 180)

These sacrifices were mostly violent, as witnessed in the *Rig Veda* when Indra says that "Fifteen in number, then, for me a score of bullocks they prepare. And I devour the fat thereof: they fill my belly full with food" (X 86.14; quoted in Griffith 916); "horses, bulls, oxen, and barren cows, and rams, when duly set apart, are offered up" (X 91.14; 926). The violence through these sacrifices was subdued from the post-Vedic times with the use of milk, curd, clarified butter, and so on.

During the post-Vedic period, there was a sudden reversal of these Vedic values and a movement away from the ideology of violence and meat eating to non-violence and vegetarianism, although the concept of purity and impurity and its relevance to the caste hierarchy remained intact. Doniger and Smith claim this ideology, which reverberates throughout post-Vedic texts such as the *Bhagavad Gita* and the *Manusmriti* (Laws of Manu), played a pivotal role in responding to the crises of traditional Aryan culture. They also postulate that the Laws of Manu consolidated and united the various Vedic schools. They state that it is an "invaluable historical witness to the forging of a synthetic common culture among persons professing the laws in the various schools" (22). Vegetarianism was a focal point that called into question all the values from ancient India.

The source of vegetarianism and non-violence is still obscure:

> it does seem likely, however, that such concepts were embedded in the larger revolutionary programme of the world renouncers or *sramanas* who were so influential beginning around the sixth century B.C.E. In each of their bands—the "orthodox" composers of the Upanishads as well as the "heterodox" groups, some of which soon coalesced into the religions later known as Buddhism and Jainism—the world-renouncers challenged the fundamental assumptions of Vedism.
>
> (Smith 21)

This has led to rivalry between these religions, particularly Buddhism and Vedism. Ambedkar, in this context, states that:

> the Broken Men[24] were Buddhists. As such, they did not revere the Brahmins, did not employ them as their priests and regarded them as impure. The Brahmin, on the other hand, disliked the Broken Men because they were Buddhists and preached against them contempt and hatred with the result that the Broken Men came to be regarded as Untouchables.
>
> (*Untouchables*, 315: Ambedkar 1979)

He further states that "they were made untouchables because they continued eating beef when the Gupta kings made cow killing a criminal offense and beef-eating a sin in the fourth century AD" (quoted in Teltumbde 379). The Guptas belonged to the upper caste, and, arguably, this is considered to be the first instance when the cow was used as a political symbol. The Guptas' influence played a very important role in rejuvenating the Vedic religion, but Buddhism and its ideology dominated for another two to three centuries. Although Buddhism did challenge the Vedic[25] worldview, Randall Collins states that "it remained more of a reform movement within the milieu of the educated religious people—who were mostly Brahmins—rather than a rival movement from outside" (quoted in Teltumbde 34). Furthermore, when major religions such as Jainism and Buddhism failed to curtail the caste system, it was questioned and resisted through oral and folk traditions, such as *Jambava Puranam*. They questioned the dominion of the upper castes and at the same time romanticized the traditions of the untouchable communities, particularly in the use of food as a metaphorical symbol.

Conclusion

Caste is hardly discussed in ecocriticism, although race and gender are popularly explored topics. As Mukul Sharma has pointed out, both caste and nature are deeply intertwined in India. This chapter has argued that food and habitat play a fundamental role in the sustenance of caste prejudice in India. Dalits were humiliated and enslaved because of their marginalized habitat, a habitat that was lifeless and barren. It contributed to their food habits. Discrimination against the Dalits has manifested in different forms in modern Indian society. Most Dalit communities are still confined to the margins of the villages, towns, and cities of India. Their habitat has not changed much over time. They live in slums and ghettos in the cities with minimal hygiene. Menial jobs, such as manual scavenging, are still done by the Dalit communities, even though this practice was banned by India in 1993. Their food habits have also not changed much. Dalit food today is still judged, and eating beef is frowned upon. Some Indian states have even banned the slaughter of cows. An important fact that needs to be considered is that the decision to ban cow slaughter is due to political and religious considerations, rather than based on animal welfare. Dalits and Muslims are beaten up and even lynched if found with slaughtered cows. On the other hand, India earns as much as four billion dollars a year from exporting buffalo meat (Malhotra), and the country is the largest exporter of buffalo meat in the world (Dhingra). This reveals the hypocrisy around animal welfare, as the export of cow meat is banned. Dalits are trying to overcome most of these prejudices and reclaim their self-respect and identity through writing and activism.

Dr. Ambedkar's three commandments—educate, agitate, and organize—have become the framework for Dalit resistance. Dalit writers are using their space to educate the world and paving the way to organize and agitate for assertion of their rights. They are representing and reinventing their identities through literature. Dalit autobiographies, specifically through sharing the suffering and resistance, are rewriting their histories. Dalits still hope their suffering and pain will be transformed into a casteless, classless, and egalitarian utopia, the realm of *Begumpura*,[26] that will give them the freedom to choose what they eat, as well as to go dancing and roaming throughout "the forests and mountains, The hills and valleys, and plains" (Sharma, *Caste and Nature*, 91).

Notes

1 The hierarchy of caste is channeled into four types: Brahmin, Kshatriya, Vysya, and Shudra. The fifth caste (*panchamas*) is outside the caste order, and, as such, they are called "the untouchables." The modern parlance for untouchable is Dalit and/or Harijan. Dalit, meaning "broken" or "scattered" in Sanskrit and Hindi, is a term mostly applied to the lower classes in India. It was first used by social reformer Jyotirao Phule. It is the preferred term in contemporary India for the untouchables. Harijan means "children of God." It was first used by Mahatma Gandhi.

2 The *Vedas* are a collection of hymns and other ancient religious texts written in India between 1500 and 1000 BCE. They include liturgical material, as well as mythological accounts, poems, prayers, and formulas, considered sacred by the Vedic religion. They are written in Sanskrit.

3 The *Upanishads* are a collection of texts of a religious and philosophical nature written in India between c. 800 BCE and c. 500 BCE.

4 The *Manusmriti* is the most authoritative Hindu code in India. It was written approximately 100 CE and is translated into English as the Laws of Manu.

5 Dr. B. R. Ambedkar (1891–1956) was a jurist, economist, social reformer, and politician, and the father of the Indian Constitution. He headed the Constituent Assembly.

6 *Chandala* is a Sanskrit word for someone who deals with the disposal of corpses and is a Hindu lower caste traditionally considered untouchable, i.e., a person from a degraded caste, whose behavior is considered to be well below standard and whose presence causes contamination.

7 *Jhootan* is old bread. It also refers to scraps of food left on a plate, destined for the garbage or to be eaten by animals. Untouchables have been forced to accept and eat *Jhootan* for centuries.

8 Since the Hindu nationalist Bharatiya Janata Party won power in India in 2014, lynchings of the country's minorities have surged. In February 2019, at least forty-four such murders between May 2015 and December 2018

were reported across twelve Indian states. Hundreds more people have been injured in religiously motivated attacks (see Human Rights Watch).

9 *Gau rakshaks*, or cow protectors, are Hindu fundamentalists who have self-styled themselves the protectors of cows. In recent years they have committed physical violence against vulnerable Dalits and Muslims, claiming they have killed cows.

10 The scientific name for the tree is *Prosopis juliflora*; the popular name is Babul. It is called the poor man's firewood in India.

11 *Murdada* – Marathi language.

12 *Hatfatka* – Marathi language.

13 *Toliv* – Marathi language.

14 *Chanya* – Marathi language.

15 Arya Samaj is a monotheistic Indian Hindu reform movement founded by Dayanand Saraswati in 1875.

16 Brahmo Samaj is a monotheistic Indian Hindu reform movement started by Raja Ram Mohan Roy and Debendranath Tagore in 1828.

17 *Cindu* literally means "vibrant step." *Cindata* comes from the community of Cindu Madiga. It is a performance through dance on popular Dalit myths, such as *Jambava Purnam*, *Yakshaganam*, and *Bhagavatams*.

18 Kamadhenu, also known as Surabi, is a divine bovine goddess described in Vedic scriptures as the mother of all cows.

19 See Thapar.

20 See Joseph.

21 *Purusha Sukta* is a Vedic Sanskrit hymn that narrates the origin of the caste system.

22 *Rig Veda* is an ancient Indian collection of Vedic Sanskrit hymns. It is one of the four sacred canonical texts of Hinduism known as the Vedas. The Rigveda is the oldest known Vedic Sanskrit text.

23 Adi-Purusha literally means First Man in Sanskrit. He is considered to be the first cosmic being. It is believed that human beings came about through him. The *Rig Veda* states: "The Brahmin was his mouth, of both his arms was the Rajanya [Kshatriya] made. His thighs became the Vaisya, from his feet the Sudra was produced" (see Griffith 924).

24 Dr. Ambedkar used the term Broken Men to denote the untouchables of Indian society. He believed that broken men are broken tribesmen who have been defeated in war and broken into pieces. In order to survive, these broken men attached themselves to different tribes. As tribes are predominantly kith and kin belonging to the same family, Ambedkar believed these broken men were always outside a particular tribal system but doing all the menial work. He believed these broken men were the modern untouchables. For a detailed discussion, see *Untouchables or The Children of India's Ghetto* in Ambedkar, *Writings and Speeches*.

25 The reservation system is a system of affirmative action that provides representation for historically and currently disadvantaged groups in Indian society in education, employment, and politics. It is enshrined in Articles 15 and 16 of the Indian Constitution.

26 *Begumpura* is a Dalit version of utopia considered to be the first one formulated in India by a Dalit, the poet Sant Ravidas (c. 1450–1520), during the Bhakti movement. This is in contrast to *Ramarajya*, an upper-caste utopia, which Gandhi propagated as an ideal nation.

References

Alex, Rayson K., and S. Susan Deborah. *Ecodocumentaries: Critical Essays*. Palgrave Macmillan, 2016.

Aloysius, G. "Law and Caste: Historical and Sociological Development." Nalsar University of Law, Hyderabad, 2018.

Ambedkar, Bhimrao Ranji. *Annihilation of Caste: The Annotated Critical Edition*, edited by S. Anand. Verso, 2016.

———. *Dr. Babasaheb Ambedkar: Writings and Speeches*, compiled by Vasant Moon. 1979. Education Department, Government of Maharashtra, 1993.

Anand, S. "Thyagaraja's Cow." *Outlook*, 8 Sep. 2003, www.outlookindia.com/magazine/story/thyagarajas-cow/221354.

Charsley, Simon. "Interpreting Untouchability: The Performance of Caste in Andhra Pradesh, South India." *Asian Folklore Studies*, vol. 63, no. 2, 2004, pp. 267–90.

Cooks, Leda. "You Are What You (Don't) Eat? Food, Identity, and Resistance." *Text and Performance Quarterly*, vol. 29, no. 1, 2009, pp. 94–110, https://doi.org/10.1080/10462930802514388.

Dhingra, Sanya. "India's Beef Exports Rise Under Modi Govt Despite Hindu Vigilante Campaign at Home." *The Print*, 26 Mar. 2019, https://theprint.in/economy/indias-beef-exports-rise-under-modi-govt-despite-hindu-vigilante-campaign-at-home/210164/.

Doniger, Wendy, editor, and Brian K. Smith, translator. *The Laws of Manu*. Penguin Classics, 1991.

Egoz, Shelley. "Landscape and Identity in the Century of the Migrant." In *The Routledge Companion to Landscape Studies*, edited by Howard, Peter, et al. Routledge, 2019, pp. 329–340.

Freire, Paulo. *Pedagogy of the Oppressed*. Penguin Books, 2017.

Fuller, C. J. "Ethnographic Inquiry in Colonial India: Herbert Risley, William Crooke, and the Study of Tribes and Castes." *Journal of the Royal Anthropological Institute*, vol. 23, no. 3, 2017, pp. 603–21, https://doi.org/10.1111/1467-9655.12654.

Gadgil, Madhav, and Ramachandra Guha. *Ecology and Equity: The Use and Abuse of Nature in Contemporary India*. Routledge, 2005.

Gidla, Sujatha. "From Malapalli to Brahmin Town." In *The Oxford India Anthology of Telugu Dalit Writing*, edited by K. Purushotham et al. Oxford University Press, 2016, pp. 182–186.

Griffith, Ralph T. H., translator. *Hinduism, the Rig Veda, Sacred Writings 5*. 1896. History Book Club, 1992.

Guha, Ramachandra. "Anil Agarwal and the Environmentalism of the Poor." *Capitalism Nature Socialism*, vol. 13, no. 3, 2002, pp. 147–55, https://doi.org/10.1080/10455750208565494.

Gundimeda, Sambaiah, et al. "What's the Menu? Food Politics and Hegemony." *Anveshi Broadsheet on Contemporary Politics*, vol. 1, no. 4, 2012, 2–3.

Guru, Gopal. "Food as a Metaphor for Cultural Hierarchies." In *Knowledges Born in the Struggle: Constructing the Epistemologies of the Global South*, edited by Santos Boaventura de Sousa and Maria Paula Meneses. Routledge, 2020.

Howard, Peter, et al. *The Routledge Companion to Landscape Studies*. Routledge, 2019.

Huggan, Graham, and Helen Tiffin. *Postcolonial Ecocriticism: Literature, Animals, Environment*. Routledge, 2015.

Human Rights Watch. "Violent Cow Protection in India." 18 Feb. 2019, www.hrw.org/report/2019/02/18/violent-cow-protection-india/vigilante-groups-attack-minorities.

Ilaiah, Kancha. *Why I Am Not a Hindu: A Sudra Critique of Hindutva Philosophy, Culture and Political Economy*. Sage Publications, 2019.

Indian Express. "In the Name of the Cow: Murder, Flogging, Humiliation of Muslims, Dalits," 5 Aug. 2016, https://indianexpress.com/article/explained/gujarat-dalit-protests-una-gau-rakshaks-mohammad-akhlaq-modi-govt-2954324/. Accessed 3 Apr. 2020.

Jangam, Chinnaiah. *Dalits and the Making of Modern India*. Oxford University Press, 2017.

Jha, D. N. *The Myth of the Holy Cow*. New Delhi: Navayana Publishing, 2017.

Jodhka, Surinder S. *Caste*. Oxford University Press, 2013.

Joseph, Tony. *Early Indians: The Story of our Ancestors and Where we Came From*. Juggernaut Books, 2018.

Krishna, T. M. *Sebastian & Sons: A Brief History of Mrdangam Makers*. Westland Publications, 2020.

Macdonell, A. A. "The Early History of Caste." *American Historical Review*, vol. 19, no. 2, 1914, pp. 230–44.

Malhotra, Jyoti. "India's Politics of Meat." *Al Jazeera*, 27 Apr. 2017, www.aljazeera.com/indepth/opinion/2017/04/india-politics-meat-170426104902909.html.

Mascaro, Juan, translator. *The Upanishads*. Penguin Books, 1971.

Olivelle, Patrick, editor, translator. *Manu's Code of Law: A Critical Edition and Translation of the Mānava-Dharmasāstra*. Oxford University Press, 2005.

Omvedt, Gail. *Seeking Begumpura: The Social Vision of Anticaste Intellectuals*. Navayana Publishing, 2011.

Purushotham, K., et al. *The Oxford India Anthology of Telugu Dalit Writing*. Oxford University Press, 2016.

Ramanujam, Srinivasa. *Renunciation and Untouchability in India: The Notional and the Empirical in the Caste Order*. Routledge, 2020.

Rao, G. Kaḷyana. *Untouchable Spring*. Translated by Alladi Uma and M. Sridhar. Orient BlackSwan, 2010.

Rauschenbusch-Clough, Emma. *While Sewing Sandals: Or, Tales of a Telugu Pariah Tribe*. 1899. Asian Educational Services, 2000.

Satyanarayana, K., and Susie J. Tharu. *The Exercise of Freedom: An Introduction to Dalit Writing*. Navayana Publishing, 2013.

Sen, Colleen Taylor. *Feasts and Fasts: A History of Food in India*. Speaking Tiger, 2016.

Sharma, Mukul. *Caste and Nature: Dalits and Indian Environmental Politics*. Oxford University Press, 2017.

———, editor. *Unquiet Worlds: Dalit Voices and Visions*. Heinrich Böll Foundation, 2004.

Smith, Brian K. "Eaters, Food, and Social Hierarchy in Ancient India: A Dietary Guide to a Revolution of Values." *Journal of the American Academy of Religion*, vol. 58, no. 2, 1990, pp. 177–206.

Staal, J. F. "Sanskrit and Sanskritization." *Journal of Asian Studies*, vol. 22, no. 3, 1963, pp. 261–75.

Stewart, Pamela J., and Andrew Strathern. *Landscape, Memory and History: Anthropological Perspectives*.Pluto, 2003.

Tak, Deepa, and Tina Aranha. "Cast(e)ing Food: Interrogating Popular Media." *Sahapedia*, 1 Apr. 2016, www.sahapedia.org/casteing-food-interrogating-popular-media.

Teltumbde, Anand. *Dalits: Past, Present and Future*. Routledge, 2019.

Thapar, Romila. *The Aryan: Recasting Constructs*. Three Essays Collective, 2015.

Vajapeyi Asoka. *India Dissents: 3,000 Years of Difference, Doubt and Argument*. Speaking Tiger, 2017.

Viswanath, Rupa. *The Pariah Problem: Caste, Religion, and the Social in Modern India*. Columbia University Press, 2014.

Afterword

Toward Shifts in Global Food Systems

Simon C. Estok

> the disciplines of literary history and cultural theory have not, in the main, taken up food studies.
>
> (Carruth 165)

In her remarkable account of "the centrality of food to accounts of globalization and U.S. hegemony that pervade the literature of th[e] period" from the First World War to the post-9/11 era (Carruth 5), Allison Carruth offers important and original analyses about relationships among narrative, power, and food. In what she terms "the literature of food," Carruth's work—truly the first of its kind—initiates a very timely conversation, one that synthesizes and brings together an enormous body of work. It is within this tradition that *Anthropocene Ecologies of Food* has sought to modestly participate, with an explicit focus on the Global South.

Food and life are obviously inseparable. I write parts of this afterword in the shadow of death, my brother having killed himself a week ago at the time of my writing, and the grief has slowed my work—as is natural. A few years ago, I saw a dead magpie on the road behind my university, its mate on the curb grieving very noisily. It brought tears to my eyes. There is a very large family of magpies (a dozen or so strong) at my university, and they are often most active when I am most active—early in the morning. They are getting food and, from what I can see from my window, sharing it with each other. They remind me of my non-exceptionality. They grieve, I grieve. They eat, I eat. Indeed, over the past sad week, I've cooked more than I did in the past month. It is because of my brother. I write in the shadow of death about food.

The celebration of life and its phases is frequently associated with food. We see this clearly in the great harvest celebrations in the world. Often in ritualized ways, food is the bridge in these celebrations between seasons and between phases of life. Food is a bond among people and a material symbol of hope. Even as they mark the death of the growing season (sometimes punctuated with visits to ancestral tombs, as with Chuseok in Korea), these celebrations—characterized by conspicuous displays of

DOI: 10.4324/9781003282976-14

excess and abundance, cornucopias of sustenance, and overflowings of goodness—affirm life.

Food is life affirming. So is sex. Indeed, the analogies between food and sex have many implications. Food, like sexuality, is obviously a very personal matter. Both have to do with real bodily penetrations. Peter Singer and Jim Mason go as far as to say that often in history, "ethical choices about food were considered at least as significant as ethical choices about sex" (3). And as with sex, food can be commodified and exploited. Fabio Parasecoli has discussed this matter in very illuminating terms:

> Food has invaded the internet through specialized websites and social media platforms that allow users around the world to post information and pictures about their meals and the dishes they cook, exchange tips about restaurants and stores, and discuss food-related issues.
>
> All over the world, these media interactions are largely dominated by what is sometimes referred to as *food porn*: a set of visual and auditory strategies—shots, camera movements, slow motion, lighting, sound, and editing—that aim to offer images of food so pleasurable and attractive that viewers lust after it, even when they are excluded from consumption. Just as in pornography, graphic, acoustic, and narrative components are meant to reproduce the physical acts of eating and savoring for spectators, often achieving comparable levels of excitement without actual satisfaction.
>
> (15–16)

The many levels at which discourses about food and sexuality intersect are worthy of more consideration than is possible here—among the associated topics are the gendering of meat and vegetables, the sexualizing of diets, meat and misogyny, and others. Some of these have been usefully addressed in this book, and many others have been addressed elsewhere. In the process of compiling the chapters of this book, with an eye to the many topics that are associated and that require attention, one thing has become very clear: Anthropocene ecologies of food are incredibly complex.

Food brings people together and has been and remains essential in the formation of personal, community, and national identities; so too does it tear communities apart. The ongoing Indian Farmers' Protest is a recent example. Huge protests have taken place in India (and in many large cities across the world within supportive communities) against the farm bills introduced in India in September 2020. To many people, these bills seem to favor corporations at the expense of private farmers. But even before the farm bills, there were food issues tearing communities apart in India.

The violence and barbarity of transnational corporations such as Monsanto have long put lives and livelihoods at stake. New corporate imperialism swallows up traditions and histories, and food is wielded as a profoundly dangerous weapon. The complexities and interweavings of food security issues with matters of culture, imperialism, and violence reveal barriers to democratic self-determination of food production and distribution. Now, as never before, the processes of identity formation face a frightening new reality. The topic of food security, a vital issue in cosmopolitanism, is one that has, in many ways, been the topic of this book. Yet, the complexities of food-based social formations require sustained and honest analysis, and this can be difficult, since food is so intensely personal.

Whatever else food security may mean in the twenty-first century, one thing is certain: global food security is no longer a guarantee. Moreover, the whole notion of self-sufficiency simply is no longer viable. And when foods are attached to notions about national identity, as they so very often are, obvious problems arise. If *kimchi*, for instance, is the national food of Korea, and if Korea is having to import enormous amounts of cabbage from China to make the *kimchi* (or if Korea is having to import the ready-made *kimchi* itself), then what does this dynamic do to the national identity of Korea? If cosmopolitanism is about integrating difference, then surely it is not about white-washing cultural variation, bulldozing unique traditional geographies, and fostering transnational corporations into positions of terrorist power that surpass anything that 9/11 perpetrators or their ilk have achieved or can achieve? Yet, these are precisely the things that have happened, and companies promoting genetically modified organisms (GMOs) are critically complicit in the ongoing legacies of colonialism. If colonialism mapped, drafted, and designed the blueprints of world domination, then globalization realizes the structures, cements the material practices, and expands beyond imagination the material and conceptual meanings of conquest: "Colonialism initiated (and globalization continues to drive) circuits of physical and virtual mobility that impact on the construction of place" (O'Brien 242–3),[1] and food has been central to these processes.

Food is very obviously a tremendously important area of research within the environmental humanities. Susie O'Brien has explained in an interview in *ARIEL* that "Food is a rich site through which to think about a number of things: environment, colonialism, culture, affect, subjectivity, among others" (Szabo-Jones 207). It is a fact that the global expansion of McDonald's, Burger King, KFC, and other meat-based fast-food companies is bad for the environment and for the people of the world in general, that meat is horrendously wasteful, that, as I explained in an article some years ago, it is "difficult to take seriously … the ecocritic who theorizes brilliantly on a stomach full of roast beef on rye" (Estok, "Theorizing" 217), that "most simply put, someone who regularly eats factory-farmed animal products cannot call himself an environmentalist without divorcing that word from its meaning" (Foer 59), and that:

> in the near future, ecofeminism and feminist ecocriticisms will need to articulate an interspecies focus within ecocriticism, bringing

> forward the vegetarian and vegan feminist threads that have been a developing part of feminist and ecological feminist theories since the nineteenth century.
>
> (Gaard 651)[2]

These articulations have begun, and some are in this collection.

Now, as never before, with staggeringly exponential increases in population, the carbon footprint of food is becoming ever more critical. A vegan diet is best for the world, but, as some of the chapters in this volume discuss (see, for instance, Moses), there are all sorts of class issues that complicate matters. As the diet of status and position, meat unfortunately sometimes becomes the diet of resistance to class bigotry—as is the case in India. Similarly, in Korea, where meat had long been available only to the wealthy, the country seems to have become mesmerized by it—especially during some of the high holidays, with galbi (cow ribs) and bulgogi (barbequed cow) gracing virtually every table in the country, the meat section of Costco as crowded as a subway, and the reek of grilled pork, fried chicken, and roasted beef always in the air. Factory farming, international trade agreements, and a rapidly growing standard of living have made meat more available than in the past. Even so, veganism is making inroads—even in Seoul.

Part of what is driving this revolution are the facts: meat wastes water, causes pollution, is unhealthy, and drives pandemics and disease. Many environment-related ills and issues (swine flu, avian flu, covid-19, deforestation, fresh-water mismanagement, methane pollution, malnutrition, and so on) owe their existence in part or in whole to humanity's fondness for meat, a fondness that often pushes (and sometimes breaks) environmental limits. There are debates, to be sure, but there are also hard facts. Meat is bad. Genetic engineering, on the other hand, garners a less definitive verdict. Indeed, the debates about genetic engineering, while important, have really taken a backseat as it has become more and more apparent that changing climactic conditions may *require* foods with resistances to extremes, foods that perhaps *don't yet exist*; moreover, as many of us lined up for genetically altered substances (mRNA vaccines) to be *injected* into our arms, the debate among scholars about genetic fiddling seems to have become somewhat muted lately.

Perhaps more pertinent than the debates about genetic engineering here is the question of patenting. Although there is, surprisingly, more than a century and a half's history to seed patenting, the patenting continues. The debate is, in some sense, understandable. Scientists who spend their lives researching and developing seeds that are more durable or bigger, or are imagined in some ways to be better than the original, are part of a long line of people in human history who have altered how foods develop in nature. For centuries, we have chosen the better crops to plant, have grafted and have selectively bred our foods, both animal and vegetable. Scientists who have spent their lives researching and developing seeds that are more durable or bigger or are imagined in some ways to be better than the original are scholars no less than I am, and when I spend my life researching and writing, I am protected by copyright laws. So, why shouldn't scientists be protected by the same laws? So the argument goes. The problem is that patenting seeds is an ethically different matter than patenting word clusters. My words will never produce birth deformities—I hope! But powerful words can deform our current food practices.

The opening line of the 2019 *Lancet* Commission's "Food in the Anthropocene" is a powerful incentive to develop such analyses that will result in material changes in how and what foods we make: "Food systems have the potential to nurture human health and support environmental sustainability; however, they are currently threatening both" (Willett et al. 447). The collective assumption behind the chapters in this collection has been that what happens with food in the Global South is vital to addressing those dual threats.

Notes

1 Much of this paragraph appears in *The Ecophobia Hypothesis*, p. 113.
2 Parts of this paragraph appear in *The Ecophobia Hypothesis*, p. 96.

References

Carruth, Allison. *Global Appetites: American Power and the Literature of Food*. Cambridge University Press, 2013.

Estok, Simon C. *The Ecophobia Hypothesis*. Routledge, 2018.

———. "Theorizing in a Space of Ambivalent Openness: Ecocriticism and Ecophobia." *ISLE: Interdisciplinary Studies in Literature and Environment*, vol. 16, no. 2, Spring 2009, pp. 203–25.

Foer, Safran Jonathan. *Extremely Loud and Incredibly Close: A Novel*. Houghton Mifflin Harcourt, 2005.

Gaard, Greta. "New Directions for Ecofeminism: Toward a More Feminist Ecocriticism." *ISLE: Interdisciplinary Studies in Literature and Environment*, vol. 17, no. 4, October 2010, pp. 643–65.

O'Brien, Susie. " 'No Debt Outstanding': The Postcolonial Politics of Local Food." *Environmental Criticism for the Twenty-First Century*, edited by Stephanie LeMenager, Teresa Shewry, and Ken Hiltner. Routledge, 2011, pp. 231–46.

Parasecoli, Fabio. *Food*. MIT Press, 2019.

Singer, Peter, and Jim Mason. *The Ethics of What We Eat: Why Our Food Choices Matter*. Rodale, 2007.

Szabo-Jones, Lisa. "An Interview with Susie O'Brien Conducted via Email between February 3 and March 1, 2014." *ARIEL: A Review of International English Literature*, vol. 44, no. 4, October 2013, pp. 205–17.

Willett, Walter, et al. "Food in the Anthropocene: *The EAT-Lancet Commission on Healthy Diets from Sustainable Food Systems*" January 16, 2019. http://dx.doi.org/10.1016/S0140-6736(18)31788-4.

Index

Note: Page numbers with an "n" denote Notes.

Ackerman, Diane 115
Adams, Carol J. 6, 123n7
Adamson, Joni 3–4
Adi-Purusha 176n23
Africa, salt fish in 97, 98, 108
agribusiness 6, 79, 114, 117, 119, 141, 142, 155
agricultural consumerism 38, 52n10
agroecology 141, 147, 148, 151, 153
agro-forestry systems 41
Agyeman, Julian 90, 93n14
Albala, Ken 3
Allchin, Bridget 22
Allchin, Raymond 22
allotreptic approach, to Anthropocene 11–12, 26n1
Aloysius, G. 160
Ambedkar, B. R. 143, 158, 160, 161, 164, 173–174, 175, 175n5, 176n24
American diet 2
ancestral diet 40
Anderson, E. N. 43
Angola 97, 108
animal sacrifices 173
animism 46–47
Anslow, Mark 92n5
Anthropocene 1, 4, 11, 51n4, 141; basic approaches to 11–12, 26n1; contextualization of 154; scientific and non-scientific approaches to 26n2
anthropotreptic approach, to Anthropocene 11, 26n1
aquatic ecosystems 100–101
Arendt, Florian 88
arisi (rice) 29n12
Armbruster, Karla 39
Arya Samaj 166, 176n15
bacalhaus 97, 99; and colonialism 100; and common people 105–106; derogatory metaphors regarding 107; in Goa 97, 107–109; as highly regarded product 108–109
Bacigalupi, Paolo 5, 112, 113–114, 115, 116, 118
Balasubramanian, P. 24
Balfour, Lady Eve 60–61, 66
Baron, Cynthia 83
Barrett, James H. 101, 102
Barton, Gregory A. 67–68, 73n9, 73n24, 73n27
Basque sailors 97, 98–99, 102
Battisti, David 120
Baviskar, Amita 73n33
beef eating: by Dalits 164–174; and food system 2
bees 121
Begumpura 176n26
Behar, Katherine 103
Benenson, Bill 79
Berg, Peter 37, 39, 41, 44, 45
Berry, Wendell 90–91, 121
"Beyond Meat" 92n4
Bhagavad Gita, The 134, 173
Bharatiya Janata Party 175n8
Bhil tribe 15, 28n10
Biénabe, Estelle 41
Biermann, Frank 141–142, 154
biodynamic farming 65–66, 73n24
bioregional culture 42–43, 50
bioregional eating 36, 38–42, 50–51; ecologies of food 42–49; intrinsic value of 41; *see also* Kodagu/Kodava people
bioregional food system 4
bioregional identity 42–43

bioregional living 45
Bird, D. K. 102
Boehrer, Bruce 103
Bolster, W. Jeffrey 101
Bondarenko, D. M. 19
Bowden, Brett 12
Bradley, Fern Marshall 72n5
Brahmadeya 24
Brahmins 23, 24, 159, 171
Brahmo Samaj 166, 176n16
Brayton, Daniel 103–104, 105, 106–107
Brazil 41
British Chatham House Think Tank 83
broken men 174, 176n24; *see also* Dalits
Broomfield, Louis 66
Buddhism 173, 174
bureaucratic corruption 144–145

Cabot, John 98
campā paddy 19
Campesino a Campesino movement 150, 151, 152
Canadian Atlantic fishery 97, 98, 99, 102–103
caṅkam literature 15, 23, 28n11
Caplan, Richard 114, 123n11
Capra, Fritjof 86
carbonized paddy 19
Caribbean 97, 108, 109
Carruth, Allison 180
Carson, Rachel 91
caste system 143–144, 158, 159, 160, 174–175, 175n1; *see also* Dalits
celebrations, and food 180–181
centralization, problems with 146–147
Ceylon, coffee production in 51–52n7
Chadwick, Alan 66
Chakrabarty, Dipesh 11, 141
Chamars 170
chandalas 160, 175n6
Charlesworth, Carsten T. 115
cheshires 115, 121
Chinese agriculture 67, 68, 73n27
Christian (ship) 99–100
civilization: and the ecosystems, relationship between 12–13; Ganges 22–23; Indus Valley 14, 23; and paddy cultivation 23
Clapp, Jennifer 124n16
class 143–144
Cleveland, David 48
climate change 119, 120, 128, 141, 142
cod 97; preserved 97–98; *see also* *bacalhaus*
Cogan, Bill 86
cōḻar 13, 20, 21–24, 26n4, 26n5
Cole, Sally C. 99
Collins, Randall 174
colonialism 182; and environmental degradation 102
commodity fetishism 104
compost 4, 57, 58, 71, 72n3, 80; composting landscapes 72n3; definition of 58–59; Howard method (*see* Indore method); Steiner method 64–66; varied methods 59; *see also* Indore method
Conford, Philip 73n24
connectedness to nature 88–89, 93n12
continuous cultivation 37, 38, 51n6
corporate imperialism 181–182
Corporation, The 91n2
cōṟu (pith) 16
cosmopolitanism 182
Counihan, Carole 36
cow 86; *gau rakshaks* 162, 176n9; *see also* beef eating
Cowspiracy 77, 83, 91n1
Crutzen, Paul J. 12, 13–14, 51n4
Cruz, Vida 126, 127
"Culture of Food, The: Literature and Society" 6–7
Curtis, Jamie Lee 79

dairy consumption 82, 83
Dalits 6, 174–175, 175n1; assertion of identity 168; beef as a symbol of resistance 164–174; and carcass of a dead cow 170–172; dependence on upper castes 160–162; dignity and self-respect 165; and environmentalism 162–163; food and habitat 159–163; menial jobs for survival 161, 167; place, memory, and identity 159; retaliation for eating upper-caste food 162; and songs 169–170; violence against 162
Dasmann, Raymond F. 37, 39, 41, 44, 45, 52n8
Dayanand Saraswati 176n15
Dear, I. C. B. 106
deforestation 12
Dellon, Charles Gabriel 107, 108
Desai, Anita 126

desertification 86
dirt 79, 86
Dirt! The Movie 77, 79, 86, 87
Discours of Voyages into Y East & West Indies 107
documentaries 78; ecodocumentaries 78, 89; food documentaries 88–89, 91; nature documentaries 89; YouTube eco-food documentaries 78; *see also specific documentaries*
Doniger, Wendy 173
Dravidian tribe 15; *see also* southern peninsula of India
Dull, Robert A. 101

Eagleton, Terry 126, 128, 135
Early Anthropocene 13–14
Earth 92n2
earth's systems, excessive human interference with 12
"Eating Cow, Becoming One" (Hanumanthaiah) 164–165
ecocriticism 3, 72n3, 182–183; early modern 103
ecodocumentaries 78, 89; toxic materiality of 89
ecofilm strategies 77
ecological disturbance, warning signs 124n17
ecological refugees 152
ecosystem people 151–152
education and employment, of farmers 151
Egoz, Shelley 159
Engdahl, William 117
England 98–100, 104, 106, 107
environmental awareness, 90
environmental education 93n14
environmental justice 117
environmental security 83
Estok, Simon C. 3, 36, 38, 103, 123n3, 124n16, 135
ethical food production 77
European fisheries 101, 102

Fagan, Brian 100, 102, 106–107
Fanzo, Jessica 1
farmers: and Indore method 68–69, 70, 73n33; mass suicides 6, 141, 142, 146, 149, 151; movements 150, 151, 152, 155, 156n7; small farmers 142, 146
farming development 82–83
farm-to-table movement 71
Fast Food Nation 77, 82, 83–84
Fasting, Feasting (Desai) 126, 132–135
Faxian 160
fertilizers 25; chemical 59; petroleum-based 80
Findhorn community 66, 73n24
Fischler, Claude 134, 135
fish and poverty 104, 105
Fitzpatrick, Joan, 103
Flow 91n2
Foer, Jonathan Safran 119
food: distribution of 126; diversity 4, 11, 14, 24, 27n7; justice 117; monism 14, 25, 27n7; and national identity 182; practices and rituals, hierarchy and resistance in 6; safety 91; security 78–79, 147, 182; and sex 181; sharing of 130; sovereignty 78–79, 148; sustainability 83
food crops vs cash crops 147–148
food documentaries 91; audience reception of 88–89
Food Inc. 77
food production 155; ecological mode of 145–146; ethical 77; industrial mode of 142, 145–146; monoculture 82; paradigms 145–146; sustainable 83–84
Food Recovery Network 86
food transformation technologies 112–113; distrust on 116; ethics of 112–113; and global warming 121; and intellectual propriety rights 118; living entities as property or as commodities 114–115; *see also* genetic engineering
foodways 132
Forks over Knives 77, 82, 84–85, 93n8
Foster, John Bellamy 102
Francis, Pope 130
Fraser, Evan 120
Fudge, Erica 103
Fulkerson, Lee 84
Future of Food, The 77, 87–88

Gaard, Greta 182–183
Gadgil, Madhav 40, 151
Galway 81
Gandhi, M. K. 175n1, 176n26
Ganges civilization 22–23
Gates, Bill 92n4
Genetically Modified Organism Exploratory Committee 113

genetically modified organisms (GMOs) 79, 93n11, 113, 182; crops 121; food 88; irrevocably serious impact of 121; multinational business 117, 122–123; paddy varieties 25; production 114; threat to biodiversity 116; vicious cycle 120
genetic engineering 112, 183; genetically engineered animals 115; genetically engineered crops 115–116
Ghosal, Anjali 25, 29n15
Ghosh, Amitav 11
Gidla, Sujatha 161
Global North 2, 5, 6
Global South 2, 3, 4, 6, 41, 141, 154, 180, 184
global warming 118, 121
Glotfelty, Cheryll 39
Goa, *bacalchau* in 97, 107–109
Graeber, David 15
Gramsci, Antonio 155n2
Great British Bake Off, The 81
Green Revolution (1960s) 25, 142, 147
Guha, Ramachandra 40, 151, 162–163
Gujarat 23
Guptas 174
Guru, Gopal 161–162

Hackett, Sophie 12
Hammer, Ed 92n5
Hanumanthaiah, N. K. 164–165
Harijan 175n1; *see also* caste system; Dalits
Harris, Jonathan Gil 103
Hastagrewilding 92n3
Hawking, Stephen 122
Helander-Renvall, Elina 47–48
Hinduism 134
hippy movement 81
Holt-Giménez, Eric 148–149, 150, 152, 154
Hopkins, Rob 92n4
Horak, Jan-Christopher 89
Howard, Gabrielle 60
Howard, Louise 64, 66–67, 70, 73n33
Howard, Sir Albert 4, 57, 59–60, 66, 71; *see also* Indore method
Hughes, Helen 89
human responsibility 141
humans and non-humans, co-agency of 12
hunger and deprivation 147–148
Hutchinson, H. B. 69
Huyghen van Linschoten, Jan 107, 108

Iberia 97, 99, 100
Ilaiah, Kancha 166–167
Inconvenient Truth, An 92n2
India: farmers' protests in 1, 181 (*see also* farmers); government's welfare measures, futility of 144–145, 151; meat eating in 2; natural resources 151–152; reservation system 176n25; village systems in 160; *see also* southern peninsula of India
Indonesia, 41
Indore method 4, 57–58, 66; field trials 70; and the Indian farmers 68–69, 70, 73n33; in large-scale agriculture 70; open-ended process 70–71; reception of 60–61; research and experimentation 62–64
industrial agribusiness, 141, 153
industrial food producers 142, 145–146
Industrial Revolution 12, 13–14
Indus Valley civilization 14, 23
insects, importance in ecosystems 121
Institute of Plant Industry 62, 70
Institution of Agricultural Technology 147
intellectual propriety rights, over living organisms 118
Ireland 82

jackfruit 52–53n17
Jainism 174
Jambava Puranam 168–170, 174
Janzen, Olaf 99–100
Japan 88
*Jataka*s 29n15
Jenu Kurubas 40, 52n14
Jepson, Paul 79

kallaṇai (dam) 21, 22
Kaplan, David 45
karikalan (King) 13, 14, 20–23, 25, 26n4
kāvirippūmpaṭṭiṉam 17, 21
Kemp, Peter 106
Kessler, Brad 130
King, Frank H. 68, 73n27
King Korn 92n2
Kirchmann, Holger 73n24

Kisan Long March 146, 149, 155n6
Kisan Mukti March 149, 155n6
Kodagu/Kodava people 4, 36–38, 39, 51n3; agricultural practice 44; and animism 46–47; and bioregional eating 39, 41, 50–51; bioregional identity 44; and black pepper 49; and cardamom cultivation 48–49; coffee plantations 4, 38, 41–42, 52n16; during colonial period 37–38; craftwork 44; cultural practices 43–44, 48; festivals 42, 45–46; food and bioregional culture 50; hunting practice and culture in 46–47, 53nn23–24; Kailpodh festival 46; lifeway 50; meat consumption in 47; multiculturalism in 52n12; native plant species/trees 40, 42; and paddy cultivation 43–44, 45, 47, 48; Puthari 45–46, 47; straw mats 44
Kolivi canal 161
Kollmuss, Anja 90, 93n14
Kondh 15
Korea 183
Krishna, T. M. 170–171, 172
Krishnan, Omkhar 25, 29n15
Kuchay, Bilal 1
Kunard, Andrea 12
Kundathbottu 40, 52n15
Kurlansky, Mark 99, 102, 104
kuṭapulaviyaṉār 22

Lancet Commission Report 126
land injury 38, 52n9
Latour, Bruno 12
La Via Campesina 155
Liebig, Justus 59, 69, 72n6
Liebig, Louise 59
Linklater, Richard 83
Lipkis, Andy 86
Little Ice Age 101–102
livestock production 82
local diet therapy 43
local food 3–4; transformation into global food 4–5
Long March, The (Waikar) 141, 142, 146, 150, 152, 154–155
Lopez, A. 80
Ludden, David 23
Lynch, Tom 39

Madigas 168, 170
Malick, Terrence 80
Malthus, Thomas 87
Manbiot, George 79
Mandanna, Sarita 4, 36, 37, 38, 40–44, 45–48, 49, 50, 51n2
Mandelslo, Jean Albert de 107, 108
mango 42, 43, 53n18
"Mango Season" (Skinner) 126, 127, 129–130, 130–131, 135
Manusmriti 158, 166, 173, 175n4
Maplahs 49, 50
March of the Penguins 92n2
Martian, The 90
Martinez-Alier, Joan 2
Martinez Torres, Maria Elena 153
Marx, Karl 102
Mason, Jim 2, 181
Matthes, Jorg 88
McLaughlin, James 92–93n8
McNeill, John R. 13–14
meat eating 2, 82–83, 128, 134; beef 164–174; impact of 183; meat-based fast-food companies 182
meatification 2
Menezes, Maria Teresa 109
Mentz, Steven 103
Mestico 107
metabolic rift 97, 102, 104
metaphor, power of 87
Mexico 41
Miller, Henry 117
millet 16–17, 18, 23–24, 27n9
Mills, Stephanie 44
Mitman, Greg 92n7
monocropping 119
monoculture 51n5, 86; farming 80; food production 82
monoscapes 29n16
Monsanto 115, 117, 123, 181
Morishima, H. 29n12
Morton, Timothy 120
Mozambique 97
mrdangam-making 170–171
Mughal Gardens, Delhi 73n33
Muller, Alexander 93–94n16
multiculturalism 39–40, 52n12
Musahars 160
"My Food, My Wish" (Shyamala) 165–166, 167

Nabhan, Gary Paul 40
Nambisan, Kavery 4, 36, 37, 39, 40–41, 43–45, 47, 49, 50, 51n1
Nanji 36, 39, 41, 43, 49–50
national identity, and food 182
native plant species 37, 38, 40, 42, 43

natural life-systems 45
naturecultures 1
nel (paddy-rice) 15, 20, 24, 28n11
Neo-*tiṇai*cene 24–26
neutral approach, to Anthropocene 11
Nevle, R. J. 102
Newfoundland 98–100, 102
New World, The 80
Nichols, Bill 93
Nigeria 97
non-governmental organizations (NGOs), environmental 90
non-violence 173
North Atlantic fishing stocks 102–103
Northeast Atlantic fish stocks 102
Northern European fisheries 101
North Sea fish stock 102
nuclear power, impact on nature 14

Obama, Michelle 72
O'Brien, Susie 182
Oka, H. I. 29n12
omnivores 152
Onge tribe 15
Oppermann, Serpil 72n3, 74
organic farming 71, 77, 84, 93n9; taste of food from 71–72; *see also* compost
Oryza nivara 28–29n12
Oryza rufipogon 28n12
Our Daily Bread 77

paddy monoculture 13, 15, 20, 24
pāṇar 17
Paraiyars 170
parasites 61–62
Patel, Raj 2–3
patents: over living organisms 118; over seeds 183–184
permaculture 80, 81
peruñcōṟu 16, 19, 23
pesticides 86, 148
Petrini, Carlo 72
Pfeiffer, Ehrenfried 65–66
Philippines 41
Pires, Maria José 105–106, 108
place-based culture 38
place-based eating 38, 40, 47
place-based identity 36, 38
place-based narratives 3–4
Pollan, Michael 72
polymers 58
poṅkal festival 23–24
Poor John 97, 98, 100, 104, 106–107
population growth 87
Portuguese, and cod fish 97–99, 102, 107–109
postcolonial cultures 97
Prabhakaran Nair, K. P. 48
Pretty, Jules 29n16
Purānās 134
PurushaSukta 171, 176n21
Purushotham, K. 161, 170
Puthari (harvest festival) 42, 45–46, 47

Quitério, José 106, 108

Rabi, Pierre 86
Rajarajan I, Emperor 13
Rajendran I, Emperor 13
Ramarajya 176n26
Rangaswamy, Jala 166
Rao, G. Kalyana 163
Rauschenbusch-Clough, Emma 168–169
Ravidas, Sant 176
Ree, Wayne 126
repeasantization 153
rewilding 79, 86, 92n3
rice: homeoarchy 20–24; homoarchy 19–20; monism 4, 25–26; monoculture 4, 11, 22, 24; monopoly 11
Richards, E. H. 69
Richardson, Ruth 90, 93–94n16
Richter, Reverend Gundert 43, 48
Rig Veda 134, 171, 173, 176n22
Risley, Sir Herbert 169
Rodale, Jerome Irving 60–61, 66
Rosset, Peter M. 153
Rothamsted Experimental Station 69
Roy, Raja Ram Mohan 176n16

Sainath, P. 6, 145, 146, 154, 156n7, 156n8
Sale, Kirkpatrick 39, 49
Salgado, Sebastião 87
Salkever, Alex 122
salt cod *see bacalhaus*
sandalwood 53n27
Sanskritization 169
"Satay" (Ree) 126, 127–128, 130, 131
Scent of Pepper, The (Nambisan) 36, 38, 39, 41, 43, 48
Schlosser, Eric 83
Schumacher, E. F. 4
Scott, James C. 18
Seaspiracy 83

Seetharamulu, Gurram 170
selective breeding 114
sex, and food 181
Shakespeare, William 98, 103–108
Shannon, Laurie 103
Sharma, Mukul 158–159, 174
Sharma, S. D. 16, 28–29n12
Shiva, Vandana 86, 87, 115, 116, 117–118, 119, 123, 145
Shudras 166–167, 171
Shyamala, Gogu 165–166, 166–167, 172
Singaravelu, S. 15, 29n13
Singer, Peter 2, 181
Singh, Kumara Suresh 160
Skinner, Michele Cruz 126, 127
Slow Food movement 71
Smith, Brian K. 173
Smithsonian Institute 124n18
Snyder, Gary 38, 40, 45, 58
social hierarchy 158
soil and soil ecosystems 71
soil-health crisis 92n5
"Song of the Mango" (Cruz) 126, 127
South America 97, 101
Southern Europeans, and cod fish 98
southern peninsula of India 4; Aryanization of food culture 23–24; denaturization of nature 22; diversity in food culture 15; Early Anthropocene 14; food hierarchy 14–18; gathering, hunting and 27–28n9; gathering, hunting and fishing in 14–15; Neo-*tiṇai*cene 24–26; partially domesticated food in 18; rice culture and Aryan immigrants 24; rice homeoarchy 20–24; rice homoarchy 19–20; wage (*campaḷam*; *kūli*) 18, 19
Spain 98
species 37, 38, 40, 42, 43, 79
Spendrup, Sara 82
Srinivas, M. N. 169
Stahel, Urs 12
Steffen, Will 13–14
Stein, Burton 26n5
Stein, Mark 134
Steiner, Rudolph, compost method 58, 64–66, 73n24
stockfish 97–98, 104–108
Stoermer, Eugene 51n4
Stokes, Kenneth M 102
structural inequalities, impact of 79
sufficiency, and bioregional living 45
Super-Size Me 92n2
survival strategy 149
sustainable food production 83–84
Svalbard Global Seed Vault 115
Swaminathan, M. S. 147
synthetic pesticides 83

Tagore, Debendranath 176n16
Taittreya Upanishad 134
Tamil culture 23; *see also* southern peninsula of India; *tiṇaikal*
technology: benefits of 147; biotech companies, campaign 117; *see also* genetically modified organisms (GMOs); genetic engineering
Teltumbde, Anand 159
Test, Edward M 99, 100, 104, 107
Thailand 41
Thayer, Robert L. 38, 39, 40
Tiger Hills (Mandanna) 36–37, 38, 39, 41–42, 43, 45, 46, 48
tiṇaikal 14–15, 16, 27n7; *kuriñci* 17, 27n9; *marutam* 14, 16, 17, 18, 19, 24, 25, 28n9; *mullai* 14, 18, 23, 24, 27–28n9; *neytal* 14, 16, 18, 19, 24, 28n9; *pālai* 14, 17, 24, 28n9
tobacco, as a food allegory 79–80
toddy 48, 53n25
topsoil 12, 79
trade policies 146–147
transnational corporations 181–182
True Cost of Food, The 85

uṇavu 29n13
United States, use of Indore method in 61
uṇṭāṭṭu 27n7
untouchable community 161–162; *see also* caste system; Dalits
Untouchable Spring (Rao) 163
Upanishads 134, 158, 175n3
upper castes food 172

Vaari of Pandharpur (pilgrimage) 149
Van Esterik, Penny 36
Vedas 158, 173, 175n2
Vedism 173
veganism 81, 183
vegetarianism 2, 3, 77, 82, 84, 134, 173
Vidarbha region, Maharashtra 141, 146, 148
Vidharba (Maharashtra), farmers' struggle in 6
Vietnam 41
Viney, Michael 81

Wad, Yeshwant D. 60
Wadhwa, Vivek 122
Waikar, Namita 141
waste management 44, 59, 60, 62, 63, 85; *see also* compost
Waters, Alice 72
weeds, importance in ecosystems 121
Weis, Tony 2
Weisman, Alan 58
Wengrow, David 15
wetlands, and caste system 159–160
Whitman, Walt 57, 58, 72, 72n1
Willerslev, Rane 46
Williams, Gordon 105
Windup Girl, The (Bacigalupi) 5, 112–123
Wiseman, Fredric 91n1

Xuanzang 160

Yerava people 47, 50

Printed in the United States
by Baker & Taylor Publisher Services